RAGGED ISLANDS

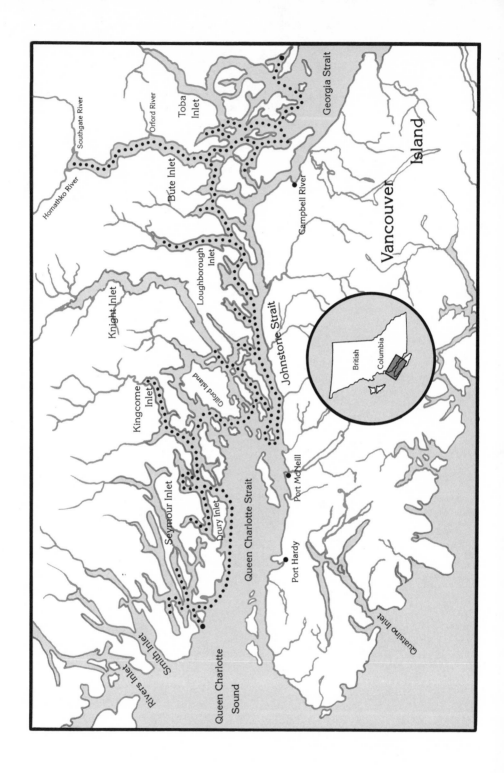

Michael Poole

RAGGED ISLANDS

A Journey by Canoe Through the Inside Passage

Douglas & McIntyre
Vancouver/Toronto

Douglas & McIntyre Ltd.

1615 Venables Street
Vancouver, British Columbia V5L 2H1

Canadian Cataloguing in Publication Data
Poole, Michael, 1936–
Ragged islands
ISBN 0-88894-718-6
1. Inside Passage. 2. Pacific Coast (B.C.)–
Description and travel. I. Title.
FC3845.I57P65 1991   917.11'31044   C91-091387-0
F1089.I5P65 1991

Text design: Robert MacDonald/MediaClones
Cover design: Barbara Hodgson
Cover photograph: Adrian Dorst
Maps: Michael Poole
Printed and bound in Canada by D.W. Friesen & Sons Ltd.
Printed on acid-free paper

For Ted

MAPS OF THE JOURNEY

CONTENTS

INTRODUCTION

Drowning always seemed a bad way to go – all those wrinkles you get from being in the water too long. Even washing the dishes without rubber gloves gives me the willies. So how would I look when I was cast ashore after a couple of weeks? Grey and pulpy with all the corners worn off.

Such forebodings had crossed my mind as I prepared to canoe alone down one of the world's most wild and deserted coasts. Drowning, to be sure, was not part of the plan. But there was no denying that I'd be travelling in dangerous waters. So why was I doing it?

To begin with, I was out of work. The documentary film business, my meal ticket for two decades, was at a standstill. The time was right for dusting off an old ambition to canoe the British Columbia coast and write a book about the experience.

At least I wasn't starting from scratch. Making films, I had seen quite a lot of the coast, though usually as a kind of travelogue framed in the window of an airplane or glimpsed from the deck of a fishboat. Year after year the coast had beckoned – surf-swept sand, island clusters, deep still inlets, snowfields, needle peaks, amber streams threading green estuaries, all without another soul in sight. And year after year I had passed it by, returning regretfully to the city.

At first that's about all I expected of the journey – scenery, quiet paddling, solitary evenings by the fire. There was also the challenge of travelling alone, testing my bush skills (from which I took much satisfaction) and my capacity to get along with only my thoughts for company, of which I was much less sure.

But when the charts were spread on the livingroom floor, my vision of the trip began to change. The British Columbia coast was much too extensive to canoe in a single summer; I would have to choose a part of it. I turned first to the northern half where the coast

1

was little developed and virtually uninhabited beyond a few towns and Indian villages. Here, surely, was the pristine country I was looking for.

But as I plotted to work out a route, I found myself overwhelmed by the emptiness of it all, by the prospect of so many deep mountain inlets and wind-swept islands utterly without a human presence. So another series of charts were spread out, delineating the tangle of land and water to the east and north of Vancouver Island. This was more to my liking. Much of this country was as deserted as the north coast, and yet a scattering of people still lived here. They were the survivors, the true coast people who had stayed on, resisting a fifty-year migration that had gathered up nearly everyone from the islands and inlets and swept them into towns.

Although I had lived in a coastal village since World War II, I was unaware of this resettlement until my father took me north on a camping trip in the summer of 1951. Once beyond the reach of roads, we saw almost no one except for the few people still living at the old steamboat stops. Wherever we camped – Buccaneer Bay, Shark Spit, Hernando Island – no other footprints marked the sand and no other boats came to anchor. I didn't understand that while our community had been sheltered by the prosperity of nearby Vancouver, nearly all the thousands of miles of islands and inlets to the north were in the final years of a long slide into depression and depopulation. Even in Georgia Strait, the most settled part of the coast, it seemed that nearly every cove had its sagging house and runaway orchard.

Years later when I returned to the coast as a filmmaker, the process had run its course. In Georgia Strait, the tide had already turned, bringing people back to the islands. But to the north, wherever I went, I followed a trail of defeat and abandonment. Homesteads, canneries, logging camps, mines and whole towns had tumbled and rotted away. More than sixty post offices had closed their wickets forever. It was an old and complicated story of booms and busts, beginning before World War I and ending in the late 1950s.

Kicking through the dust of shattered dreams, I often wondered what had gone wrong. None of the traditional explanations – the withdrawal of steamship service, the closing of canneries, distance from markets –fully satisfied. There were deeper causes, things of the heart and mind. Many people came here looking for the last frontier, for a final chance to play out their freebooting fantasies of man-against-the-wilderness. They had no real interest in settling down. Others tried hard to make a home but were never at ease with the gloomy winters and stifling press of mountains and rampant growth. Yet there were always a few hardy individuals who hung on, people who felt neither alienation nor the urge to cut-and-run. They built and planted well, achieved a measure of harmony with their surroundings and lived contented lives.

In the 1960s and '70s the back-to-the-land movement brought a new wave of settlers to the coast, most of them young and city-bred. They were long on idealism and short on skills, and after a winter or two in the rain, nearly all of them pulled out. The few who persisted fit comfortably into the old patterns of settlement, reviving abandoned homesteads, fishing, tree planting, making a living however they could.

I observed this return to the coast with an envy that verged on resentment. People from all over North America were doing what I – who was raised here with my feet in the water – was too bound up with career and security to do. Between film jobs I dabbled unsuccessfully with growing Christmas trees and fishing crabs, trying to establish an economic footing for moving out of the city. None of it worked, of course, because the commitment was lacking; I wasn't prepared to take the plunge. Finally, at the end of the 1970s, my family grown and marriage dissolved, I moved back to the Sechelt Peninsula, though it was hardly a return to the coast; fast ferries had transformed the community into a suburb of Vancouver. And I was still making films, which took me away from British Columbia for weeks or months at a time.

So this trip was to be a surrogate of sorts for the move I never made. Hunched over my charts, I laid out a route that would give me a sample of what I had missed, beginning on the deserted mid-coast, traversing the shores of Queen Charlotte Sound and winding through

3

the inlet country to the south. It was a mix of the wild and the sparsely settled coasts, alternating days of solitary paddling with encounters with loggers, fishermen and homesteaders. I wanted to know what kind of lives these people led. Why had they stayed on when so many others had left? What had I missed by not joining them? And was it really too late for me to make the move?

In the lengthening days of spring I set to work building a canoe for ocean travel, accumulating gear, questioning tugboat skippers and fishermen about who was living on the coast, and mining libraries for the little history that had been written about the places I would be going to.

The hardest part was saying goodbye. Recently remarried, I had moved back to the city and was just getting to know my twelve-year-old stepdaughter, Ashely. My wife Carole put on a brave face when we parted, though she was deeply fearful that I might drown in some God-forsaken inlet. As things turned out, she was very nearly right.

On an evening in mid-July I loaded my canoe and a mountain of gear onto a fish packer at Vancouver and headed north.

1

From the dark wheelhouse only the faintest light of false dawn was visible on the water beyond the bow of the fish packer, *Sea Harvest*. Captain Dick Hansen eased back on the throttle and cut our speed to dead slow. His face caught the luminous green of the radar screen.

"We're getting close," he said, moving aside so that I could see. "That's Fox Island and there's the narrows just beyond."

I made out two blurry shapes and a thin, dark line between them. The shapes were the points that form the entrance to Slingsby Channel, and the slot between was the dangerous Outer Narrows, about a mile dead ahead. This was the western gateway to Seymour Inlet, where I planned to begin my three-month journey south. We ran on in silence. Dawn began to show through the windows, and I stepped out on deck. Fog hovered low overhead. In the distance on both sides of the boat, grey cliffs were edged below by a white line of surf and above by the black of the forest. The sea was smoked glass, heaving slowly on a long flat roll from the open Pacific.

My luck was improving. Three days ago I had arrived here aboard another packer, the *Ocean Endeavour*, after a 250-mile run north from Vancouver. A gale was driving twelve-foot swells out of the northwest. For as far as I could see to the north and south, an unbroken line of surf thundered in on cliffs and islands that looked as if they had boiled up out of the sea. The bay in front of the Outer Narrows was a minefield of reefs and breakers. In such a sea there was no chance of unloading my canoe and gear. And so we went on, fifty miles farther north to Smith and Rivers inlets. For two days and nights I had stayed with the *Ocean Endeavour* while she picked up salmon from the gillnetters. The westerly blew round-the-clock, and I paced the deck like a caged animal, wondering if I would ever get into Seymour Inlet. But last night after midnight, the wind began to drop. Working under floodlights, my canoe and gear were quickly transferred to the *Sea Harvest*, which was about to leave for Vancouver.

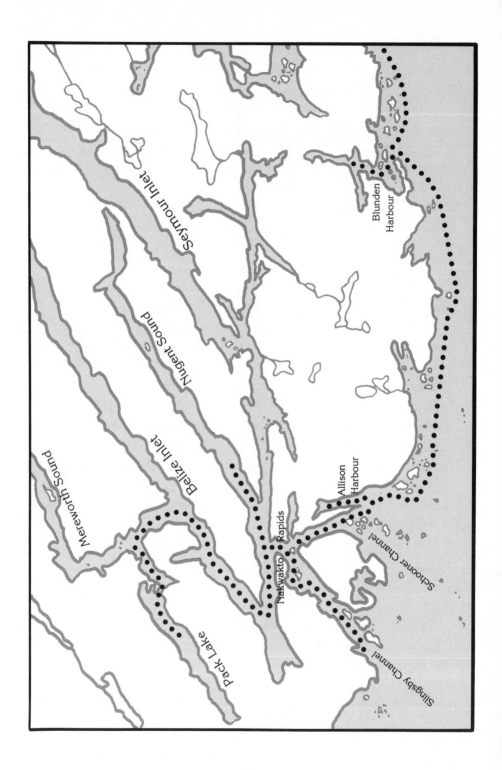

Seymour Inlet

Nugent Sound

Belize Inlet

Mereworth Sound

Pack Lake

Nakwakto Rapids

Allison Harbour

Blunden Harbour

Schooner Channel

Slingsby Channel

Now, after a five-hour run, Dick Hansen was peering into the gap where the Outer Narrows split the cliffs. "It doesn't look good," he said, handing me the glasses.

This was not what I wanted to hear; I was hoping we could get through the narrows into the shelter of Slingsby Channel to unload the canoe and gear. One look with the binoculars queered that idea; the ebb tide from Seymour Inlet was piling head-on into the ground-swell, turning the narrows into a chute full of steep, breaking waves. I had been forewarned about Slingsby Narrows; the government's normally phlegmatic guide for mariners spoke of fast tides and "extreme danger." When the ten-knot ebb collides with storm waves from the open Pacific, the sea stands on end. Years ago a surveyor trained his instruments on the breakers and claimed to have measured a wave of seventy feet from trough to crest. In this dawn of grey stillness, the narrows was on its best behaviour, but it was still no place for a packer loaded to the scuppers with fish.

Dick unrolled a chart. "Maybe there's some other place we can get in out of the swell." He knew I'd rather not be be left bobbing on the open Pacific for three hours until the turning of the tide let me through the narrows. If a wind came up in the meantime, I would be caught without shelter. Off to the south the chart showed another entrance to Seymour Inlet, called Schooner Channel. It would be ideal, but the approaches were dotted with crosses and stars and patches of blue, which in the language of charts meant sunken rocks and reefs. Dick shook his head. "I wouldn't want to take her in there. I've never been here before."

We looked in the other direction, north of the narrows. Just around the first point, a slim arrowhead of water cut into the shore, labelled Vigilance Cove. Dick referred to another larger-scale chart. "It's deep," he said, "I can get you in there."

Dead slow, the packer nosed up to the very head of the cove. On either side the cliffs pressed so close that Dick had to work the boat back and forth to turn her. A deckhand dropped the anchor and we lowered the canoe into the water, tying it alongside. Then, as Dick and the deckhand passed things down to me, I fitted them in place:

three watertight boxes of food and equipment, ten gallons of gasoline, an outboard motor, five gallons of water, cooking pots, two
tarps, a rucksack of clothing, sleeping bag and a miscellany of fishing
rods and other gear. The load seemed preposterous for one canoe, yet
I knew it would all fit because I had done a trial loading in the garage
at home. But now, hurrying to let Dick get on his way, I botched the
job and finished with a clutter of loose gear on top. It was not a sight
to inspire confidence; without my weight in the stern to balance the
450-pound load, the canoe looked perilously bow-heavy. To make
matters worse, the spray tarp wouldn't fit over my sloppy packing.
It was meant to snap down tight around the gunwales, sealing all but
the stern seat against any waves that broke over the canoe. As I
struggled with it, Dick disappeared into the cabin and returned
bearing an oilcloth package. "I think you'd better take these," he said,
grinning slyly. "We have to get new ones, anyway. They're out of
date." Inside were six marine distress flares. They were a welcome
addition to the two small flares I had bought for the trip.

The *Sea Harvest* faded away into the fog like an overexposed
photograph. Long after she was gone, the sound of her engines hung
over the cove, melding gradually into the faraway whisper of surf.
Close around the canoe, kelp heaved and slithered on the rise and fall
of the groundswell. The sea gurgled under the cliffs, and somewhere
back in the forest, beyond the mist, a winter wren poured out a
torrent of tiny notes.

The extent of my isolation began to dawn on me. I was almost half-
way up the British Columbia coast, 150 miles from the nearest road
to the south, and more than 100 from the closest road to the north.
But those were air miles, straight lines that bear no relation to the
tortured water route travellers here must follow. This coast is a crazy
quilt of inlets, islands and passages with 16,500 miles of shoreline, all
crumpled into the 600 miles between Washington and Alaska. Only
in three places – the south coast in the Vancouver area, the mid-coast
at Bella Coola and to the north around Prince Rupert – do roads
connect with the outside world. Much of the rest of the coast is
crosshatched by logging roads, none of which break through the

8

mountain barrier to the east. To the west the towns and roads of northern Vancouver Island were less than thirty miles away. But between me and the island lay the open waters of Queen Charlotte Sound, which only a suicidal idiot would attempt to cross in a canoe.

Somewhere out there in the fog, fishing boats, tugs and perhaps even the occasional freighter were traversing the sound, though there was little chance that any of them would turn in to Seymour Inlet. It had long been closed to salmon fishing, and towing companies had told me they hadn't brought a log boom out of the inlet for years. The only post office and store, at Allison Harbour, was abandoned in the 1950s. The marine chart, normally dense with detail, showed soundings for only a small part of the inlet. All the rest – an enormous complex of fjords, sounds and lagoons – was a white blank, adumbrated only by dotted lines along the shore. Up-to-date information of any kind about these waters was hard to come by. In the 1930s and '40s the Anglican Church Mission boat *Columbia* called here many times, and its log recorded visits to at least a dozen logging camps, big and small. Now, as far as I could determine, there was no one left in all the more than 150 miles of waterways.

It had started to rain; not the rain of clouds and drops, but the drenching mist of summer fog which drifts on the slightest breeze and finds its way under any covering. The air was raw with the breath of an ocean that was, in this third week of July, only a few degrees warmer than its mid-winter forty-six degrees Farenheit. Shivering, I pulled on raingear, tilted the motor out of the water and began paddling to get warm.

Outside the shelter of the cove, the canoe lifted her red hull to swells lumped up by the current from the narrows. Her trim was perfect: slightly high at the bow, with enough of the stem in the water to hold a course into the wind. I heaved a sigh of relief; the canoe was not maimed, after all, by the addition of a transom and motor. I had done violence to her elegant lines (taken from a Peterborough rib canoe)*, by lopping off the stern, but there had been no time to make a trial run with all the gear during the crescendo of deadlines and tearful farewells that filled my last days in Vancouver. Now, with her trim in good order, the moment had come to determine how the canoe would perform. At the mouth of the narrows, I put her to the test.

Keeping to the quiet water within a yard or two of shore, I paddled around the point until the tidal race was only a couple of canoe lengths ahead. The ebb was slowing, though still making seven knots or more, and the breakers had subsided to long streaks of foam, riding the backs of the four-foot waves. Easing ahead, I caught the pull of a strong eddy and shot into the narrows. The canoe sliced deeply into the first wave, then rose to the next and rode smoothly over the crest, buoyant and responsive to the paddle, despite her heavy load. I held the bow upstream for a moment, then let it fall off slightly to the right, so that the canoe sheered sideways across the current and into the biggest waves in the middle of the narrows. Canoeists call this ferrying, after the cable ferries that once employed the same principle to cross swift rivers. I dug deep with the paddle, heaving the stern to the left. Instantly, the bow came around to the right. With two more strokes, the canoe spun end-for-end and sped away down the rollers.

I could not have wished for more; she was as stable and responsive as any canoe I had ever used. But she was a canoe nonetheless and a questionable craft for ocean travel. A kayak would be faster and more seaworthy. It would also be cramped as a coffin and carry so little I'd be forced to live like a chipmunk on nuts and raisins for three months. I had opted for comfort and convenience, a choice I would question during some lively times on the water.

Killing time until the tide turned, I coasted along the shore to the north of the narrows. Black and bone-coloured granite bulged

---

* See Appendix for a description of the canoe and list of gear.

abruptly out of the sea and sloped steeply into the forest. The fog had lifted above the treetops, unveiling low hills of spruce, hemlock and yellowish-green cedar, prickly with the bleached spikes of dead snags. At the clifftops the trees were stripped of limbs on their weather sides, their tops shattered and thrown back into the forest by winter gales. Lower down, on the west-facing slope of every headland, matted salal and spruce lay permanently wind-flattened, as if a great hand had brushed over the land. Offshore, islets trailing pennants of ragged trees looked as if they had been knocked back on their haunches by the blasts from the Pacific.

In the winter on this open coast, plumed combers charge through the reefs, wind tears the words from your mouth, surf bays beneath the cliffs, and for weeks on end, the horizontal rain drives in from Queen Charlotte Sound. It is no place to be shipwrecked. The cliffs are split by impassable surf-swept gorges, and the undergrowth rises high and hard as a wall at the edge of the rainforest. Once, cut off by high water in such a place, I crawled through salal for two hours to cross a point I had walked around in two minutes when the tide was out. Anyone cast ashore here is rescued where they land, or they are not rescued at all.

In the last of the ebb, the waves in the narrows were down to a long, glassy roll. Deprived of its rapids, the Outer Narrows dwindled to an innocuous strip of water, flowing sedately between walls of dull rock and runty trees. I started the motor and ran through.

Ah yes, the motor. We must speak, however reluctantly, of the motor, a 1.5 hp British Seagull that had caused me pangs of conscience. Of course, it was a gross violation of every canoeing canon about sweat and ecology. But without it, I wouldn't see much in one summer on this coast of daunting distances. And there would be headwinds and long tedious stretches where paddling was pointless. Perhaps partly as a balm for my conscience, I had rigged a tiller to steer the motor with my knees, so that I could continue paddling, adding a knot to the five knots made by the Seagull. And if this were not atonement enough for my sins, I resolved to use the Idyll Smasher, as I called it, as little as possible; it was smokey and possessed of a furious roar out of all proportion to its eggbeater size. With it running, I would see little and hear even less of the birds and animals of the coast.

A mile above the narrows I went ashore on a point of pink granite and cooked porridge over a sulky driftwood fire. I sat on the grub box with the weighty *Sailing Directions, British Columbia Coast* open on my lap to consider what lay ahead. Five miles farther on, Slingsby and Schooner channels joined and entered Seymour Inlet through a passage just 300 yards wide. Twice a day on the ebb tides, water from the entire Seymour network of inlets – four inlets all told, encompassed by 700 miles of shoreline – forced its way through this gut. And twice a day on flood tides, the sea rushed back in. The resulting tumult of waters was Nakwakto Rapids, one of the most spectacular of the dozens of tidal streams on the British Columbia coast.

The *Sailing Directions* advised that currents reached sixteen knots, "one of the highest rates in the world," and warned mariners to enter Nakwakto only at slack water, "taking care that the calculated time is accurate, because at no other time is it possible to navigate these rapids safely." There was a final cautionary note: "The duration of slack is about six minutes."

Timing was the trick of it. If I got too close to the rapids too soon, I risked being sucked in by the current. Too late, and the ebb tide would throw me back. But for the few minutes at the turning of the tide, Nakwakto would be as placid as a duck pond. I looked up Nakwakto in the Current Tables at the back of the tide book. The next slack was more than four hours off.

I repacked – this time finding a place for everything – and pushed out into the three-knot current of Slingsby Channel. Weary from sleepless nights on the packer, I lay back, intending to snooze and drift with the tide. In a few minutes I began to shiver. The air was raw, even though the fog had lifted to form what weather forecasters call marine cloud. Reluctantly, I took up the paddle. For an hour the shoreline dragged by, rocky and monotonous, until an island-strewn passage opened on the left into Treadwell Bay, within sight of the rapids. Traditionally, boats wait here for slack water. There are two entrances, a boat passage on the eastern side of Anchor Island, which nearly fills the mouth of the bay, and the much more constricted western passage, where I had turned in. Here the current coiled lazily through waterways hardly wider than the canoe, floored with shell and sea stars of red and electric blue. Hemlocks leaned over the water, trailing beards of grey lichen, like Spanish moss in a sycamore swamp. I poked along, watching the bottom go by and dozing a bit. Meantime, the current had died away, and by the time I came to my senses, it was flowing in the opposite direction. Slack tide wasn't due for nearly half an hour in the rapids, but here it seemed to have come and gone already. Quickly, I started the motor and headed for the boat passage.

Out in Slingsby Channel the ebb tide had clearly begun. The canoe plowed into the current and bogged down. Paddling hard, I steered into slower water close to the west shore and picked up speed. Ahead now I could see the narrows. From aerial photos, I recognized Tremble Rock, an islet the size of a house, jutting up in the middle of the passage. When the tide is running full tilt, it trails two white plumes of immense waves, like a ship cutting through the sea. But now, with the current just beginning, Nakwakto seemed unexceptional: the land to either side low and solidly timbered and the shoreline a tumble of dark rock. No lofty cliffs framed the narrows like the Gates of Hell, as I half-expected of the most notorious rapids on the coast.

On the west shore, just downstream from the island, I found my way blocked by a line of fast water curling in a white wave off the point directly ahead. I would have to cross to Tremble Rock and try to make my way to the top of the rapid from there. As I angled out into the faster water, the current piled into the left side of the bow, driving the canoe across the gap and into the eddy behind the island. I idled there for a moment, reading signs that bore the names of tugs and fishboats that had passed through the rapids over the years. Long ago an Indian burial box was suspended in the trees, no doubt providing the occupant with a tumultuous ride through eternity. Now I could see no trace of it.

But what to do next? Upstream from Tremble Rock, the water was beginning to show a definite slope where it ran down from the inlet. The rapids were gaining speed, forming humps and valleys that would soon become white water on either side of the island. Already the current was too strong to buck; I would have to find a way to sneak up the side, or drop back and wait more than five hours for the next slack.

There was no chance on the west side, but on my right to the east there appeared to be slower water in a cove just below the head of the narrows. To get there I would have to cross 200 yards of fast water. Working as far as possible up the eddy next to the island, I opened the throttle and, paddling my damnedest, nosed out into the rapids. The current slammed into the side of the bow, and the canoe yawed to the right. Pitching and rolling, I reached wide with the paddle and brought the bow back up into the current. The canoe steadied and began slicing cleanly through the waves. For a moment I imagined myself going ahead at a great clip. But when I glanced at the island, it was apparent that the canoe was barely holding its own against the current and making no progress at all towards the cove. I angled more to the right, increasing my lateral speed across the current, but at the cost of dropping downstream. The game now was to reach shore before the canoe was swept down into the rough water below the cove, where I could see white foaming over a reef. Turning slightly more upstream, I dug deep with short, grunting strokes. The canoe slowed her backward slide, edged in to shore and caught the tail of the eddy at the bottom of the cove. The rest was easy. Riding the back current to the top of the narrows, I slipped through behind a kelp bed into Seymour Inlet.

Drifting offshore, well away from the pull of Nakwakto, I gave some earnest thought to the lesson I had just learned: when running tidal rapids, get there early and don't trust the tide book. Tugboat men had warned me about this; the tide tables are generally reliable for the height of tides, but there are too many natural variables to predict the timing of tidal streams with consistent accuracy. On this day the prediction for Nakwakto was out by more than half an hour.

In its western reaches, far from the mountains to the east, Seymour Inlet looks more like a sprawling lake than a coastal fjord. The water is a benign blue, untinted by the glacial flour that clouds many of the biggest inlets a forbidding green. The soft lift and fold of the hills belong more to eastern woodlands than the fractured coastal mountain country. Even the tides are unlike the ocean; Nakwakto so restricts the flow that their range is less than five feet, a third the height of tides outside in Queen Charlotte Sound. And the rapids themselves leave you with a strong impression of having come upriver into a lake system. On the chart Seymour Inlet resembles a pitchfork with four crooked tines pointing to the east and Nakwakto entering from the west, where the handle would be. But this is an eagle's-eye view. On the water, with the line of sight closed by bends in the passage, I could only imagine the labyrinthine branching of sounds and lagoons which probe thirty and forty miles back into the mountains.

As the summer westerly swept the last rags of fog from the sky, I crossed to the shore opposite Nakwakto and turned left towards Belize Inlet. My intention was to go part way up Belize then north into Mereworth Sound, where the chart showed many islands and a large lake very close to tidewater. But right now I wanted to make camp.

For two or three miles I scouted every point and cove without finding a single break in the narrow band of rock between the sea and tangled undergrowth. Trees crowded so close to the water that their limbs were cropped in a straight line at the high tide mark. Almost to Belize the brush pulled back grudgingly from a ledge, leaving room for the canoe and a tight camp. But the rock fell away nearly vertically into deep water, which would make for awkward loading on the low tide in the morning. And so I went on.

In country like this one should be grateful for any patch of open ground level enough to lie down on. And yet it's always tempting to look for a nicer beach or view, or a place better supplied with fresh water or wood. If you are too choosy, you go on. And on and on, passing up perfectly adequate spots, until you run out of light and end by hacking a miserable camp out of the bush. Often as not when you set out in the morning, you pass the beach of your dreams just around the next point.

Drifting on Belize Inlet, I scanned the shore with binoculars for two miles to its western end and all the way round to the east, where the inlet stretched away so long and straight that it blurred in haze. Nowhere for as far as I could see in any direction was there another place to camp. I turned back, pleased enough with the place I had found.

Late in the afternoon I woke from a nap in the grip of an iron resolve: to get rid of my excess baggage, all the redundant and self-indulgent junk that should have been left at home. In no time I had turned out the contents of every box and pack and spread them far and wide for sorting. The camp resembled the scene of a plane crash. Things of real utility I repacked. The rest I set to one side: oil for the outboard, all but two of Dick's flares, tinned milk and bully beef, bottles of ketchup and other goodies too bulky or heavy for a canoe trip. But what to do with it all? I was too much the ecological boy scout to merely chuck it into the bushes. Instead, I built the lot into a cairn on the highest point of the rock so that the next visitor would find a little cache of goodies. At least, the non-perishables would still be usable.

Pleased with myself, I drew on the cache to make corned beef hash, heavy on onions and ketchup. But as I ate, I began to have second thoughts. Perhaps I had been a bit hasty. After all, this journey would be much longer than any previous canoe trip I had made. Maybe I did need more than the customary rice, bannock (premixed for the trip so that I only had to add water), oatmeal and tea. Yes, it would be a good idea to take back just a few of the things. And so, with failing resolve, I pulled the cairn apart. Before long, everything was back in the boxes, save for four flares and two cans of oil. No sense, I told myself, leaving things that will only spoil.

Disillusioned with housekeeping, I made a seat on a foam mattress with the grub box for a backrest, and sat to watch the day wind down. The camp had a fine aspect, southwest across Seymour Inlet to a hog-backed ridge and northwest up the path of the setting sun to the end of Belize Inlet. At sundown the west wind died away, and in the stillness, Swainson's thrushes called from the woods. The sky was full of golden light, glancing from the sea beyond the horizon. A night breeze dropped from the hills and spread a herringbone ripple over the water. In front of the camp, a mink pulled a silver arrow through the kelp, and once, far off, a loon called.

I thought of my first solo camping trip, when I was eighteen or nineteen. A boat dropped me off at a creek mouth, with enough food to last a week. I put up my tent, ate a lumberjack's supper and went to bed. In the night I woke and felt an unease which, by dawn, had grown into something close to panic. Abandoning most of my gear, I walked out to the nearest road. My excuse: the tent leaked. In truth, I was petrified at the prospect of spending a week in my own company. Now, thirty years later, what sort of travelling companion would I find myself to be? Many times since that first ignominy, I had been alone in the bush, though never for more than a day or two. I expected there would be down days when I hungered for company. But I knew also, from living alone for five years in a backwoods cabin, that solitude – on the good days – is the ultimate self-indulgence.

Feeding cedar chips into the fire to make a quick flame, I brewed a billy of tea: Jasmine for sweet dreams and a tranquil gut. Just before dark, when the water had turned midnight blue, a sharp, shrill whistle sounded from beyond the point towards the rapids. More whistles followed, and two river otters came riding along the outside of the kelp on the current of the flood tide. Swimming low in the water, they looked at first like young seals. But when they dove, their humped backs and thick, arched tails stood out in silhouette against the afterglow. Another whistle sounded and two more otters rounded the point. The two pairs met in front of the camp and played chase-me-Charlie, round and over and under the kelp. Suddenly they came to a dead stop, periscoped their heads towards the fire and dashed off in the direction of Belize Inlet, tail nipping and wrestling as they went.

In the night I was visited by a dream that had been haunting me in recent weeks. I was paddling outside a dangerous surf, looking for a way in to the beach. The waves rose higher and higher until I had to either run through the breakers or swamp at sea. The canoe coasted faster and faster down the front of the combers, and no matter how hard I tried to keep it straight, it always broached and rolled. Sometimes the dream ended as I foundered amidst a flotsam of smashed canoe and ruined gear. Or I swam through the surf, only to find myself marooned on a beach of black sand. Day after day combers thundered in from the ocean, and my food supplies dwindled.

I lay awake, damping down anxieties. The shore of my nightmares was clearly the twenty-five miles to the south of Seymour Inlet, much of it wide open to the Pacific swells. It wasn't all that bad, I told myself; there were a few places to take shelter. And I would bide my time and wait for the right weather to run the open stretches.

A cold wind had come up from the west. Clots of fog flew past the face of the moon and vaulted over the ridges into the inlet. By dawn it would plug every passage and lagoon, all the way back to the mountains. I pulled a shirt, like a nightcap, over my head and went back to sleep.

2

The British Columbia coast is a chameleon land, given to dramatic transformation. Under the sun it nurtures a wild beauty in its mountains and extravagant growth. In rain and fog it takes on a dark malevolence, like an exotic fruit gone bad. On the open coast the miasma is dispelled by the exuberance of wind and wave, and in the mountains, by the energy of lift and thrust. But in the deep, closed inlets, it can be suffocating. Belize Inlet is such a place.

Fog squatted low over the water when I turned into Belize and headed inland along its south shore. Within a few yards of the canoe, everything – trees, water, shore – blurred and vanished. The only sound on the dead air was the slow drip of moisture from limbs overhanging the water. Rank moss clogged the underbrush and swarmed up into the trees. Here was the scene of the classic Gothic tale about a man and a woman shipwrecked on a shore overgrown with a strange spongy lichen, which proved to be addictive when they began to eat it. Spots of the stuff grew and spread on their bodies until they realized, to their horror, that many of the mounds of lichen around them had humanoid shapes.

With a swoosh of pinions, a ghostly grey raven landed overhead on the spike of a cedar snag, then followed the canoe, hopping from tree to tree and clacking like a New Year's noisemaker. I slapped the paddle on the water, and it flew off into the mist, trailing a dry rasping of wings.

I had been paddling for more than an hour when a breeze from the west began to ripple the water. Within minutes the fog was moving inland, tugging strands like cotton candy out of the ravines. The sun broke through, tearing the mist to shreds and sending it eddying up the mountainsides on the warming air. Crossing two miles of open water, I turned north into the mouth of Mereworth Sound. Abruptly, the looming walls of the inlet gave way to softly moulded ridges, mottled with the shadows of wandering clouds. Broad valleys opened on creeks that shone with the tender green of new grass. Sheltering from a freshening north wind, I followed the lee of a string of small islands paralleling the western shore. As I rounded the last of them, I caught sight of a white speck on the water, far ahead. For a moment, I doubted my eyes. But when I looked with the binoculars, there was no doubt and no reprieve. Another boat was in *my* inlet!

19

In no time the speck grew into a speedboat, which slowed and stopped beside the canoe. Two women, both in their sixties, told me they had come north from Seattle in a yacht that was anchored in Village Cove, a few miles ahead.

"We're lookin' for prawyuns," one of them barked in the voice of a sargeant-major. She was square-jawed and mannish, with a disconcerting habit of closing one eye whenever she spoke. "We've done real good, but we want a bunch for the freezer." Prawn traps were heaped up behind her.

The boat around the point turned out to be five big yachts, all with outboard runabouts that were buzzing around the cove. I learned from one of the boaters that new charts had recently been published, giving soundings for all of Seymour Inlet. Until this year, fear of uncharted waters had kept all but the most venturesome away. Regretfully, I paddled out of the cove, leaving behind a long gravel beach, with a creek trickling from a tunnel of cool shade under the alders. There could be no peaceful co-existence with the boaters; noon was still an hour away and heavy metal rock was blaring from their outside speakers.

Across the sound from Village Cove, near the head of a deep bay, the water turned the colour of strong tea. The stain was tannin, issuing from a lake which the chart showed just to the north. Many coastal lakes carry this tint, leached from cedar swamps and peat bogs. I followed the stain into a stream that ran deep and slow between grassy banks to a sunken ledge, barely covered by a glide of brown water. With the tide near full, I hauled the canoe easily over the ledge and into Pack Lake. The water was warm and tasted slightly brackish, like many coastal lakes that are fresh at the surface but salty underneath, a legacy from the last Ice Age when they were connected to the sea. As the glaciers retreated, the land rose and the entrances to these lakes were lifted above all but the highest tides.

Logging was taking place somewhere on the lake. On the way into the estuary, I had passed a floathouse that was obviously occupied, and here at the outlet of the lake timber was rafted, awaiting a tide high enough to carry it downstream to the bay. Seymour Inlet was apparently not as depopulated as I had been led to believe. Around the first point gaps appeared on the hillsides where trees had been pulled into the water. It was logging with a light touch; the country was unscarred by clearcuts or roads, and the lake was still attractive, stretching away, wind-ruffled cobalt, six miles to the west. Not far from the outlet I came upon a raft of timber with a seaplane tied alongside and a man sawing logs, soaking himself with water thrown up by the chain. Three other men stood near the plane, watching him. One of them, wearing green Sears catalogue work clothes, came over to the canoe. This was Charlie Chilson, a small-time logger, or gyppo as they are called on the coast.

"Come on by the house this evening," he said. "I haven't got time to talk to you now."

Late in the afternoon I tied the canoe beside Charlie's small three-room house. Back of the building was another much larger float bearing, among other things, a bunkhouse, a woodpile, a heap of boom chains, spools of cable, gasoline barrels and a shed housing a generator. A much-patched tugboat lay alongside. The scene was a throwback to the 1950s when thousands of loggers lived on floats in the days before prefab trailers and fly-in logging camps. The great advantage of the float camp was portability; to move to a new timber claim the logger simply untied from shore and towed his entire establishment away. In some places, aggregations of float houses came together in water-borne villages, complete with boardwalks, gardens, stores, schools, hotels, dancehalls, even – it is said – a baseball diamond. Though proof of the ball field is elusive, the biggest village afloat, Simoom Sound, did manage a badminton court.

Charlie came noiselessly along a trail from the lake and walked a log out to the float. In the house he made coffee on the propane stove and sat at the table, gathering his energy to cook supper. Lean and greying in his late fifties, he looked tired. His wife was away, he said, "outside" visiting. He was cooking for two of his sons, who were working with him, and for the scaler who had flown in to grade his logs. I told him I was surprised to find anyone living in Seymour Inlet. "Actually, we haven't been here that long," he said. "Just a couple of years and only a month or two here at Pack Lake. But this is the second time around for me."

Charlie Chilson was eleven when he first came to Seymour Inlet in 1940 with his father, who was also a logger. By the time he was fourteen he was working full-time in the bush. Twenty years later, when his own kids were in their early teens, he left the inlet in order to give them a better education than he had.

"We had been sending the oldest boy to a private school in Vancouver," he said, "and it was costing me two hundred and fifty dollars a month. With the other two boys coming up to school age, we just couldn't afford it. We had no choice. We had to move into town." For the next twenty years Charlie lived in a Vancouver suburb, working as a logging foreman and coming home weekends to his family. The money was good, though he never liked the city. "There were just too damned many people. You could never get away from them." Three years ago, against all odds, Charlie came back to Seymour Inlet to pick up where he left off. "I had a twenty-five-foot boat and not much else. Me and my son, Ken, lived on it and worked to get our own outfit, while the rest of the family stayed in town."

They worked in Allison Sound at the head of Belize Inlet, slowly scratching together the nuts and bolts of a logging operation. Charlie built an A-frame – two logs raised upright on a raft in the shape of a huge A, with a winch and engine – to pull timber down off the hillsides. (It was this device which accounted for the cosmetic logging I had seen in Pack Lake.) The A-frames had their heyday in the 1940s and '50s and then died a natural death for want of good timber within reach of the water. They were replaced by "power logging," a costly business of roadbuilding and clear-cutting with huge machines. But Charlie found timber close to the water in Pack Lake, and three months ago he had towed his float camp down the inlet. He was turning the clock back thirty years, defying trends that had driven nearly all the small loggers out of business. He was an anachronism, a nostalgic throwback to a time that was supposed to be dead and gone.

Charlie started supper, moving about the kitchen with the assurance of someone long practised at cooking for crews of men. "You know," he said, "I haven't made a goddamned cent in three years. Everything costs so much in here – over four hundred dollars return to fly out – and if we need a load of heavy stuff brought in by water, it costs more than a thousand dollars. So we go ourselves in the tug."

Although Charlie had expected his costs to be high in such a remote inlet, he could not have imagined that his income would be so uncertain. The timber is mediocre and he never knows what he'll be paid for it when it is towed to Vancouver and put up for sale. "You've got to trust a broker to sell your boom for you, but they're just looking out for themselves. It's easier for them to sell your logs cheap."

His two sons – a third, married son was in town for a few days – and the scaler came in to eat. Charlie put roast beef, mashed potatoes, carrots, salad and gravy on the table and apologized for forgetting to cook another vegetable. The scaler, a porcine man with a purple face, ate hugely and carried on an arcane monologue about a new system for grading logs. No one, Charlie included, knew what he was talking about.

Outside in the afterglow, an owl was trilling in the woods towards the lake, and I regretted for the hundredth time that I never learned to identify them by their calls. I spread my bedroll under the porch roof to avoid the dew. Charlie's big, amiable dog cold-nosed me on the cheek and settled down by my side for the night.

Moving about the kitchen in the morning, Charlie looked much thinner in a T-shirt than he had in work clothes. His hands seemed too big for his body and his shoulders had the stooped look of someone who has lifted too much too often. Unprompted by anything we were talking about, he began telling me about a brush with death he'd had many years before, when he was living here with his father. He had been away several days in the boat and nearing home, he ran into ice on the water. It was a mere skim which the boat easily broke a path through. He kept on, without realizing that the ice was becoming thicker and cutting into the hull. Before he knew what was happening, water rushed in and drowned the engine, and the boat sank under him.

"I got pretty close to an island before she went down," he said, "but I couldn't swim against that ice. It was too thick to break with my hands and every time I tried to get up on it, it broke under me. Then I saw a glove on the ice – I don't know how it got there, but it must have come from the boat. I reached out and took hold of it. It was frozen to the ice, and I pulled myself out." Lying as flat as possible to distribute his weight, Charlie inched his way to the island, breaking through once again just before he reached shore. With no way of making a fire, his clothes froze stiff as sheet metal as soon as he crawled out of the water. The island was close to the float camp, though round a point and out of sight. His only hope of survival lay in attracting his father's attention.

Breakfast forgotten, Charlie was standing by the table, talking into space, lost in the horror of that afternoon.

"I can't remember anything from the time I got out of the water until I found myself at the far end of the island. I yelled for help – I don't know how long – before I realized that I was yelling in the wrong direction. Somehow I got back where I came from and then I hollered and hollered for hours until my voice just gave out and I could only make a little whisper."

In the floathouse, Charlie's father heard nothing. But the family dog had been barking all through the afternoon on the end of the float, looking out towards the point. Near dusk, Charlie's father decided he had better investigate. He got into a skiff and broke a path with an oar through the ice to the island.

Charlie went on: "He nearly didn't find me. I didn't know where I was any more. I was crawling in the bush and he would never have seen me if I hadn't knocked a rock loose. Dad heard it and came and found me just before dark. I guess he was almost too late."

As I loaded the canoe, I wondered about Charlie's future here. Without his sons, he would be hard-pressed to carry on. The night before when his youngest son came in from work, I asked him how his day had gone. "The shits," he snorted, and clumped off to the bunkhouse. Young men his age no longer live in logging camps; they work their ten or twenty days and fly back to town where the action is.

I retraced my route past the slumbering boats in Village Cove and down Belize Inlet, which was stuffed again with morning fog. At the first night's camp, my discarded cans of oil stood out like a red and white beacon; they would not stay there long with so many boats in the inlet. Passing Nakwakto, I kept to the opposite shore, a half mile from the rapids, which were two hours into the flood tide. Even at that distance, a boil as broad as a house erupted under the canoe and sent me scurrying into shallow water next to the beach. A mile past Nakwakto I turned east into Nugent Sound in search of a boat logger who Charlie Chilson said worked here seasonally. Apparently, this was not the season; his floating shack was enisled by a mat of tree limbs and tops that no boat had penetrated for some time. Boat loggers make this sort of mess when they pull trees off the shore and trim them in the water, which is less work than trimming them on land, as they are supposed to do.

Nugent Sound was narrower and less monotonously straight than Belize, and I was tempted to follow it to its end. But I had to make a decision: I could wander all summer in the immensities of Seymour and its companion inlets, or move on to the south, where I was more likely to find people who lived on the coast year-round. There were, in fact, a few other people in Seymour Inlet – Charlie Chilson had put their number at eight – but all were boat loggers who worked here only sporadically. It was not fertile ground for the kind of encounters I was looking for. I turned back towards Nakwakto.

On the way into Nugent Sound, I had passed a peninsular knoll on my left, ringed by twenty-foot cliffs, in the center of a small bay. Perhaps an acre in area, it was treeless and overgrown with apple-green thimbleberry bushes, the unmistakable sign of an abandoned Indian village. Twin beaches of fine gravel curved around the bay from either side of the isthmus that joined the knoll to shore, and a

25

creek trickled down from the forest. This was Tigwaksti, once the main winter village of the Nakwakto band, a branch of the Kwakiutl people. I went ashore to look for carved house posts, said to be still lying at the edge of the forest, but impregnable thorn bush covered all of the old village site. I scrambled up onto the knoll and found open space between the berry bushes – black currants, twinberries and thimbleberries, all bearing heavily and all sprung, most likely, from fruit the Indians brought here.

Tigwaksti has been abandoned for barely a hundred years, and yet little is known about its history. Although there is no direct archaeological evidence, the Nakwaktos – and perhaps others before them – must have lived here for centuries or even millenia. (Digs immediately to the north and south of Seymour Inlet date habitation back 2000 and 9000 years respectively.) Sheltered from storm winds and well supplied with food from Nakwakto Rapids and the salmon streams in the inlet, the site was ideal for a winter village. The scanty records suggest that as many as a thousand people may have inhabited the big cedar houses that once stood around the bay. The bluff was used only as a place to dry berries and fish and as a redoubt when the village was attacked.

Defence must have been a preoccupation in Tigwaksti. The village was off by itself, away from the center of Kwakiutl population farther south, and close to the route of raiding parties from the north. Almost every year, usually in the summer, Haida or Tsimshian warriors swept down on villages to the south, particularly Salish communities around Georgia Strait. It was a kind of ritual warfare, without territorial objectives or booty, except for slaves and, occasionally, a high-born captive for ransom. Its real objective was a spirit quest, in which the attackers gained psychic strength from the dangers of the journey and the life force of people they killed. The dangers were considerable. A foray against the Salish took the raiders deep into enemy territory, where many things could go wrong – and frequently did. The party might be detected or rebuffed by the defences of a village. Or the homeward trip could turn into a harried retreat through a gauntlet of hostile tribes. And it was not sufficient for the warriors merely to save their skins; if they came home empty-handed, they would be scorned by their people. So there was always a powerful motivation to strike elsewhere to recoup the losses of an abortive raid. Tigwaksti, isolated and close to the homeward route, must have been a favourite target.

Sometime around 1850 a party of Tsimshian warriors from the village of Kitkatla slipped through Nakwakto Rapids under cover of darkness and attacked the village at dawn, killing many people and setting fire to the houses along the beach. The Nakwaktos fought back from their defensive position on the bluff, led by a renowned warrior named Nandzi ("Great Grizzly"). Single-handedly, he killed several of the attackers, and the Tsimshians retreated, taking with them a number of slaves. Tigwaksti had been saved, though it would soon succumb to greater disasters.

In 1862–63 smallpox swept the entire northwest coast, carrying off at least a third of the Indian population. Although no record survives from Tigwaksti, the Nakwaktos could hardly have escaped. And then, five years later, a raiding party from the village made an abortive attack on a trading schooner in Queen Charlotte Sound. One of the traders, armed with a Henry repeating rifle, waited for the Indians to fire their primitive muskets, then shot them all in their canoes before they could reload. The Indians had never seen a gun that could be fired more than once without reloading. The Henry rifle held fifteen rounds, one for each Nakwakto that was killed. The loss must have been crushing to the dwindling population of the village. Around 1885 the last of the Nakwaktos left Tigwaksti, just as the first white loggers and fishermen were moving into Seymour Inlet.

At the end of the beach, where the thorn bushes petered out, I walked back into the forest, looking for some trace of the massive houses. Nothing remained, of course; everything in Tigwaksti was built of wood, which the rainforest soon reclaims as its own. There was not even a feeling that people had once lived here, no trace of psychic energy to twitch at the corners of the mind. If ghosts still tramped Tigwaksti, they came with the driven rain on winter nights. Likely no new houses were built after the 1860s, at least twenty years before a remnant population moved permanently to one of their summer villages on Queen Charlotte Sound. Tradition maintains that they left because Tigwaksti was too vulnerable to attack, though the new village was at least as exposed. More likely it was simply that Tigwaksti was too isolated, too lonely for the few people who were left.

Over the bluff, two ravens shot across the sky, clacking and rolling on their sides. Bumblebees droned in the hot grass and a squirrel rustled under the bushes, gathering berries for the winter.

3

In the middle of Seymour Inlet, Bonaparte's gulls lifted like blowing snow from the top of an islet. Crossing to the Nakwakto side, I could see the white of the rapids a half-mile ahead and hear their distant roar. I wanted to get as close as possible, though I was wary of being sucked into the backeddy that was certain to lie off the near point at the rapids' edge. Cautiously, I paddled closer until the eddy was just ahead, wheeling round and round like an enormous plate with a freight of driftwood, seaweed and foam cast out of the rapids. Dividing the eddy from shore was a narrow band of bull kelp and quiet water. Slipping through the opening, I went on almost to the tip of the point and tied onto a kelp bulb as big as my fist. Not two canoe lengths away, Nakwakto charged past, filling the air with mist and thunder. With the tide only an hour past full flood, waves still peeled off the sides of Tremble Rock and rampaged into the inlet. Half-way to the far shore I could see white water flung into the air by rips and whirlpools.

Someone once watched these rapids around the clock for a complete moon cycle, painstakingly noting the time and height of the tides. Such observers were hired by the Canadian government to record tides all over the coast, providing the foundation of local knowledge on which the tide tables were built. But for all their careful columns of numbers, predicting the tides has never become a precise science. Hydrographers have a saying: all tides are local. On this coast their science is confounded by so many local variables, their punctilious plotting of sun and moon is knocked cockeyed. Wind, water temperature, ocean currents and even salinity can warp the tides out of their predicted pattern. Usually the deviations are too small to notice, but for a tugboat with a tow, a twenty-minute shift in the time of slack water in a place like Nakwakto can bring disaster. The bottom of these rapids is said to be paved with spilled logging equipment.

The most dangerously capricious tides occur in slots like the Outer Narrows of Slingsby Channel, where the ebb piles directly into the ocean swells. Constantly changing sea conditions strongly influence the tides in these places. The worst of them is perhaps Lituya Bay in Alaska, where the early French explorer La Pérouse lost twenty-two men who made the mistake of expecting the tides to behave predictably. They were sucked into the breakers by a twelve-knot current and two of the three boats were never seen again. The officer in charge of the surviving craft said they were caught by an unforeseen current that wasn't there when they sounded the narrows on previous days at the same stage of tide. "It must be inferred," he wrote, "that the violence of the current was owing to some peculiar cause, as the melting of snow, or strong gales of wind, which had not reached into the bay, but unquestionably blew with violence in the offing."

A decade later Captain Vancouver's men were surprised by the tide in Loughborough Inlet. In the middle of the night they "were hastily roused from their repose by the flowing of the Tide, which had risen so much higher than they expected and rushd upon them so suddenly, that every person got completely drenchd."

In Vancouver's day any Indian who committed such a blunder would have been laughed out of the village. Tides were the ground-swell rhythms of the coastal natives' lives for 10,000 years, and they clearly knew how to foretell their times and range. But how? The ebb and flow of the sea on this coast is far too complex to predict by a simple reading of the moon. We'll never know; the aboriginal knowledge or intuition, or whatever it was, has not survived. Indians read the tide tables like everyone else today when setting their nets and digging for clams.

Nakwakto is never still. In the six minutes of so-called slack, when the tide changes direction, vagrant currents wander about as if uncertain which way to go. And the surface is broken by patches of nervous water that tremble as though hit by shock waves from beneath. Around the canoe, kelp fronds hung straight down for only a moment, then streamed away on the beginning of the ebb. Eddies the size teacups formed along the outside of the kelp bed. Across the narrows the inlet appeared to be sloping to the left and sliding sideways out to sea. Paddling over to Tremble Rock, I let the tide take the canoe down, snake-fashion, on the sinuous course of the currents. Half-way through the rapids, the view opened on the left into Schooner Channel and right into Slingsby Channel, a swath of rumpled silver leading straight to the afternoon sun. I bore left, past two green knolls marking the site of another Indian village, perhaps an outpost of Tigwaksti, built here as a fishing station. Everywhere on the coast, tidal rapids were known by the Indians to be places of spectacular abundance, like cold upwellings at sea. Farther back, at the edge of the woods, a fisherman's shack sagged in the underbrush. Someone had taken the windows, leaving black sockets staring out to sea.

Below the abandoned village I moored to a bulb at the edge of a kelp bed and tied a silver spoon onto my fishing line. I had to be quick; the rapids were picking up speed, yawing the canoe. I flipped the spoon upstream and let it sink as it came down on the current. Instantly, a fish struck. The rod bent and jerked violently, then straightened as if the fish had slipped the hook. This was to be expected of rockfish, which are not esteemed for their fighting qualities. But supper was my interest, not sport; without ceremony,

I hauled in a silvergray rockfish. I threw it back, and two of its bony brethren, before a copper rockfish lay in the bottom of the canoe, olive brown, washed with a lovely copper-pink and yellow. I clubbed it and twisted out the hook, keeping well clear of the spines on the back which inject a toxin that causes pain as bad as toothache.

I had trouble getting loose from the kelp. The current had gained speed, increasing the drag of the canoe so that my mooring was pulled far underwater. Every time I hauled up on the line the canoe sheared dangerously across the current, and I had to let go before the knot was within reach. With no way of replacing it, I was determined not to cut the rope. Again I tried, hauling line fast (an awkward business when the canoe is pointing downstream and the rope is behind you) until the shear wave hissed uncomfortably close to the gunwale. Throwing a quick turn of the line around the thwart, I reached as far as I dared over the stern and slashed with a knife through the kelp. The rope snapped free and the canoe lurched crazily to the opposite side, teetered then righted itself and shot away downstream.

Once into Schooner Channel I felt the tension drain from the pit of my stomach. Nakwakto was no place for mistakes; if I had dumped the canoe or swamped, I'd have lasted only minutes in the frigid water that is brought up from the depths by turbulence. Drifting with the three-knot current, I lay back in the sun and dozed.

The seaward end of Schooner Channel opened onto the maze of islands and reefs where Dick Hansen had wisely declined to venture with the *Ocean Endeavour*. To the west the approach to the channel was blocked by Murray Labyrinth, a cluster of precipitous islands, standing black against the late sun. Ahead, to the southwest, the way seemed clear. But through binoculars I saw the telltale swirls of white where shoals lay hidden. In the salty parlance of the *Sailing Directions*, this was "foul ground."

I turned left into Allison Harbour and soon wished I hadn't. It is a pinched kind of place, long and narrow, shelving up from a muddy bottom at its end to a patch of boggy ground. Rainforest rose like a wall from the water, shutting out all sight of the open sea, the sunset and the surrounding hills. Going slowly, I searched in vain for traces

31

of the store that was here until the early 1950s. The buildings must have been towed away, or perhaps they collapsed and the forest repossessed whatever clearing there had been. Even a bit of open ground for a camp was hard to find, and I had all but given up when I came upon a granite point near the head of the inlet.

Allison Harbour was a place of eerie stillness. No sound came from the sea, so far from the open water. Few birds sang, and even they fell silent as soon as the sun had set. I moved away from the hiss of the fire and sat, listening. At first I heard nothing. But tuning my hearing down, I began to catch the understorey of sound – the tiny spit and crackle of shoreline exposed by the falling tide; the friction of water on rock; the faint scratch and click of insects; perhaps even the stir and sigh of growth and decay. These are the base notes that give depth and texture to the soundscape. They are also the first sounds drowned out by man-made noise which now throbs over much of the earth. Millions of people never hear these background sounds, never realize how impoverished the sound tapestry is without them.

Allison Harbour was alive with echoes. My journal from that evening reads: "Every sound rebounds from the trees across the water with startling fidelity. The crackling of the fire comes back as a large animal moving through the brush. A minute ago I caught myself tip-toeing around the camp, cowed to silence by the clang of pots and the crack of the axe. If I stayed here very long, I'd be talking to myself."

At dark the fog crept in, muzzling the echoes and clamping the inlet in damp silence.

Dawn broke slowly in the fog. Loading the canoe, I moved about with the flashlight long past the time of daylight on a clear morning. Overnight, fog rain had drenched everything not under cover including the motor, which I had neglected to wrap in plastic. Coughing and complaining through a dozen pulls on the cord, it started reluctantly, belching steam.

Outside Allison Harbour, I groped along the coast to a passage between the Southgate Group of islands and the mainland that would cut a mile off my route. At the entrance, the motor stalled in rafted kelp and I forced the canoe ahead with the paddle for another quarter hour, only to find the way blocked by a reef exposed on the falling tide. Backtracking, I took the long way around.

South of the islands, the chart indicated a deep bay, which I decided to cross. I turned into the fog and immediately lost sight of land. Steering a course by the set of the swells was easy enough, though I felt strangely disoriented. There was no horizon, or sensation of movement – unless I looked at the water by my side – or any sound, except for the directionless drone under my ear protectors. Space travel must by something like this; my world was my ship, bearing me on towards places unseen and unknown. A surreal bald eagle flapped out of the void, circled the canoe twice and faded away through lighter and lighter shades of grey. After a while I lost track of time; without any land to measure my progress, I seemed to be running on and on. Then, suddenly, kelp sprawled in my path and, farther off, an outline of cliffs and ghostly contortions of trees.

Close by another groups of islands, I shut off the motor and stood up to get the kinks out of my legs. The groundswell was down to a lethargic roll, gurgling in fissures under the rocks, without enough energy to make a breaking wave. I could hear a boat engine way out in Queen Charlotte Sound and, ever so faintly, what I took to be the moan of a foghorn. The chart decreed otherwise; the nearest lighthouse at Pine Island was nearly ten miles out in the sound, surely too far to hear. Such stillness was hardly what I expected, for I was smack in the middle of the coast of my nightmares, wide open to the swells of the Pacific. But close behind me was a reminder that this was no place to linger in a canoe. At the head of a cove on the island, a nearly vertical ravine was rammed full of driftlogs and smashed wood, thrown high above the tide by storm waves. I started the motor and moved on.

I was wary of the westerly that blows most afternoons at this time of year. Even a low swell could cause me trouble if I were forced ashore by the wind. There were no beaches – the sand was all to the north of Seymour Inlet – only steep pitches of boulders between the cliffs. A landing could be managed in bad weather by two people, one to keep the canoe off the rocks while the other unloaded. Alone, the best I could do would be to try to hold the canoe with an anchor while I unloaded. But a canoe anchor is necessarily light and certain to drag in even a moderate swell. Heavily loaded as she was, the canoe was certain to be holed if she came down off a wave onto the boulders, despite her double-thick bottom.

When the Indians travelled this coast two centuries ago, they were able to shelter behind a protective belt of kelp that grew parallel to the shore for hundreds of miles. The kelp put a damper on the waves, tripping the breakers and flattening the whitecaps. Although kelp is still unevenly spread over the coast, the sheltered lanes vanished at least a century ago with the disappearance of the sea otter, which was hunted to extinction in British Columbia for its pelt.*

Kelp and sea otters are symbiotic; otters feed on spiny urchins which, in turn, feed on kelp. Where there are otters, the urchins are kept to a minimum, and the kelp flourishes. Where there are no otters, the urchins graze the kelp down to bedrock, creating a kind of undersea wasteland known as urchin barrens, where little of anything grows. Much of the subtidal North Pacific has been in this state since the otters were exterminated.

In 1972 sea otters from Alaska were transplanted to the Bunsby Islands on the northwest coast of Vancouver Island, after two unsuccessful attempts. Following a decade of precariously slow growth, the colony has recently increased to more than 500 animals and expanded its range along the island coast. Urchins have virtually disappeared from the sea floor around the Bunsby Island and magnificent kelp forests have overgrown the barrens, providing food,

---

*The sea otter, *Enhydra Lutris*, is often confused with the river otter, *Lutra Canadensis*, despite marked differences in their appearance and habits.

shelter and spawning grounds for a vastly more diverse and productive community of life. On the surface dense rafts of kelp buffer the ocean swells and create a lane for travel close to shore. Given time, sea otters should find their way back to all their former haunts on the open coast. (They never inhabited the inlets.) However, they will never be secure as long as oil tankers – currently more than 800 a year – ply the waters off British Columbia. Even a minor sheen of oil on the water is enough to destroy the insulating capacity of the otter's fur, which is its sole protection against the cold. Otters are the only marine mammal without a layer of blubber. If their fur is soiled, they die within hours.

With the fog lifting I began watching for the entrance to Blunden Harbour, which opens to the south and is not immediately apparent when you are coming from the north. In fact, there was a second entrance, a backdoor through a narrow passage, leading directly to the head of the harbour. I tried it first, wallowing about in kelp and finding the passage high and dry. Laboriously, I hauled myself clear. This was not my day for shortcuts.

The front door, a mile farther on, opened onto twin islands that screened much of the harbour within. This is where the Nakwakto people came when they left Tigwaksti, settling in a village which they called Ba'a's, across the bay from the entrance. As I rounded the islands, the site revealed itself as a strip of shell sand, gleaming white in watery sunlight. A photo from about 1900 shows six traditional Indian houses built close together along a boardwalk with steps running down to the beach. Long before Ba'a's was abandoned in the mid-1960s, the old houses had fallen and been replaced by a row of split-cedar shacks. Now even these were gone – burned, it is said, by the government – and the site was overgrown with native crabapple, berry bushes and tall stalks of pink fireweed. Massive roof beams and a thick adze-scalloped post jutted out of the bush above the beach, the only visible remains.

In their last years here, sickness and alcohol wore the people down until they were too few to call themselves a village. They had no school, and access to health care was difficult. For these and other reasons – mainly administrative convenience – the Indian Affairs department pressured them to move to Vancouver Island. When they left Ba'a's, the Nakwaktos had dwindled to four families. A little more than a century before, the Hudson's Bay Company had placed the Nakwakto population at just under 2000.

It is easy to understand why the Nakwakto people were reluctant to leave this place. The harbour, dotted with small islands, narrows attractively to a passage leading to a tidal waterfall and a lovely salt lagoon. On either side of the village the forest steps back, leaving a verge of tall grass. On a solitary islet an Indian burial box is cradled in the spreading arms of a spruce. When I paddled beneath, the wind was soughing through the tree, gently rocking the coffin. No wonder the Indians were appalled by the missionaries' suggestion that they bury their dead in dank holes in the ground!

At low tide the flats in front of Ba'a's go dry across to the twin islands. This was the village larder; clams keep a steady stream of water jets rising over the beach. From my camp on the midden shell in front of the village I watched as the tide came in. Eight great blue herons spaced themselves along the shallows, still as stones. An osprey hovered, fixed in the sky like a kite on a string. Where the seagrass creased the water, an Arctic loon surfaced with a fish wriggling in its bill, then released and recaptured it twice, like a cat playing with a mouse. The osprey plunged, missed, and rose again, shaking silver from its wings.

When I remember Blunden Harbour I think of red-throated loons. They come in high and fast from Queen Charlotte Strait, circling and calling overhead in a staccato *gork-gork-gork* which echoes across the flats. Then they make their long descent, winging three or four times around the bay, calling and calling as they come down to a landing as smooth as a rocket returning from space. Male and female often land far apart and carry on a dialogue that draws them gradually together. Back and forth across the bay, pairs con-

36

duct a rapid antiphonal chant, locking their voices together in tight oscillation, like Eskimo throat singers.

In the afternoon an old black fishing boat anchored in front of the village and a young woman rowed ashore in a yellow plastic dingy with two small children. They picked berries for a while and then she came along to my camp. She was fair-skinned and freckled, but with the features and rusty tinge to her hair of a coast Indian. We talked about the weather and the berry picking and then she asked: "Do you have permission to camp here?"

I knew that many of the old village sites were now closed to visitors without authorization from the Indian bands that own them. I didn't know whether Ba'a's was one of them. I waffled: "Well, I'm staying out of the village – I have no interest in digging or taking anything."

"But do you have permission to camp here?" she insisted, polite but firm.

"No," I confessed, "but no matter where I camp in British Columbia, I'm on Indian land." I was referring to the fact that the provincial government has refused for more than a century to concede that the Indians have rights to the land, despite Indian treaties in every other Canadian province and territory. The British Columbia government resorted to racist legislation and, in more recent times, a series of rearguard actions in the courts.

I offered to move my camp. "No, no, that's okay," she said, "I just wanted you to know that we still think of this as our village."

Her name was Colleen Hemphill, and her great-grandmother had lived in Ba'a's. That evening she came ashore with her husband, Bob, and his mother, Marion MacGillivray, a short and very merry Kwakiutl. We sat by the fire and talked about what had become of the Nakwakto people since they moved from Ba'a's to a new village called Tsulquate, built on the edge of the town of Port Hardy on Vancouver Island.

"The problem at Tsulquate," Bob said, "is that people from several different abandoned villages were thrown together there. It has been very hard for the people who came from here to keep any sense of themselves as a distinct community."

37

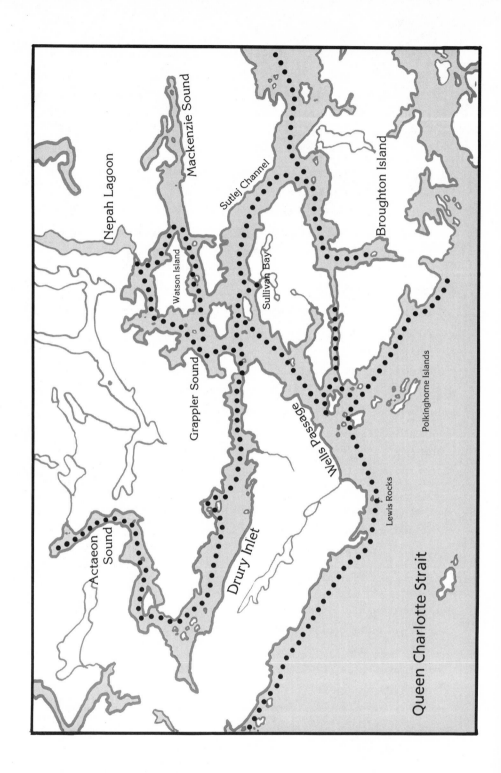

38

"They're outvoted when they want to do things their own way," Colleen said. "They've lost control of their lives and there's a lot of frustration and social problems. Some of them talk about moving back here, but it's too expensive. And there's no way to make a living."

Like many Indian people, Colleen and Bob live in a never-never land between the bush and the city. They tried Vancouver for a few years. She went to university and he did courtroom sketches for a television newscast. ("The news is mostly trivia, and they think it's the whole world.") But they found the city cold and unfriendly and they went back to Port Hardy, where he has an art studio and she is an advisor on Indian local government. They have thought about moving into Tsulquate. "It would be nice to live amongst our own people," Colleen said, "but you lose a lot of your privacy." They have never lived in a place like Ba'a's, yet they sense some roots here that have been severed from their lives. They talked about building a cabin in the old village, "a place where we could come weekends – it's so beautiful here, so peaceful."

At dusk Colleen rowed out to the boat and came back with three tins of salmon, lightly smoked and home-canned. They contained thin strips from the salmon's belly, the richest and tenderest part. I hoarded the last tin until the very end of the trip.

At first light I left Ba'a's, paddling quietly so as not to wake Bob and Colleen, asleep on the deck of their boat. At the islands, I looked back; the shell beach glowed a dull bone colour, and the mast light on the boat made a pinprick in the fog.

4

Ten miles south and east of Blunden Harbour a chain of treeless islets called Lewis Rocks steps out from the mainland into Queen Charlotte Strait, marking the division between two strikingly different kinds of country.

Drifting by the outermost islet, I looked across an immense sweep of ocean and island on three sides. Low on the southern horizon the islands enclosing the bottom of Queen Charlotte Strait melded together in a line of monotone grey. Across the strait to the west, Vancouver Island dipped northward over the horizon until only the highest hills could be seen, thrusting like shark's teeth from the sea. To the northwest, towards the open Pacific, the Deserters Islands hung in supension over a horizonless sea at the edge of the fog. Southeast to northwest, all was seascape, the land pushed back and flattened to insignificance. The fourth side, to the east, was all landscape – ridges, points, bluffs, peaks – thrown together in a convulsion of forest and stone and ice. There seemed to be no room for the sea, and yet, unseen in the deepest creases of the land, inlets probed to the feet of the faraway mountains, cloud-lost and brooding under their snowfields.

Imagine Vancouver Island as a fat 250-mile-long cigar lying parallel to the British Columbia mainland. The southern half and a bit at the north end are separated from the mainland by the open waters of Georgia and Queen Charlotte straits. In between, a bump on the cigar presses towards the mainland, pinching the waterways. Now, fill this constriction with several thousand islands, large and small; carve up the land with six long inlets and a maze of arms, sounds, channels, passages and lagoons; dump in four sizeable rivers and countless lesser streams, and you have the most confused and confusing stretch of coast on the entire North Pacific. This was the country I would travel for the next two months.

A line of rain squalls was approaching from the southeast, blanking out the islands at the bottom of the strait and drawing a slanting grey curtain over the mainland. Wind came ahead of the rain, ruffling the leads of still water within the kelp rafts around the canoe. Three black oystercatchers circled the islet and struck out across the strait, trailing a skein of shrill calls. Pulling on raingear, I struck out for Wells Passage, the northernmost entrance to the labyrinth ahead. Inland now, the mountains were fast disappearing under lowering cloud. Already, at the heads of the inlets, rain would be hissing down through the cottonwoods, raising mist over the glacial water. I had mixed feelings about this country. While I would be rid of the groundswell and perpetual summer fog of the outer coast, the inlets would be oppressive if the weather turned bad, with days of straightdown rain and dank stillness. I hoped for a break from the weather: a hot dry summer.

In the middle of Wells Passage wind and rain came scudding over the waves and flicked my battered cowboy hat into the water. I clapped it on again, taking a cold shower down the neck, and steered for the shelter of a loose group of islands south of the passage. In their lee, the wind fell off, though the rain came down harder. It was time for a dry camp and a fire, but the islands were inhospitable knobs of granite, mop-topped with runty timber and salal. I started the motor and set off on a long search for a camping spot along the south coast of Broughton Island. Doubling back after three or four miles, I followed the shore all the way round to Carter Passage on the north side of the island. On and on through the rain I went. Nowhere could I see a place to haul out the canoe and make even the smallest of camps.

The chart, as usual, was not much help. Charts are for tugs and fishboats and yachts, not for people who have to go ashore to lie down every night. They don't differentiate between beaches of sand, rock or mud, and they care even less whether the ground above is overgrown or clear. Charts become really valuable only after you have made the trip and marked in all the things they don't tell you.

I turned back into Wells Passage, intending to look into Tracey Harbour, farther inland on the right. There was said to be a logging camp in Napier Bay, at the head of the harbour; maybe I could pitch there on a float for the night. Approaching in mid-channel was a salmon troller, idling towards Queen Charlotte Strait with his poles spread like skeletal wings. He was standing in the well at the stern, puffing on a pipe. Staying outside his lines, I hollered across to him, asking about Napier Bay.

"No, there's nothing there," he yelled back. "They moved over to Hopetown Pass. That's their show you can see up on top." He pointed to a raw gash of new logging, high on a ridge several miles inland.

If Napier Bay was like every other abandoned logging camp I'd seen, it would be a mess of cable, oil drums and derelict machinery. I decided to pass it by; better to sleep like a beast in the bush than to spend the night in a garbage dump. Running beside the troller, I had dropped back beside mile-long Dickson Island, which I had already searched for a camping place. Now, on its north side, facing onto Wells Passage, I noticed a thread of water leading between the cliffs and a row of treed islets. I shut off the motor and coasted into an opening barely wider than the canoe. Inside, around a blind corner, was one of those invaluable places worth marking on a chart. Tucked between the cliffs and one of the islets was a pocket of deeper water leading to a granite sill that sloped gently into the water, making an ideal canoe haul-out. There was dry wood, shelter from all winds and plenty of room for a camp. The only drawback was a complete lack of cracks in the rock where stakes could be driven to anchor the tarp, which I used as a lean-to in preference to a tent. No matter; I would anchor it to gear boxes and boulders, if I could find any.

Late that afternoon I paddled through the passage behind the islets and found myself looking onto Queen Charlotte Strait. The sun had come out and flat-bottomed clouds drifted north in the wake of the rain. Away off towards Vancouver Island, a toy seiner inched south on a glassy sea. From behind me I heard a loud chittering. A flock of sanderlings swept round the shoulder of the island with a rush of wings and shrank to a wavering cloud of pepper on the horizon.

Two miles out in the strait I paddled into the Polkinghorne

Islands, an aggregation of reefs and lesser islets clustered at the side of a long, rugged island. It seemed a good place to fish for my supper; the chart showed a bottom of shoals and drop-offs, the sort of ground favoured by cod. And kelp sprawled in every direction, also a good sign. At the first of these kelp beds, I lowered a cod jig over the side and stripped line off the reel until it found bottom. Winding in two or three turns, I began jerking the rod up and down to make the jig twirl and flash erratically, like an injured herring. After only a few pulls a fish hit and I heaved up on the rod. Instantly, a geyser of spray erupted behind me. I spun around and braced for the heavy pull and reel-screaming run of a big fish: this was the typical flight of a coho salmon, dashing to the surface at the first prick of the hook. But the spray had hardly settled when I saw that I'd been fooled by a harbour seal which had been lying hidden in the kelp fronds and had bolted when the canoe drifted almost on top of it. Meantime, the rod was still jerking, and I reeled in a rockfish too small to keep. Twisting the hook free with the gaff, I watched the fish angle down into the kelp forest.

The flight of the seal had probably sent the cod into their hiding places, where they would be difficult to entice with an artificial lure. I moved on to another group of reefs and lowered the jig. Ten, twenty, fifty times I worked the rod up and down. I took in line and moved into shallower water. Still nothing. Then I heard the breathing – a wet, wheezing sound, somewhere very close. At last, I spotted the seal, hiding under a mat of bulbs and fronds, given away by the movement of its nostrils, opening and closing with each breath. I slapped the paddle hard on the water, setting off not one but four simultaneous eruptions in the kelp and a fifth in the open water behind me.

On the way to the next kelp bed, two more seals joined in the fun, and all seven followed close behind the canoe. I shouted and beat on the water, but my antics only encouraged them. Even before I dropped the jig over the side, I could hear breathing all around me, like a dirty phone call in the night. This, I knew, was an unwinnable game. I turned back towards the camp, weighing the relative merits of tuna with rice, or rice with tuna.

Although I regretted the cod, it was good to have the seals around. They would enliven many an empty mile in the days ahead. Only a decade or two ago they were scarce and wary all over the coast.

Harbour seals were hunted for bounty in British Columbia waters from 1914 to 1964. The kill averaged about 3000 animals a year and more than doubled in the Depression when the $2.50 bounty was one of the few sources of cash on the coast. Despite the bounty, their numbers held steady at about 40,000 until a commercial hunt for pelts began in 1963. Five years later, when the hunt was stopped by the fisheries department and seals were given legal protection, their numbers had plunged to 12,000. They have since multiplied to about 80,000, which is thought to be close to their aboriginal population.

The bounty was originally offered in the mistaken belief that seals and sea lions make serious depredations on salmon stocks. Steller sea lions were bountied a year before the seals and suffered even worse abuse. After 1940 the Canadian airforce bombed and strafed sea lion rookeries, and the navy shot them up for artillery practice, ostensibly as a wartime emergency measure in aid of fishermen. But more than a decade after the war, the military was still pounding away at the rookeries. In 1958 the fisheries department mounted machine guns on the foredeck of some of its bigger patrol vessels and for the next eight years hit every major rookery on the coast. By the time the slaughter was outlawed in 1968, the Steller population had dwindled from more than 13,000 animals to about 3500. Unlike the seals, they have never recovered.

To some extent the Stellers have been replaced by a northward movement of California sea lions into waters around southern Vancouver Island, where they were almost unknown before the 1960s. This migration, combined with the increase of harbour seals, has revived the cries of the fishing industry (which now includes a powerful lobby of sportsfishermen and resort owners) for a kill. But this time there is a difference. Analysis of the scats of seals and sea lions has revealed that no more than ten percent of their food is salmon. These findings won't mollify the fishing lobbies, whose real agenda, behind a smokescreen of specious concern for salmon, is to rid themselves of competition from seals and sea lions. Sportsfishermen become irate when seals appear and the fishing goes off, and many commercial fishermen are quick to shoot seals or sea lions that take fish from their lines or foul their nets. With or without scientific justification, there could still be another round of slaughter. Politics, not science, will decide.

Sundown brought a sharp change in the weather. As I paddled in from the Polkinghornes, wind patches appeared on the water and rapidly joined to form waves. The fogbank in Queen Charlotte Sound broke apart, sending towers of mist up the strait, like tall ships with fire in their sails. The sun went down red behind the hills across Wells Passage, and the temperature plummeted. I pulled on a sweater and paddled hard to outdistance the needling cold at my back. The wind was out of the northwest, bitter as the ice fogs of the Aleutians. On Dickson Island the waves slapped at the base of the cliffs, jostling into the narrow passage. The canoe bounced through the cross-chop at the entrance, rounded the bend and glided soundlessly into the still pool. The first bright stars in the night sky trembled on the black water.

I sat late by the fire that night, snug in my pocket of granite. An entry in my notebook reads: "The din of the waves is hushed to a whisper here, and the gale overhead barely stirs the flames. I'm eating bannock hot from the frying pan with soup and sharp cheddar cheese that's getting green around the edges and tasting better every day. Across the pool firelight flickers eerily over the cliffs. It's easy here to conjure up ancestors huddled in awe around the first captive flame."

I wondered about the seals out by the Polkinghornes. How did they pass a night such as this? Rocking half asleep in their kelp rafts behind the islands? Or shivering on the reefs in fear of killer whales? In fact, no one knows more than the barest outlines of these animals' lives. Yet we killed them for fifty years on the presumption that we understood how they fitted into the natural order.

The bounties on seals and sea lions were by no means the first in British Columbia. Wolves and cougars were bountied as early as 1869, and the list expanded steadily over the next fifty years. Hawks and owls were trapped and poisoned in the name of protecting game birds, and bald eagles were shot to preserve salmon.* By the turn of the century strychnine was being widely used against coyotes, wolves, cougars and golden eagles.

In the late 1940s the B.C. Game Commission decided that the bounty system wasn't killing off enough animals. Moreover, wolf scalps and cougar ears had a way of getting out the back door of the game department, to be claimed for bounty again and again. Beginning in the winter of 1949 a campaign of extermination was launched against predators in general and wolves in particular. Pellets of meat impregnated with a deadly new poison, 1080 (sodium fluoroacetate), were dropped from airplanes onto muskegs, frozen rivers and lakes all across the northern and central regions of the province. The scale of the program was enormous. By the mid-1950s hundreds of thousands of baits were being scattered around B.C. every winter from nearly 2000 "poison stations." In the spring the pellets that had not already been eaten by wolves, birds and any number of other species floated down the rivers and washed ashore on the lakes, spreading their deadly and persistent toxin on and on through the ecosystem.

---

*While British Columbia encouraged the shooting of eagles, it never offered a bounty, as did Alaska. Between 1917 and 1953, 130,000 bald eagles were killed for the 50-cent (later raised to $2) reward. Long before the bounty was lifted it was known that eagles on salmon streams feed almost exclusively on spawned-out fish and do no damage whatever to the runs.

The Game Commission decreed that the only animals worth preserving were livestock, fur bearers and species classified as game. Everything else was dismissed as "noxious vermin." In the 1960s growing environmental consciousness checked but did not end the poisoning. Today, guides and ranchers still use poisons, and the Wildlife Branch (which replaced the Game Commission in 1963) continues to wage war against wolves and other predators.

All through this century of killing, new species were being introduced into the province. British gentlemen farmers imported songbirds, deer, game birds, hares and fish in an attempt to create the ambience of English country life. Complaining that the Pacific salmon would not rise to the fly, sportsmen introduced English brown trout and Atlantic salmon. Most introductions followed a pattern common for exotics, flourishing for a time and then dropping to remnant populations or dying out altogether. Others, like the Atlantic salmon, never caught on, despite dozens of transplants of fry and eggs from New Brunswick and Scotland. We can count ourselves lucky; Atlantic salmon carry diseases unknown on the West Coast, and the transplants were carried out without quarantine.

Most of this tinkering with nature was pointless as well as dangerous. But in a few cases, introductions had the potential to fill a gap in B.C.'s fauna. Lobsters, for instance, were not to be found anywhere in the North Pacific, and ten unsuccessful attempts were made to transplant them from the Atlantic. A report survives from the first Canadian effort (the Americans had their own failures) in 1895. Six hundred lobsters were trundled across the country for seven days in a refrigerated railway car, swaddled in seaweed and ice against the summer heat. At New Westminster, the surviving lobsters (more than half had already died) were hurried aboard a tug that was to carry them out into Georgia Strait. But the Fraser River was in flood and, in the words of the report:

"We steamed over 100 miles from five o'clock in the morning til nine at night but could not find the water sufficiently salt anywhere. The whole Straits of Georgia being quite high coloured with floating sediment from the Fraser River."

47

They ended up at Nanaimo, on the far side of the strait. Some of the lobsters were enclosed in a net, where they soon died, and the rest were dumped over the side, never to be seen again. Subsequent transplants were more sophisticated, though no more successful. Finally, in the 1960s, the fisheries department made a last do-or-die attempt at a place called, prophetically, Useless Inlet on the west coast of Vancouver Island. More than 5000 lobsters were flown from the East Coast and for two years they went through all their normal life stages, breeding, moulting and hatching young. But the young died off quickly and the older lobsters in the basin dwindled by attrition. After three years the experiment was laid quietly to rest. Bureaucracies bury their dead without ceremony.

I went to Fatty Basin to film the experiment on a cold day in the winter of 1967. My one clear recollection is of a mink on a floating log, eating a lobster that must have cost the taxpayers of Canada $100 a pound.

While the lobster transplants were failing, another potentially useful introduction, the Japanese oyster, was succeeding, perhaps too well. When seed oysters were first introduced from Japan in 1914, they were not expected to reproduce in the cold local waters. The idea was simply to raise them to maturity and sell them in place of the native oyster, which was too small to be commercially valuable. And so it went, seed coming from Japan year after year, until the hot, dry summer of 1932 when the waters of Georgia Strait became unusually warm and the oysters spawned freely. In 1942 the warm oceanic current, El Niño, moved north off British Columbia, causing the oysters to spawn again, this time much more heavily. Then in 1958 another El Niño resulted in a huge spawning that plastered Georgia Strait with oysters from one end to the other. It was hailed as a magnificent gift from nature, but the jubilation may have been premature.

In a remarkably short time Pacific oysters have become the dominant species on miles of Georgia Strait shoreline. Succeeding generations grow on the shells of their precedessors, accumulating layer on layer until most of the intertidal zone is densely covered.

Experience elsewhere suggests that the shell will accumulate indefinitely, forming "oyster reefs" a yard or more deep, where the community of plants and animals is reduced to species that can co-exist with oysters. And there could be even more unwelcome changes in the making.

As a youngster in the early 1950s I camped with my father on a sprawling expanse of flawless sand on Marina Island in upper Georgia Strait. Thirty-five years later I returned to find the beach clumped with mussels and sea lettuce growing almost solidly in the tidal watercourses and more sporadically on the higher, dryer parts of the flats. Turning up the mussels I found that they were all rooted to oyster shell – half shells, fragments of shell and live oysters. It was probably brought to the beach by boaters, who shucked the oysters and threw the shells overboard. Some of the shell undoubtedly carried small oysters, which have grown and multiplied. Now, the once-lovely beach at Marina is probably doomed, and there is no telling how many others will follow. Certainly all but the biggest, most exposed beaches (where oysters don't survive the waves) are at risk. So far, oysters have not spread north of the cold tidal rapids that form a temperature barrier against drifting spawn at the top of Georgia Strait. But sooner or later they will be planted all over the coast on shell discarded by boaters. No doubt they will thrive; oysters grow as far north as Ketchikan, Alaska. And they will likely reproduce, as well, in some of the shallower, warmer lagoons. Unfortunately, the predators (especially the oyster drill *Purpura clavigera*) that could check the inexorable spread of the oyster were left behind in Japan.

The fire was down to embers and it seemed a bother to scrounge in the dark for more wood. The lean-to, I decided, was not worth the trouble of putting up; the westerly blew unabated, a sure sign of good weather. Spreading my mattress and blankets on the rock, I was gone in minutes into deep space beyond the waning moon.

Nothing brings a person to his senses like cold rain in the face at three in the morning. There was no warning, no preliminary drizzle, just a few fat drops and then the cloudburst. Cursing my sloth, I groped for the flashlight and stumbled, bare ballocks, into the rain. There was no point even dressing; my rainsuit was stuffed somewhere into the bottom of a pack and my hat . . . well, God only knew where it might be. Certain of a dry night, I'd left the gear scattered everywhere. I found a poly sheet in a puddle in the bottom of the canoe and threw it over my bed. Barking my shin on the grub box, I pulled the gear together in a heap, tore it apart again to retrieve a tarp from the bottom of the pile, rebuilt the mound and covered it. Boxes on either side of the blankets raised the poly sheet enough to let me crawl under. Things were a bit soggy, though I slept soon enough and woke only once; the poly had sagged and the rattle of raindrops on the plastic sounded like someone making popcorn on the side of my head.

The day did not begin auspiciously. I awoke in a puddle. Without a groundsheet (more sloth) the foam mattress had sopped up water streaming down the slope of the rock. The unanchored tarp had blown half off the gear, soaking a chart and one of my notebooks, now turning to mush. At least the rain had stopped. I boiled coffee and built up the fire until steam rose from my wet jeans. A bright spot appeared overhead to the east and quickly opened a rent of yellow sky in the clouds. When the sun came out, I spread clothes and bedding to dry, then opened the soggy chart by the fire and went over the route ahead. I'd go first to Sullivan Bay, six miles to the east. It was certain to be a pesthole of yachts at this season, but there would be a phone to call home. After that I would turn back to the northwest, into Drury Inlet, in search of a former Czech freedom fighter who fished there for prawns.

The day was looking more promising.

5

At first sight Sullivan Bay appeared to be a place of some consequence. Acres of floats and spanking white yachts took up much of its east side. But as I drew closer, it became apparent that there would not be much left when all the boats had gone south for the winter. Inside the point on the left was a small store, a cottage, a fuel shed and a public laundry, all on floats. Except for some fuel tanks in the trees behind the store, there was nothing on shore.

Forty years ago Sullivan Bay was one of those names that young men dropped into the conversation to show they had been up the coast, where the real loggers logged. It was a gyppo community, bustling year-round, with a store and post office and even, for a while, a restaurant. The Union steamships called here on their weekly trips through the raftcamp country. But with the eclipse of A-frame logging by fly-in camps, the gyppos departed for greener slopes, and Sullivan Bay had little reason to exist. Today, a few loggers and fishermen still come in for their mail, and the liquor outlet – a counter at the rear of the grocery store – stays open all winter. Now it's a drowsy sort of place, except in July and August.

In all those acres of floats, I could see no place for a canoe to tie up. The few open berths were for paying customers; even as I looked for a spot, three more yachts were turning in from Sutlej Channel. I tied at the fuel dock and was digging out my gas can when one of the newly arrived yachts swung in towards the space I was occupying. It reversed hard, then maneuvered back and forth, revving its engines and kicking out a lot of sternwash. I stuffed my puny can back in the canoe and pushed off. Out on the very end of the seaplane dock, I found a place to slip in behind the float.

Sullivan Bay tries hard for the ambience of the suburban yacht club. White trousers, deck shoes and peaked caps with gold braid for the men. Lounging suits and designer sunglasses for the women, worn to backdeck coffee klatches, while the men are out fishing. To which has been added an overlay of cutsey-poo: floats with names like Spud Row, Herring Strip, Hoochie Row, and buildings labelled Santa's Summer Sack (once a gift shop?), Sullivan Bay Brig (wooden bars in the windows) and Fish Alley (the fish cleaning shed). The sign on the scale is, of course, Weightwatchers. The boats are mostly from Seattle and Portland, with a few from San Francisco and points south and one, unaccountably, registered in Blackfoot, Idaho. Many are more than 100 feet long, million-dollar cream puffs with calfskin furniture, rosewood bars, home entertainment consoles and navigation equipment that would do credit to an ocean liner. Some of the biggest yachts function as floating hotels, berthed here for the summer for fly-in fishing parties, mostly from Seattle. Many have speakers for their radio-telephones mounted outside, and the air crackles with the mindless roger-wilco chatter that men cannot resist whenever they have a chance to play with a two-way radio. I had tuned it out, like a radio commercial, when a panicky voice boomed over the floats. A sportsfisherman had hooked a halibut "at least a hundred pounds" somewhere out in Queen Charlotte Strait. He wanted advice on how to get it into his runabout. Instantly, the airwaves were jammed:

"Don't bring that thing in the boat. It'll break your legs"..."Have you got a gun?"..."You gotta tow it into the beach and kill it with an axe"..."No, the line will bust"..."You got a knife? Stab it in the head"..."Lasso it around the tail"..."Naw, you gotta get the rope through the gills"..."Even if you think it's dead, it can still break your legs"..."No foolin,' those things are strong...."

Several boats offered to come to the fisherman's aid, but he vanished from the airwaves and was heard no more. There followed an extended debate about landing halibut and a final word, expressing what was on everyone's mind: "He must have lost it. Otherwise, he'd be on the air braggin' about it."

On a float near the head of the bay, I found Pat Finnerty, the proprietor of Sullivan Bay, unloading cedar planks, ferried on a raft from a portable sawmill anchored nearby. His hands were streaming blood from cuts inflicted by the broken strands of a rusty steel cable.

"It's nothing," he shrugged, "I couldn't find my goddamned

gloves." An intense man in his forties, Finnerty has a deeply tanned, mobile face that clouds with anger or creases with laughter in an instant. The planks were for new floats he was building to expand the marina. We were standing on one of them. "A float like this would cost $75,000 built by a contractor," he told me. "That's because of the goddamned unions. Who the hell can afford that?" He spoke in machine gun bursts, his temper flaring up and dying like a grass fire.

He took me on a tour of the marina, which was filled nearly to its capacity of 100 yachts. I observed that most of them were from the United States. "Ninety-nine percent American," Finnerty said, "and I'd just as soon the Canadians didn't come at all. They're so goddamned cheap, they complain about everything and they won't spend a cent. The sailboats are the worst. If they come in and say anything like 'Look at all the Yanks,' I tell them to get their goddamned ropes off my floats and get the hell out of here right now. If it wasn't for the Americans there wouldn't be a goddamned thing on this coast."

The store was a madhouse, packed with boaters shopping early before the fresh fruit and vegetables sold out for the day. Fishermen were buying wine and whiskey by the case. Everything was priced in Canadian money and the customers all paid with American bills, credit cards or traveller's cheques. Pat Finnerty's wife, Lynn, behind the one cash register, calculated the exchange and wearily explained it to customer after customer. Although I was loath to burden her further, I wanted to call my wife, Carole, on the radio-telephone, which was behind the counter. After three tries she reached the operator, who added my name to the list of callers waiting for a free line to Vancouver. A half-hour later my call went through. There is no privacy on a radio-telephone; while only Carole could hear what I was saying, she could be heard by anyone on the coast who happened to be tuned to the same channel. In the store her voice blared from a speaker.

"So where are you anyway and why haven't you called?"

I glanced around; everyone was listening. I wanted to yell, "She's only kidding." Instead, I turned my back on the audience. We caught up on mutual news for a minute or two and then Carole said, loud and clear:

"Listen, why aren't you here to perform your bedroom duties?"

"Hey, you're on the public airwaves," I hissed into the phone. This just encouraged her.

"Boy, do I need you. Right here, between the sheets."

There were sniggers behind me. I didn't mind the hundreds of anonymous fishermen and tugboaters listening in, but the live audience made me cringe. "I'm in a store," I told her, cupping my hand around the microphone. "There are a lot of people here."

"Well, that's their problem. If they don't like what they hear, they shouldn't be so damned nosy."

"I know, it seems like a long . . ."

"Little man, you get your butt home here or I'm going to start inviting in some of those fishermen who are listening."

There were fond farewells and a promise to call more often. I hung up and turned to face the audience, itching to explain: Carole is no tough ball-buster; she's gentle and kind and likes to make jokes. But everyone was pointedly occupied with their shopping.

I was late. I'd been two hours waiting in line for groceries, gas and the phone in Sullivan Bay, and now the wind was beginning to blow. Crossing Wells Passage ahead of the worst of it, I nipped into the shelter of Stuart Narrows, island-clumped and pinched in the middle like an hourglass. With the motor shut off, the tide whisked me through and into the lee of Leche Islet, where I stopped to reconnoiter Drury Inlet, stretching ten miles of wind-hammered silver to the west. Drury is an anomaly among coastal inlets, which almost without exception open to the *west* and run back into the mountains. Drury's mouth faces *east*, while the head of the inlet is just over a low rise of land from Queen Charlotte Strait, where the wind was now whistling in from the Pacific.

I put on a full suit of raingear, despite the warm afternoon. To make any progress against the wind I would have to use the motor, and that meant getting a snoot full of spray. For a short distance beyond the island the tide held back the waves; then the current slowed and soon the canoe was burying her foredeck in the white-caps. Although the canvas cover shed the water, spray was caught up by the head wind and thrown back in my face. It found a gap no bigger than a Looney dollar at the throat of my jacket and poured in, soaking my chest and dribbling unkindly down to my crotch. Two miles along the north shore I turned in gratefully to Jennis Bay, a crescent of sheltered water, screened from the inlet by an island that nearly fills its mouth. Two sailboats with Canadian flags snapping in their rigging were anchored on the left, taking refuge, perhaps, from the wrath of Pat Finnerty in Sullivan Bay. To the right a floathouse slumped crookedly on its waterlogged raft by the side of a log dump. Nestled behind an islet straight ahead was a white building (a workshop, not a house, as it turned out) on a float piled high with oil drums and prawn traps. Atop a brushy bank a house of cedar shakes looked comfortably out from the shade of an alder. This was the home of Milan Pesicka, the prawn-fishing Czech who, it was said, had fled his homeland only a jump ahead of the Russians in 1968.

I climbed the stairs from the beach and went round to the back of the house, past a small vegetable garden that was doing poorly, except for lettuce and the ubiquitous zucchini. A blonde woman in her late twenties came to the door and introduced herself as Pam, Milan's wife. Her eyes were blue and her skin as clear as porcelain.

"Milan is up at his traps, but he'll be back pretty soon," she said. "Come in. I'll make tea."

While her two girls, aged one and three, tumbled around me, Pam talked about the train of events that brought her to Jennis Bay. She came west from Ontario in the mid-1970s, a flower child straight out of high school, and drifted into one of the hippie havens on Texada Island in Georgia Strait.

"I was working in a bar and going nowhere fast until I met Milan.

He had a boat. Neither of us had any ties, so we lived on board and just wandered around the coast."

For the next four years they led a gypsy life, digging clams and fishing for a living. The boat was cramped and damp. And so, seven years ago, they moved ashore in Jennis Bay in the last surviving house of a one-time logging camp. Somewhere along the way, Pam got religion. The house reflects her peregrination: macramé on the walls and Biblical injunctions posted over the sink.

We heard the sound of an outboard and Milan skimmed into the bay in a herring skiff, an open, flat-bottomed aluminum boat, twenty feet long and half as wide. Running wide-open almost to shore, he turned with a flourish and cut the motor at the last second. Clean-shaven and natty in an Icelandic pattern ski sweater, he didn't look like a fisherman just coming off the job. He had a cherubic hand-someness, round-faced and brown-eyed, with a deep tan and wavy chestnut hair. Up at the house he peeled down to a purple singlet and jeans and prowled the house in sock feet, looking for beer. Aside from recently bottled homebrew, still green and yeasty, there was only one store-bought bottle, which he downed in a few gulps.

I asked about Czechoslovakia. Milan looked embarrassed. "Actually, I wasn't in Czechoslovakia when the Russians came. I'd just finished high school and I was on holiday in Paris. I was enrolled in a film school in Prague and I wanted badly to go back. But the door was open all over the world for Czech refugees, so I just got on the magic carpet and came to Canada."

After nearly twenty years in this country, Milan still speaks with a trace of an accent, which gives him a faintly cosmopolitan air.

"For years I was ashamed of how I got here and I guess that's how these stories about freedom fighters got around; I didn't want to talk about it. But I can see now that I was just a kid and it was a tough decision." Because his father was an officer in the Czech air force, Milan knew when he came to Canada that he might never see his parents again. "I didn't realize then how much I hurt my parents. Parents love their children. Children just love themselves. At that time when you left an Iron Curtain country without permission, it was final. For my parents, it was like I was dead."

Pam called us to dinner and Milan passed around a joint before we sat down. Pam took a couple of drags, pulled her chair up to the table and bowed her head to say grace.

Milan wanted to be a journalist when he first came to Canada, but his English wasn't good enough. Instead, he drifted west to British Columbia in the early '70s and got caught up in the back-to-the-land movement. Six families joined together to pre-empt a homestead at the head of Toba Inlet. They cut cedar shingles and shakes for sale, fished prawns and salmon, and tried their hand at farming.

"The land was really good but just about everything else went wrong," Milan recalled. "Grizzlies killed the animals, and the women were always afraid for the kids. The road got snowed in so deep we couldn't get out half the time. I was away fishing all summer and couldn't keep things together. A few of us were busting our asses and the rest of them were sitting on theirs."

After three years the families quarrelled and the community collapsed. Milan lost everything except a herring skiff and a small engine.

"I had no tools to start anything else and I was flat broke. I spent all that winter camping on the beach under a tarp and digging clams for beer money. But, you know, I liked it. I got an airtight heater and I'd close the tarp all around and get in there with a good book and a bottle of rum and have a damned fine time."

There was a caged restlessness in Milan. All through the evening he kept jumping up and pacing the floor. Repeatedly, he searched the same cupboards for beer before settling for homebrew and two more joints.

Milan has a twelve-year-old daughter, Rebecca, by a previous marriage. When I arrived, she rowed me to shore from the float where I tied the canoe. She talked easily and handled the boat with skill; she was in her element. Now, when I tried to talk with her, she was painfully self-consicous. Shyly, she told me that Jennis Bay was fine, but she wanted to be with other kids her age and go to a regular school. When Rebecca had gone off to bed, Pam spoke quietly: "We're worried about her. She's a year behind in her correspondence studies and she really should have some friends her own age. If she stays here she could grow up to be a country bumpkin."

Milan would like to send her to spend a year or two with his mother in Czechoslovakia. "This is a good place for young kids," he said, "but there comes a time when they have to get out. When I look at the people around us, I think of Thomas Mann's *The Magic Mountain*. Everyone here is living in a kind of sanatorium where you don't have to deal with the real world."

Nearly hidden by a group of islands at the head of Drury Inlet, reef-strewn Actress Passage leads into Actaeon Sound, which twists away to the north. Prawns and shrimp move through the passage on their migrations between the inlet and the sound, making it a productive though difficult place to fish. Prawn traps are easily snagged on the jagged bottom or swept away by the current. Milan fishes here because nobody else wants to. The reefs and tides are his defence against the big freezer boats that roam the coast with a thousand or more traps, cleaning out the prawns wherever they fish. They avoid tight places, like Actress Passage, that steal their traps and cramp their juggernaut style.

Anchored in a cove part way through Actress Passage, Milan has a makeshift float of logs and an old tugboat, which he uses as a home-away-from-home while he's working his traps. When I tied alongside I was assailed by the stench of putrid fish wafting from buckets of bait which were "ripening," as Milan put it, to better attract the prawns. We loaded bait into the skiff and ran out into the middle of the passage, where he hooked up a buoy marking the end of a line of traps. Holding the boat into the current to take the tension off the line, he started his winch – an ingenious contraption of car parts and scrap metal, held together by rope, wire, and inner tube – and the drum rumbled into motion. As each trap came over the side, Milan shook the prawns into a bucket and stuffed bait into a wire basket inside the trap. Anything else caught in the trap – mainly small crabs and sea stars - went into the basket and was smashed down with a stick so its odour would spread through the water and attract the prawns. He doesn't relish this part of the job.

"This is a butcher business. I feel sorry for all the little creatures that have to die to get those precious prawns. I've been meaning to look into getting some kind of artificial bait. But of course something has to die to make that too because it all comes from some animal or fish."

Milan re-set the line, running into the current and spreading the traps as far apart as possible to avoid tangles. The dozen traps had yielded more than twenty pounds of prawns and shrimps, a very good haul for the season. The prawns would bring him $3.25 a pound, the shrimps a dollar less. The next two lines were more typical of mid-summer; ten pounds in one and almost nothing in the other. It was a far cry from springtime fishing when the traps come up heavy with jumbo prawns and there are sometimes glorious $600 days.

Milan uses only 130 traps. "If I go beyond that, the fishing runs downhill pretty fast. I guess it cuts into the breeding population. But I wonder whether it's worth protecting. One of these days, I know, someone is going to move on me and clean this place out."

While we were at the lines, a chunky ketch-rigged sailboat putted slowly into the passage and tied alongside Milan's tug. She was dark green, with a lot of varnished woodwork above and *Runaway Girl* painted in script across the transom. Milan took me aboard to meet Mason Gray, a round ball of a man with a pot belly and bullet head bristling with silver hair, shorn almost to the scalp.

"Mason has come for a little party we have every year," Milan said.

"We're going up to the head of the sound to eat prawns and drink a few beers with Walter Rudd [the watchman at a dormant logging camp]. Would you like to come along?"

"Sure," I said, "but I feel like a freeloader with nothing to contribute."

"Oh, hell, don't worry about that," Milan said. "We've got everything; I supply the prawns, Mason buys the beer and Walter takes care of the bullshit. What more do we need?"

Mason sat me down at the galley table while he split cedar kindling on the floor with a hatchet, in preparation for making tea. He did everything with great deliberation, lighting a fire in a tiny cast-iron stove, pumping water and warming the teapot, talking all the while about his life as a seaman, or sailor, as he prefers it. In the 1920s and '30s he fished for cod out of sailing schooners in the Aleutians. When the war broke out, he got a chance to crew on a four-masted square-rigger out of Seattle, taking a load of lumber around Cape Horn to South Africa. The ship had no auxiliary power and was possibly the last American commercial voyage entirely under sail.

"The ship's agent told us there was a chance we wouldn't get paid." Mason chuckled at the understatement. "But I wanted to sail around the Horn, so I went anyway. Of course, there was no money when we got to Durban. But by that time America was in the war and I was in no hurry to go home. I was having a great time – the beaches are beautiful there – until the U.S. Consul put up the money to send us back to the States." In a framed photo on the cabin wall, Mason stands before the massive main mast of the square-rigger, swaddled in old-fashioned foul-weather gear. He sported a pencil mustache and wore eyeglasses with small, black rims which gave him the appearance of a young James Joyce.

Every year in April Mason sets out from Seattle and sails north, taking several weeks to get to Alert Bay, the home base for his summer cruising in the inlets. "If the wind isn't right, I just wait a day or two until it is. I'd rather not use the engine. I like to sail." It is late September or even into October before Mason heads south again.

We heard the distinctive drone of a Beaver floatplane and stepped out on deck to see it bank over the cove and disappear beyond the point on its landing run. It had come to take Milan's prawns to Vancouver Island. He stood on the edge of the float, listening, and not until he heard the plane touch down did he lift the first sacks of prawns out of the water. Time was critical; the longer the prawns are exposed to air, the lower the rate of survival. And there is no market for dead prawns. Working quickly, he shook the prawns gently into plastic tote boxes and loaded them aboard the plane. Within ten minutes of the time it landed, the Beaver was airborne again. In Port McNeill, across Queen Charlotte Strait, the buyer would be waiting to rush the prawns to tanks of sea water.

Late in the afternoon Milan's ponderous tug brought us to the logging camp at the head of Actaeon Sound, an assortment of trailers, workshops and trucks thrown together on a shelf of gravel cut out of a hillside. There were no houses, gardens or other signs of settled habitation, though the camp had been here for decades. The place was deserted, except for Walter Rudd, who lived in a floathouse near the head of the dock. His bullhorn voice came down to meet us:

"Machinegun the bastards on the beaches. If you let the sons-a-bitches get a foot in the door, you'll never get rid of them."

Walter was pronouncing on events of the day, in this case the illegal immigration of Sikhs who recently landed in lifeboats on the east coast of Canada. When we stepped inside, he was sitting across a big slab table from Mason, facing the open door, a can of beer clamped in a hand the size of a rump roast. He ignored us.

"Sure they'll let 'em stay, gutless bloody politicians. You wait and see, they'll breed like rats and the whole damned tribe will be on welfare. And who's paying for it? You and me, that's who."

Walter is cut from the whole cloth of logger legend: rough, tough, hard drinking and loud talking. Over six feet, he has arms like stovepipes, a big square face, bulbous red nose and jaw of stubbled granite. His wiry grey hair stands up where no comb appears to have passed in living memory. Despite his sixty years and sagging gut, Walter is still a formidable man.

Without the niceties of introductions, he barked at me, "Now what kind of bullshit are you going to put in this bloody book?" Mason, had wasted no time in telling him what I was up to.

I had been primed for this moment by Milan. "Walter likes to be outrageous," he warned me, "but it's all bluff, and he's really a pretty good guy. Give the old bastard some of his own, then he'll respect you."

But there was no need to fend off Walter. Before I could say anything he was already back on the immigrants, only this time they were "goddamned DP's [displaced persons] all wanting to get into the best country on earth." Milan, who had brought two beers from the kitchen, took this personally. "Maybe you'd talk a different line, Walter, if someone was pointing a gun at *your* fat head."

"Look," Walter said, thumping the table, "there's five billion people in the world and it's only going to be seven years before there's six billion and they all want to come here."

"Ah, come off it," Milan scoffed, "this is a big country and there's all kinds of room."

"Huh," Walter snorted, "They've been saying that ever since Jacques Cartier arrived and they'll still be saying it when we're up to our necks in immigrants."

Abruptly he jumped up and turned on the television. "Oh, shit," he said, "I missed it." Walter is a current affairs junky, hooked on television news and a dozen magazines and newspapers that arrive every ten days on the float plane with his mail and groceries.

Mason, who doesn't see a newcast for six months at a time, was grinning slyly at Walter. "You know, Walter," he said, "I hope they've got TV in hell so you can still get the news when you're dead."

"So do I," Walter trumpeted, "so I can be watching when they hang that son of a bitch of a president of yours."

Walter sat down and packed a wad of Copenhagen snuff inside his lower lip. Unlike most users of snoose, as the loggers call it, he didn't spit. Every half hour or so he packed in a fresh wad and washed the noxious juice down with beer. I was in awe; my one encounter with chewing tobacco was followed within minutes by a spectacular eruption of puking.

Milan set a kettle of steamed prawns in the center of table and everyone fell to. Everyone except Walter. He called his dog, a brown nondescript in tangled sheep's wool, in from the float. It sat beside a tortoiseshell cat and the two of them waited with perfect decorum to be fed. Walter picked out the biggest prawns, shelled them meticulously and fed the cat and dog by turns. They ate slowly, daintily, for twenty minutes before they'd had their fill. Only then did Walter shell the first prawn for himself.

Milan had been chewing all this time on the immigration question. "You know, Walter, all this stink about immigration really comes from the unions because they're scared shitless of competition from people who aren't afraid to do a day's work."

This was a red flag for Mason. "Now just a minute. All you people from Communist countries are the same. You're against the unions because you've never been in one."

"So what, I know what the unions do to a guy who wants to . . ."

"You know bugger all. I worked hard for forty years and if it wasn't for the union, I'd be sleeping under a bridge somewhere." Mason pays only thirty dollars a month for his room in a Seattle retirement home run by the seamen's union.

Walter is also a good union man. "Mason's right, all you DP's are the same. You're hardly off the boat and you want to change the country. The unions aren't the problem. It's bringing people in from countries where they don't live like we do. Hell, they come here and live like rats – fifty people in a house. No wonder they work for less!"

"Yes, that's right," Mason sighed, "the niggers have ruined America."

I slept on the floor of one of the camp trailers, close to the open door, away from the bunkhouse stink of cigarette butts and damp mattresses. It rained in the night, hammering down on the aluminum roof. In the overcast dawn, I prowled the workshops and trailers, killing time until Milan got up. A notice from the camp superintendent was posted on one of the doors:

RECREATION ROOM CLOSED
UNTIL FURTHER NOTICE

The memo beneath spoke of "unacceptable behaviour" and "damage to company property." Mixing boredom and beer, the loggers had smashed the place up.

Milan surfaced, a bit subdued but in good spirits, and we started down the sound into the rising sun. I marvelled at his recuperative powers; he'd downed nine beers (the cans were lined up like soldiers in front of him) and smoked two joints by the time I left the party. He talked of going back to Czechoslovakia for a visit now that the political climate was changing, but didn't sound very serious about it. "I'm pretty content right where I am. I must be because I've been here seven years and, with my character, that's a long time." I wondered if Milan knew how inexorably the odds were stacked against him: a five-fold increase in prawn boats and a seven-fold rise in the catch in the past ten years. Every fishery on the coast was being ground down to a subsistence level.

The last clouds drifted east, and I sat out on the front deck, drinking in the rain-washed morning air. Down through the pellucid water, schools of fingerling herring flashed away from the boat.

"It's too nice a day for pulling traps," Milan announced when we tied up at his raft. "I think I'll go home and take the kids to the lake for a swim." Some of the prawn lines had already been down three days, a day longer than they should have been. He threw a few things into the herring skiff, swung out of the cove and disappeared between the islands, flying so fast and lightly over the water that his boat scarcely left a wake.

64

6

On the north shore of Drury Inlet an eagle soared over a bluff on the first updrafts of the day, then broke off its circling and dwindled to a speck across the inlet. I paddled on and had forgotten about the eagle when I chanced to look up at the bluff, now very close. Backlit against the shadows in the trees, two tufts of eagle down descended in slow circles through the golden morning air and landed, curved side down, just in front of the canoe. As I passed between them, the feathers turned and began to sail, like tiny coracles, on a breath of air too faint to stir the surface.

I felt that I had received a benediction. The spreading of eagle down on the water is the most ancient and universal symbol of peace and welcome on the northwest coast. In 1774 when the Spanish explorer Juan Perez blundered onto the Queen Charlotte Islands, his ship was circled by two Haida canoes, each with a chief dancing in the bow and spreading eagle down on the water. My welcome was less grand, but appreciated nonetheless because I was having one of my doubting mornings, an aftermath perhaps of Mason's beer. Was I going to the right places, doing the right things? Or was this trip all a silly self-indulgence that would end in nothing? I took the eagle down for the good omen it was and my spirits soared, though I could not have said why.

Outside Stuart Narrows I stopped to talk with a man from Bellingham, Washington, who was filleting cod on the back deck of his yacht. When I stood up to stretch my legs, I saw that he had five big plastic tubs heaped with fish, many times the legal limit. He was filling his freezer with a year's supply. When I observed that he had taken quite a haul, he stalked into the cabin without a word and closed the door.

I turned north into Grappler Sound and landed beside a white cliff that leaned past the vertical, high over the water. An apron of smooth pebbles ran round its base, providing the first good canoe haul-out since Blunden Harbour, other than the stone shelf by Dickson

Island. The Indians must have beached their canoes here and they would certainly have given the place a name, though, not surprisingly, the chart was blank at this point. Charts, I was coming to realize, are not just about coastal geography; they also make a statement about the difference between European and Indian experience of this coast. Nearly all the white man's place names were superimposed on the country from elsewhere, paying homage to friends, patrons, ships, race horses, actresses, pets, poets, mistresses and fondly remembered parts of the homeland. (Some have a fine, if unconscious, irony. Simoom Sound gets its name via a British troopship from an Arabic word meaning hot, dry wind. More than a hundred inches of rain pelts down on the sound every year.) The original Indian names conveyed something about the place itself: "the forest where bark gets peeled in the spring," "where the seagulls hatch" or "spring salmon feeding close to the cliffs." Other names were purely descriptive: "the creek where there is grass when the tide goes out" or "marks on the rock like a school of herring." Many of the names were onomatopoetic, echoing some natural sound like a waterfall or wave breaking on the beach. Every cove and point and hill and even the reefs and shoals under the sea had their names. Taken together, they documented a relationship to the coast which was altogether distinct from the white man's.

Europeans saw this coast as an opportunity to trade, or fish or log and, all going well, to settle down in a new homeland. But if things didn't work out, they could always move elsewhere. For the Indians, there was no elsewhere; land and identity were inseparable. Every tribe saw itself as a distinct people, made only in its traditional territory. Loss or destruction of the homeland was tantamount to self-destruction, and the land and sea were therefore known and valued – and named – with an intimacy that Europeans have never experienced here. Protecting these traditional territories was a network of private ownership which covered every square yard of the northwest coast from goat hunting tracts in the back-country mountains to the rich longshore fishing grounds and out to sea as far out as the eye could see. What was owned was not the land or beachfront or cod reef itself but the right to hunt, pick berries, fish or gather whatever the territory produced. These were not so much rights of private property as authority for the chief to *direct* the use of resources in order to conserve the fish runs and rotate harvesting pressure throughout the homeland. The governing principle was mutual dependence between man and nature. Felling a tree or catching a fish was an act of spiritual exchange, to be done with restraint, humility and gratitude. The Indian was given physical sustenance in return for releasing the spirit of the tree or fish to invest the next generation. Waste, greed or abuse of a creature or its habitat would annul the covenant and deprive man of the things he needed to survive.

Well before the end of the nineteenth century, Indian ownership was swept aside by the European idea that anything not nailed down was common property. First come, first served was the new ethic. The result is illustrated by the fate of the great salmon runs, the mainstay of the native economy. Despite widespread use of weirs that were capable of intercepting every fish and destroying the stocks, the Indians had sustained the runs for centuries. Yet less than twenty years after the white man's canning industry began, the catch on all the major salmon rivers peaked and went into permanent decline; the Sacramento River by 1883, the mighty Columbia by 1895 and the Fraser in 1901. Cannery operators in Alaska fenced off the mouths of rivers with gillnets, decimating every major run in the southeast part of the state by the turn of the century. Meanwhile, Indians in British Columbia were forced to destroy the last of their weirs in 1911 because, it was said, they were damaging to the runs.

With everything up for grabs to the first-comer, like the man I had seen stuffing his freezer with cod, the abundance of the coast is fast disappearing. For the commercial fisherman, the struggle to survive has put a grim face on what was once an attractive way to make a living. There have been ugly confrontations on the beaches between rival gangs of clam diggers. "Creek robbers" seine illegally in remote estuaries, extinguishing remnant races of salmon in a single set of their nets. Debt-ridden fishermen build bigger and faster boats in a fleet already ten times over capacity. Even in remote Actress Passage, Milan Pesicka lives in the shadow of competition that could destroy his livelihood.

Whenever I stopped in some nameless cove or creek, I wondered what the Indians called it and what the name would have told me about the place. Almost all that knowledge is gone. Even the few aboriginal names that survive have lost their meaning for most of the Indians, whose native languages were suppressed in church-run residential schools. For all but a handful of the oldest people, the ancient voices of the land have grown faint.

At the head of Grappler Sound I paddled through a narrows into Kenneth Passage, which bends around the north side of Watson Island to the mouth of Mackenzie Sound. My plan was to by-pass the sound because it contained a fishing lodge and many tourist boats, and return to Grappler Sound through Hopetown Passage south of Watson Island. Along the way I hoped to find Henry Speck, an Indian artist who lived in the passage.

Kenneth Passage is cut deep between hills of fir and hemlock which give the country a darker, bolder green than the bilious cedar forests in the western reaches of Drury Inlet. Its turnings between the islands open sudden vistas of distant points and ridges. On the north side I detoured into a cove to investigate the sound of falling water and a line of foam rushing from a break in the shore. The gap opened into a tumble of rapids bounding down a boulder staircase under overarching trees and a shroud of mist. This was Roaringhold Rapids, the outflow of Nepah Lagoon, one of the largest tidal basins on the coast. Thirty years ago a young man from a logging camp in the lagoon attempted to shoot the rapids, rather than wait for high slack. In the backwash where the waves piled into the sea, his boat capsized and he was drowned.

At the east end of Watson Island, in the narrows leading to Hopetown Passage, the water turned brick-red, obscuring the bottom just a foot or two beneath the canoe. The cause was a plankton bloom, thickest at the pinch of the narrows and thinning gradually as the passage opened to the west. This was my first encounter with the so-called red tides, though I had heard warning bulletins on the ship's radio on the trip north from Vancouver. The danger was slight – only two or three of the more than twenty different types of red plankton render shellfish poisonous – but there is no telling the safe varieties from the lethal ones by sight. Travelling alone, I couldn't risk a dose of paralytic seafood poisoning; clams had been off the menu since the beginning of the trip and would not be restored for another six weeks.

Where the plankton thinned and finally disappeared I passed three islands on the north side of the passage, each flagged as former Indian village sites by a topknot of berry bushes. Behind the islands was Hopetown Village, consisting in its entirety of six houses – four yellow, one bright blue and the newest and biggest unpainted – standing in uncut grass between a beach of shell sand and the beetling brow of Watson Island. On the rock tip of one point, a splash of colour resolved itself into wreaths of plastic flowers arranged inside a cedar shelter, bearing the inscription:

1887-1979
Chief Fred Williams
'Sheltered in the Arms of God'

This was the backwater where Henry Speck had carried on a successful career, far removed from the galleries and commissions that have lured many other Indian artists to the city. I was arriving unannounced – after failed attempts to reach him by radio-telephone – and uncertain of my reception; someone living in such isolation might well be jealous of his privacy. On the float a man was helping a boy rig a fishing rod. I asked if Henry Speck was in the village. "You're lookin' at him," he said, grinning broadly.

We sat in the sun on an overturned boat, talking about the train of events that brought him to Hopetown. "It was the usual thing – there was a woman involved," he chuckled, crinkling deep creases at the corners of his eyes. "My wife is from Hopetown. When we came here the village had been slowly dying for years. There was only one house left – that little yellow one down at the end."

The big new house is Henry's. He has been doing very well; everything he produces sells readily and he is often working against a backlog of orders.

"Of course, I was pretty well established as an artist before I came here. I started carving and painting in Alert Bay and after a few tough years, I had no trouble selling my work. But time became the problem – too many interruptions – and I had to get away someplace where I didn't know so many people."

In moving to a small village, Henry was returning to his roots. He grew up in Turnour Island, one of the villages shut down in the 1950s by the centralization mania of the Indian Affairs Department. The edict still rankles.

"They just forced us out. Sure, there weren't many people left, but we liked it there. It was our home. Some of our people had a lot of problems after they were moved. Problems with alcohol, families breaking up. And it was all unnecessary, nothing but a power trip by Indian Affairs."

Two boys and a girl sauntered down the float and joined us; any visitor is a novelty in Hopetown. Henry introduced them as his children, and they asked me a lot of questions, making small jokes with a self-assurance surprising in kids who live in such isolation. They were tanned to dark mahogany and wore identical white T-shirts, silkscreened in one of Henry's intricate designs. He looked pale beside them, his skin nearly white from long hours working in the studio. His thinning hair is curly, his nose flattened and bent and his squat frame retains the bunched strength of the logger. Unlike some of the best Indian artists, who were trained in their craft from childhood, Henry worked in the bush for many years and became an artist only when his employers wanted him to move away from his home country.

Walking behind the houses, we passed a patch of rank grass with a trace of base paths where the kids had been playing scrub. At one time every coastal community had such a field: any ball hit out of the infield was a homer and the game was much delayed by wrangles about ground-rule doubles and infuriating searches for the ball. "Yeah," the oldest boy said, "we lost the last ball we had. We're going to get another in town."

Henry's studio was a small, impeccably tidy room facing south towards greening slopes of logged land a mile across Hopetown Passage. Prints and masks lined the walls and his many carvings-in-progress took up much of the space around the perimeter of the floor. An elegant loon's head, painted turquoise, orange and black with green abalone shell eyes, lay drying in the sun by the open window. Henry took a mask down from the wall and showed me how the loon's head fitted on top. "I was up until one-thirty this morning working on this," he said. "It's for a guy on a yacht over at the resort."

Glowering from the back wall was a beautifully carved and painted Crooked Beak of Heaven, one of the biggest and most spectacular of the masks used in the Kwakiutl winter ceremonials. I said it brought to mind a Crooked Beak carved by Willie Seaweed of Blunden Harbour, the Kwakiutl master carver who died in the 1960s. Henry didn't take this as a compliment. "People have said that before, but I don't copy Willie Seaweed. I have my own style."

Backpeddling hastily, I explained that I meant that the rigid design conventions of traditional northwest coast art can make the work of one artist look similar to another. It's a creative box some artists have found so restricting that they are driven wild with frustration. I asked Henry how he solved the problem, but the question had no meaning for him; the old rules are his strength and his inspiration, the codex that carries the wisdom of ancestors. From his perspective as traditional artist, the significance of a mask or painting lies not only in its originality but also in its effectiveness in invoking insights and emotions shared by his people. The expression is *tribal* rather than merely *personal* as in the European tradition. The West Coast artist Emily Carr came close to the matter in describing a D'Sonoqua (Wild

Woman of the Woods) mask she saw in one of the Kwakiutl villages: "The power that I felt was not in the thing itself, but in some tremendous force behind it that the carver believed in."*

"I asked Henry about his printmaking. In the early 1960s he was one of the first northwest coast artists to make silkscreen reproductions of his paintings. I remembered a series depicting creatures from Kwakiutl mythology, and later, a number of complex, brilliantly coloured designs, two or three of which were displayed in the studio. "I haven't been painting much, " he said. "Carving takes up all of my time."

Henry's eldest boy brought in a half-finished Hokhokw, the huge supernatural raven mask used in the Kwakiutl cannibal bird dance cycle. It was carved with absolute assurance, and the pencil layout of the unfinished parts flowed over the wood so cleanly that it seemed to be printed. Beaming with pride, Henry's kids stroked the silky cedar and sniffed its exotic scent of old growth. The mask is a potent metaphor for the presence of evil in the world; the Hokhokw cracks the skulls and eats the brains of people lured to the house of the cannibal at the north end of the world. Henry grew up in the presence of old people who still felt the power of these symbols. But what force could they have for his children or their generation? Wasn't it the function of the artist to recast the old symbols in contemporary terms before they die away? We talked around these things and didn't get very far. Henry saw no need to reinterpret. What mattered was respect for tradition, fidelity to the old forms. He pointed to the impressive cultural revival taking place in Alert Bay, the heart of the Kwakiutl nation. "The young people are rediscovering their past," he said. "They will understand it."

On the wall over Henry's work table hangs an enlarged colour photograph, actually a poster, of a group of Kwakiutl men in ceremonial dress, most of them in their sixties or older. "That's my grandfather, Jack Peters," Henry said, indicating one of the elders. "Those were strong men."

---

* *Klee Wyck*. Toronto. Clarke, Irwin & Company, 1971, p. 36.

They were the survivors, the last of the men who brought the Kwakiutls through the anti-potlatch laws, the assaults on the language, the influenza epidemic of the 1920s, the affliction of alcohol, the daily affronts of official and unofficial racism and the despoilation of their traditional homeland. They had faced extinction – the Kwakiutl population didn't hit bottom until the late 1920s – and lived on. Now, most of them were dead, though the picture had been taken only a few years earlier.

With the Kwakiutl population now growing rapidly, I wondered if other people might move back to Hopetown, or perhaps to some of the other abandoned villages. Henry was doubtful. "It costs too much to build a house out here, and unless you've got some way of making a living like me, you'd have to be away working a lot of the time. No, I can't see it happening."

The new houses in Hopetown create a false impression. With the exception of Henry, the few families hang on a thread of seasonal fishing and unemployment insurance. The village could die at any time. If it does, a period of habitation longer than many of the cities of Europe will be broken. "Some people from the university excavated back there beyond the ball field," Henry told me. "They went down through more than two thousand years of old fires and tools and I'm not sure they ever got to the bottom. People have been living here for a long, long time."

On the way out I asked the kids how they were passing their summer vacation, and they pointed to a stack of video cassettes. *Bridge on the River Kwai* was the favourite; they had screened it at least half a dozen times. Two of the boys came along to see me off and we marched down the float together, whistling Colonel Bogey.

The traditional Indian art of the northwest coast has a message for our age. Running like a spine through the melded images of man and beast is the insight that all life is indivisible and interdependent. The identical insight is the foundation of the modern science of ecology, but there the similarity ends. Ecology is an academic discipline, often compromised by economics or politics, while the Indian belief was a way of life, all-encompassing, consistent and uncompromising.

For the past century the Native land-use ethic has been cooped up in tiny reservations. Now it may well be revived through land claims suits currently before the courts. Indians have a strong case in law and history, especially in British Columbia, where no treaties have ever been signed with the federal government.* Some bands have declared their intention to replace our system of common property ownership with control by hereditary chiefs on their tribal lands. They would like to manage their resources holistically, linking responsibility to opportunity. The privilege of catching fish, for example, would be tied to conservation and rehabilitation of salmon streams. Logging would become husbandry, rather than merely harvesting, with the forest managed so as to preserve its biodiversity, not simply to produce wood. They intend to recreate a truly sustainable economy, which would exclude the absentee companies and bureaucrats that now exploit the environment under the oxymoronic rubric of "sustainable development." It would be a local economy, based on local knowledge and local control, with the benefits going to local people, both native and non-native. They have learned that control by outsiders leads to an exhausted environment, loss of autonomy and, when the chips are down, jeopardizes even their right to exist as distinct peoples.

In the past two decades British Columbia Indians have regained some of their lost entitlement to land and resources, especially salmon. But in their own communities the jury is still out on the question of whether they can return to the ecological sensibilities of their ancestors. After a generation of exposure to the consumer

---

* The British Columbia Supreme Court decision of March, 1991, dismissing all land claims of the Gitksan and Wet'suwet'en, was received by native people throughout the province as a devastating setback. But in fact, B.C. courts have almost invariably ruled against Indian rights, only to be overturned by the Supreme Court of Canada. It is widely believed in legal circles that the Gitksan-Wet'suwet'en decision will be substantially altered on appeal.

society, it remains to be seen whether the young people in particular can find their way back to the ethic of co-existence with nature still emanating from the intertwined images of traditional artists such as Henry Speck.

Poking along the north shore of Hopetown Passage, I passed islets rimmed with patches of white shell, spread like tablecloths beneath the overhanging cedars. Across Grappler Sound the brimming tide edged up the flanks of the white cliff where I had stopped that morning, drowning all the pebble beach save for a strip just wide enough to slide the canoe between the boulders. I made an awkward camp amongst the driftlogs, then scrambled roundabout through the woods to a perch on the clifftop. Dusk filled Hopetown pass and scaled the three red peaks of Mount Stephen, standing alone above the darkening hills like outriders from the Coast Range, miles to the east. Away in the far distance, towers of cumulus mushroomed over snowfields sprawled around the head of Kingcome Inlet, where I was headed tomorrow.

7

On the way down Sutlej Channel I braved the mob at Sullivan Bay, hoping for a loaf of homemade bread or some fresh fruit from the store. But I had been dawdling in camp and it was nearly noon. The store, of course, was sold out.

Around the point, boats were scattered all down the channel. I stayed near shore, keeping my distance from the traffic, until a thunderous convoy of thirteen yachts passed close as I cut across the mouth of a bay. Some of them slowed when they saw the canoe, and I waved my thanks, though they needn't have bothered. As long as I kept my distance and gave their bow wash time to flatten, the canoe

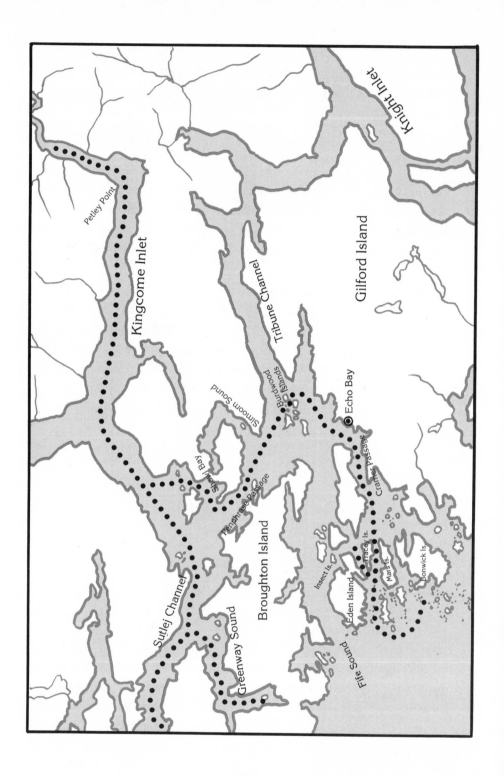

could weather any wave they put out. There was danger only in getting caught too close – as I was about to discover.

Doubling a point, I saw what appeared to be a converted sea-going tug a half-mile ahead. Through binoculars she looked beamy as a barge and very low in the water. Her upperworks gleamed with brass and mahogany and an American flag snapped at the mast. Tumbling ahead of her blunt bow was a wall of white water, peeling waves like breakers off to either side. The tug was well away from shore; even if she didn't slow down, there would be ample room to keep clear of her wash. I kept on, not paying much attention. Then suddenly, when the distance between us had closed by half, the tug changed course and angled sharply for the point I had just passed. I was trapped, too late to turn back and too close to shore to get away from the waves. I could only hope the tug would slow down; there was a man on the flying bridge who couldn't miss seeing a bright red canoe.

I turned towards the tug and shut off the motor; the impact of the waves would be less if the canoe was nearly dead in the water. The tug bore down fast and churned past at full speed, no more than twenty-five yards away. The man on the bridge looked down on me as if I were a piece of driftwood then turned away without a sign of interest. Waiting for the waves, I could see twin streaks of propwash jetting from under the tug's stern; two engines and two propellers were driving her squat hull through the water. As the waves came on, I felt like a body surfer looking up at a comber about to break on top of him. The canoe climbed the first wave, toppled over the crest and buried two-thirds of her length in the second. She rose sluggishly, streaming green water from the spray tarp and dumped an icy bucketful into my lap. Close behind came the stern waves, but they were mercifully flatter and only the front deck went under. Pitching in the backslop off the cliffs, I shook an impotent fist at the man on the bridge. He didn't even glance back to see if I were afloat.

My pants were soaked and water was squelching around in my rubber boots. And now it began to rain. I would have to beach the canoe and partially unload to get dry clothes. The next two miles of the Broughton Island shore offering no place to land, I turned into

Greenway Sound. Despite paddling hard, I was getting colder all the time. With the wind picking up and rain rattling like shot on the spray tarp, I was looking now for a place to camp. A floating resort came into view, promising coffee and shelter from the downpour, but I went on by. Another hour dragged past with no place to haul out before a passage opened on the right and I paddled into a nearly land-locked cove. Embedded in the mud bottom were two streaks of rusted iron, the remains of the rails for a boat haul-out, which I followed to the head of the cove and up onto a gravelly beach.

I threw up a lean-to, hung my things to dry by the fire and, thrusting dry socks into wet boots, went off to investigate what appeared to be an old homestead. The rails of the boat haul-out ended in crumbled rust at the base of a stone wall that had been built at a cost of great labour to shore up a bank of midden soil. The heavy boulders had been raised head-high, though many were now fallen and sinking into the slumping earth. Set back from the top of the bank stood three maples, strangling in English ivy, and farther back, in a depression where a house had once stood, tin cans rusted to filagree poked through the leaf mould. Beyond the house on rising ground, a half-dozen apple trees had run wild, trunks riddled by sapsuckers and branches sprouting grey leaves of staghorn lichen. Purple bear droppings, full of blackberry seeds and undigested apple, cobbled deer trails through the bracken under the trees.

The animals had been in possession of this little clearing for a long time – forty years at least – and yet I felt, as I always do in these forlorn places, like an intruder. Not an intruder in the sense of trespass and property, but an interloper, snooping into a diary of failure and abandonment. And back of the defeat were older, fainter echoes of hope and fulfillment in the stonework and cleared land; caring and love in the apple trees and the flower gardens gone to weeds; a dream of independence in the isolated cove. Futility was there in the bedrock bulging everywhere through the grass, and mocking irony in the fecundity of the clam beach, the only true and lasting potential the place ever had.

I turned over the garbage for some clue to the history of the homestead. There was nothing, of course; this is a secretive coast, where little survives the creeping mould. No parish chronicle of births, deaths and marriages was ever kept. Settlers usually arrived without official knowledge or assistance, scattering over the coast like straws in the wind. Usually, British Columbia was not even their first choice. Most immigrants landed first in the Prairies, Eastern Canada or the United States, where fares from Europe were lower and prospects for farming and work looked better than on the West Coast. But many of them drew bad land or crop failure, or discovered that America, The Land of Opportunity, was hard-nosed and co-opted by cattle barons, railways and coal capitalists. They came to British Columbia down on their luck and desperate, acting on information that was misleading or wrong, often willfully so. Many ventured onto the coast with no clear idea where they were going and only the most fanciful notions of what they would do when they got there.

Those who did come directly to the West Coast tended to be British and middle class, more at home in the Little England of southern Vancouver Island than rooting stumps out of the ground in some upcoast inlet. Homesteading was more likely to be the choice of workingclass people who laboured in mill or farm or logging camp to make a grubstake before they set out on their own.

I sat under the edge of the lean-to, making bannock and trying to imagine what chain of circumstance had caused the people who settled this cove to choose a place of so little promise. Were they seduced, like so many others, by romantic nonsense about the coast? In Britain before before World War I, they would have had access to a dozen or more "footloose in the colonies" travel books on British Columbia, written by gentlemen adventurers. It's hard to believe that these jaunty accounts of wing-shooting eagles and thrashing saucy Indians influenced many would-be immigrants, except in their glowing descriptions of the agricultural potential of the land. Francis Poole (no relation to the author) visited the Queen Charlotte Islands in the 1860s, and wrote that the arable land was "not only extensive beyond all present calculation, but rich beyond description and, better still, wholly unappropriated. It seems to be crying out to the personifiers of civilization, 'Come and farm me, and I will return you a hundredfold.'"

Published in a vacuum of accurate information about the region, such accounts contained just enough truth to make them credible, especially to someone down on his luck and looking for the New Eden. Small plots could indeed be cleared almost anywhere on the coast and the acidic soil conditioned to grow a variety of crops, but not in big acreages. It is gardening country, not farmland.

The provincial government did nothing to set the record straight because it was ardently courting immigrants from wherever it could get them. Every other province and the federal government had the same objective, and so, rather than compete, they joined together in a massive campaign to recruit immigrants from Britain. In his memoir, *Confessions of a Tenderfoot* (1913), Ralph Stock – traveller, journalist and sometime homesteader – described the scene in London at the turn of the century. The metropolis, he wrote,

> was plastered from end to end with flaring posters, representing fields of yellow grain and herds of fat stock tended by cowboys picturesquely attired in costumes never heard of outside the covers of a penny dreadful ....Unctuous gentlemen met you in the street with six-page pamphlets, imploring you to come to such and such an address and hear the fortunes in store for a man of initiative who would take the plunge and emigrate to Canada.

The pitch was cleverly designed to play upon the agricultural depressions, chronic unemployment and lack of social mobility that frustrated millions of Britons. The lush farm scenes of the posters – many of them beautifully executed – promised undreamed of wealth and independence with captions that hammered home the message: "Canada Offers Free Farms" . . . "Tremendous Crops in Western Canada" . . . "Happy Homes, Healthy Climate, Bountiful Harvests – UNDER THE FLAG," or simply "There's Elbow Room Out There."

80

Pamphlets featured letters sent to relatives in the Old Country from contented settlers in Canada. When the supply of letters was insufficient or wanting in fervour, hacks were hired in Canada to write effusive testimonials in the name of settlers. Successful immigrant farmers – "returned men" – were brought back to Britain and sent from town to town to extol the virtues of the Canadian soil and climate. Likely none of them had ever seen the British Columbia coast.

Although much of the propaganda put out by other provinces was truthful and sober in tone, British Columbia tended to inflate its claims. It was, of course, the most difficult province to sell; in addition to high fares and dubious farmland, the colonial clique of British merchants and gentlemen farmers wanted only the "right sort" of immigrant. The wrong sort were slum riff-raff, landless farm labourers and working men infected with radical notions about trade unions. Consequently, the government in Victoria closed the door on the mass immigration schemes that brought whole shiploads of working class immigrants into other provinces. Labouring under such restrictions, the province's Agent General in London, Malcolm Gilbert Sproat, felt the need to write a booklet for immigrants that grossly exaggerated British Columbia's agricultural potential. Working from imagination, he produced a map shaded in broccoli green to denote arable land where sheer-sided mountains plunge into inlets and the islands are solid rock. There is no telling how many immigrants set off up the Inside Passage, Sproat's official government map in hand, in search of the fanciful farmlands.

In the orchard at dusk a doe and her yearling fawn watched unafraid from the edge of the clearing when I came looking for apples. She was no bigger than a setter, dwarfed like deer on many coastal islands by inbreeding and overpopulation. The trees were barren, except for one still bearing a few runty apples, which I brought down with a stick. Between rain splits and scab, the yellow skin was starred with

81

the white spots of the Bellflower, an American variety from the past century.

The place had its charms. The cove was sheltered from all weathers, yet open enough at the mouth to frame the hills across the sound. A belt of clean sand lay between the gravel and the soft bottom at low water; there would be swimming here on summer afternoons when the tide rose over the hot beach. But none of these things put food on the table; whoever lived here must have had a thin time of it.

It made a world of difference *when* the settler arrived on the coast. In the early years good farmland was, as the advertisements claimed, free for the taking. But all the best, most accessible land was pre-empted before the turn the century, leaving latecomers to settle for hardscrabble homesteads like this one. Less than three percent of the land was arable, and much of that was put beyond reach of the immigrant by the profligate land policies of the government.

In 1883 British Columbia began subsidizing railway companies with large blocks of granted land. Sniffing a bonanza in the making, promoters incorporated more than 230 boondoggle railways, tying up over thirty-five million acres of grant land. An additional fourteen million acres were given to the Canadian Pacific Railway. And for good measure, the government alienated eight million acres in timberland at fire sale prices, much of it in coastal river valleys with good agricultural soils. By the time the timberland and grants for the bogus railroads reverted to the Crown, the peak years of immigration were long past. The CPR lands, at least, were for sale, though that was cold comfort to settlers who arrived short of money, expecting to pre-empt free land.

All through these years when British Columbia's best farmland was tied up, settlers were pouring into Canada as never before or since. Immigration increased steadily from the 1890s to a peak of more than 400,000 in 1913, an enormous influx for a nation of scarcely eight million people. In the same period within North

America thousands were cut adrift by Prairie crop failures, a depression in the 1890s, the playing out of the Klondike gold fields, a financial panic in 1907 and a severe depression the following year. A good many of them made their way west to wait out the hard times in the soft coastal1climate. In1908, an English immigrant, thrown out of work in the B.C. interior, described his arrival in Vancouver:

We soon learned that things were in a shocking state there. Thousands of men walked the streets and holdups occurred frequently . . . . At the docks men were packed together in hundreds around the freight sheds looking for work, whilst the trains brought in hundreds more.*

To people in such a plight, a homestead free for pre-emption was a godsend. No matter that much of the pre-emptable land was up the coast and the government could tell them nothing about it because it had done no systematic surveying. They went anyway, rowing and sailing north, tramping over every island where there might be a pocket of arable land and pushing far up into the river valleys.

The best land was on the alluvial flats of big mainland rivers like the Klinaklini, the Homathko, the Southgate, the Toba and the Kingcome. Thousands of fertile, stone-free acres awaited the plough, though none of it could be farmed without dyking to hold back the winter storm tides and spring freshets. Building a dyke was an enormous undertaking, far beyond the resources of a homesteading family. Only a farming community like the Danish colony at Cape Scott or the Norwegians in Bella Coola could assemble the necessary manpower. Or so it was believed – until the Halliday family homesteaded on the Kingcome River.

In the spring of 1893 two brothers, Ernest and William Halliday, stopped overnight in the Indian village at Alert Bay on their way to northern Vancouver Island, looking for land. A missionary told them about magnificent open grasslands at the head of Kingcome

---

*A.D. Chalmers, "The British Emigrant in Canada – the Dark Side," *Travel and Exploration*, 1909.

Inlet. The next morning they set out in a rowboat on the two-day pull to Kingcome.

I like to think the Hallidays first saw the delta of the Kingcome River as I did when I came to it on an August morning. Since daybreak the inlet had been plugged with low cloud. After four hours of paddling I was bored by the sight of grey water and mountains lopped off at the knees. I was following the north shore, skirting a cliff that soared, sheer as a skyscraper, hundreds of feet to the first ledge. At mid-morning the cloud began to lift. As the cloud pulled back three and then four thousand feet above the cliffs, vast plates and bowls of granite emerged, planed so smooth by ancient glaciers that no plant could find a foothold. And higher still, streams came down out of the mist and over the stone in a tracery of foam.

The cloud had climbed clear of the peaks but not opened yet to the sun, casting the inlet in dreary light. With its river valley blocked from view by a sharp bend, Kingcome looked as if it might dead-end disappointingly in mountain walls and impassable creeks. Then, rounding Petley Point, the entire sweep of river and delta opened before me, just as a shaft of sun struck the flats. The sunlight spread like a prairie fire, transforming the river from grey to milky green and racing through the grass to the base of the mountains, miles across the delta. Keeping close to the cliff I paddled into the rivermouth until the current was too strong to buck, then ferried fifty yards across to the tip of the delta. At the top of a mud bank, I waded waist-deep into a sea of grass, spangled with purple vetch, milfoil and yellow flowers I couldn't name. The grass stretched inland for a mile without a tree, and as far again through gently rolling glades before the forest closed in. The river looped right through the flats then back to the left and disappeared into the narrowing valley around the flank of Kingcome Mountain, which towered over the south bank, craggy and belted with glaciers.

Tying the canoe at some decrepit floats on the left bank, I walked up onto a dyke. A field of overripe hay stretched to the west, pale as straw. Beyond, a road crossed over a bridge and watermeadow to a brown two-storey house on rising ground, commanding the farm-land below. A massive ridge rose straight from the backyard. This was the Halliday homestead.

That first summer when the Hallidays arrived here they built a log cabin, planted a garden and fruit trees, and smoked salmon for the winter. They brought in cattle and turned them out to graze on the flats. The winter of 1893-94 was unusually severe. Fierce winds howled down the valley from the glaciers, the river ran ice and the flats were under snow for weeks. The starving cattle pawed the frozen ground and browsed the bushes like deer. By spring it was obvious that the Hallidays would have no farm unless they dyked the river out of the fields and grew hay for the winter. And so, equipped only with shovels, homemade wheelbarrows and an endurance now hard to imagine, they built 500 feet of dyke, enough to enclose a small hayfield.

William Halliday moved on within a year or two, and Ernest, with his wife Lily, began a long struggle to make a living from the farm. He brought in horse-drawn machinery and extended the dyke to enclose more land. The couple started a dairy herd, raised beef and once a month for the next fifteen years, Ernest made a four-day rowboat trip to and from Alert Bay to sell meat for ten cents a pound. They bartered and swapped with other homesteaders who had moved onto the delta and with the Indians in Kingcome Village, two miles upriver. Although there was always plenty to eat, they never had enough cash to buy the gasboat they desperately needed, or staples or clothes for their growing family. By 1908 they were ready to pack it in. But just as they were about to leave, a big logging camp opened a mile upstream providing the Halliday's with a market for every-thing the farm could produce. Before long, steamer service came to the head of the inlet, Ernest got his boat and, in 1918, he and his sons built the house I could see now across the fields.

In the afternoon when the wind was up and a red-tailed hawk hunted over the dyke, I crossed the hayfield and went on through a graveyard of farm machinery to the house. Seen close up, it aged years. The shingles were gap-toothed and the front stairs too rotten to climb. Hydrangea, red climber roses and briars ran wild over the fences. Back of the house, seedling trees marched down from the forest like scouts of an invading army. A sign on the wall proclaimed, in the official red on white of Canada Post: Kingcome Inlet V0N 2B0. The Hallidays ran the post office out of their house for eighty years, down to 1986. Now the place was apparently abandoned.

Late in the afternoon I camped on the riverbank upstream from the floats and treated myself to a scrub and plunge in the glacial river. With temples throbbing and mosquitoes at work on my tender parts, I lay in the sun, revelling in the ecstasy of fresh water after days of saltwater camping and teacup baths on waterless islands. An hour or two before sundown I walked up onto the dyke. The Halliday farmhouse was already in deep shadow under the ridge; in winter-time it must have been a damp and unhealthy place. Two of Ernest and Lily's seven children died young of tuberculosis and there had been illness since in the family. Perhaps sickness played a part in the demise of the farm, though the obvious causes were economic; its market dried up when airplanes began supplying the logging camp in the 1950s.

As the wind died away and the alders ceased rustling, the faraway rumble of creeks and waterfalls drifted down from an ampitheater, high in the saddle between Kingcome and a sister peak. With the glasses I could see cataracts tumbling from the aquamarine mouths of ice caverns all round the base of the cliffs. The snow had gone only recently from the tilted floor of the basin, and the alpine meadows shone with the tender green of early summer.

Sitting in the firesmoke at dusk to thwart the mosquitoes, I heard the mutter of an engine from downstream. The mast of a boat moved through the grass, and a fishboat rounded the bend, riding the crest of the flood tide against the current. It passed the floats (where the water was very shallow) and went on upstream towards the logging camp dock. The boat belonged to Alan Halliday, the last member of the family to live on the farm.

Next morning in the kitchen of the old house, Alan Halliday, a stocky, bushy-browed man in his sixties, nursed a mug of coffee by the side of a massive cookstove. The ranch had been sold and he had come to clean out some things he wanted to take away.

"After all these years, it's kind of sad to see the place go out of the family," he said. "But I couldn't keep it going myself. My legs got so bad I couldn't chase the cattle any more and none of my kids were interested in living here."

The farm had been bought by a nature trust which planned to return it to its wild state as a breeding and resting place for waterfowl. Alan was skeptical. "There used to be thousands and thousands of ducks here and at least two hundred Canada geese on the flats every winter. But they won't come back, hell no, they haven't been here for years." Alan walked slowly to the window (he has a pronounced limp) and stood looking out across the hayfields and grasslands. "Last night I came all the way up the river and I saw six mallards. That's all. No, they won't come back."

A panel truck pulled up and disgorged a half-dozen Indians who stood around the back yard talking with Alan. They had come from their village upriver to see him about some piece of machinery he was leaving behind. But in the manner of natives, nothing would be said about it until they were ready to leave, and then almost as an afterthought. First came the small talk and joking. Although Alan had been a neighbour and perhaps even a friend of these men for most of his life, there seemed to be a guarded distance between them. The farm, after all, was on land the Indians considered their own, and resentment must have come down the generations from the time when William Halliday, as Indian Agent and magistrate in Alert Bay, earned the enmity of all the Kwakiutls for his zealous prosecutions under the notorious anti-potlatch laws.*

After the sound of the Indians' truck faded away, the old house was enveloped again in silence. I realized then how isolated Alan must have felt in his last years here, with his children grown and gone, the other homesteads all abandoned, and the families at the logging camp replaced by shift workers. The farm became a lonelier place in its last years than at any time in its history.

Alan fathered six daughters and two sons. One of them, Randy, was sleeping upstairs in the old house. At one time Alan hoped that he might take over the farm but nothing came of it and now, thirty-eight years old and unemployed, Randy had come to look at another piece of land that was for sale across the river.

"I think he feels bad now that he sees the place going out of the family." We were sitting in the kitchen and Alan had lowered his voice, as if his son might hear. "But Randy isn't easy to talk to. I don't know what he's thinking. I was hoping he'd say something to one of his sisters."

I left Alan rummaging about on the sagging back porch for things he wanted to salvage.

Across the river in front of the camp a seal swam slowly upstream, searching under the cutbanks for spawning salmon. There would be very few. The Kingcome salmon were decimated years ago when seiners set their nets in front of the rivermouth and cut off the runs. Alan Halliday had been angry when he talked about it that morning.

"There aren't two percent of the salmon in the river that there were when I was young." he said. "Not two percent, and it was just plain greed."

---

* The potlatch was outlawed by the federal government from 1884 to 1951, because it was considered to be an obstacle to Indian integration into white society. Despite jail terms and confiscation of ceremonial regalia, the ban was defied by the Kwakiutls and other Indian bands.

Kingcome was not unique; rivers all over the coast suffered a similar fate. As the runs declined, many canneries shut down or moved their operations into Vancouver, depriving the settlers of seasonal work. Other jobs disappeared when trail-making was abandoned by the forest service and fire fighting was taken over by specialists. Part-time work in the bush became harder to get as gyppo loggers went out of business and the big companies did their hiring in town. But none of these things – or all of them together – fully account for the failure of settlers to take hold on the coast. The Halliday ranch, for instance, could still turn a good dollar growing beef, if someone were willing to live there. More subtle factors, things of the heart and mind, also played a part.

One can be perceived in old photos of settlers from the peak immigration years before World War I. On picnics and holidays they dressed as if they were stepping out in Edwardian London, the women in ruffled blouses and wasp waists, the men stiff in their dark suits and high collars. The turnout was remarkable for people living in shacks without running water or bathrooms, but it was an effort that had to be made. For the English immigrant, pride of place in the world was demonstrated by matters of taste – dress, speech and manners – and of character – steely reserve and grit. These were the lifelines, the essential connections to the great civilizing Empire that would keep barbarism at bay, even in the most remote corners of the globe. But there was a price to be paid. Overweening pride and the stigma of "going native" blinded many immigrants to local knowledge and custom often better suited to the country. Captain Vancouver's men dragged their futile seine and never once tried trolling, while the Indians all around them caught salmon with simple hooks and spoons made of mussel shell. Settlers rowed laboriously up and down the coast and rarely resorted to the much faster Indian canoes. Many a coastal household spent precious cash on tinned beef, while dozens of native seafoods were never tried. Some nationalities adapted better than others: the Scandinavians, accustomed to a fish-heavy diet and skilled in the crafts of the sea; the Japanese who appalled their white workmates in the logging camps with the bizarre seafoods they dredged up from the tides and ate with evident relish. But in the end what settlers ate or how they did things counted less than how they *felt* about living on the coast. Coming as they did from pastoral lands and denatured cities, they were overwhelmed by rampant nature, untamed and untamable. Only their precarious clearings in the bush looked anything like a civilized land, anything like home. They were permanently estranged, trapped on alien ground between the glowering mountains and a cold, capricious sea.

Rupert Brooke came to the British Columbia coast in 1909 and quickly moved on. He wrote: "To love the country here is to embrace a wraith. The air is too thin to breathe. A European requires haunted woods, the friendly presence of ghosts. Here one is perpetually a first-comer."

In fact, there were haunted woods and ghosts, too, though they inhabited the Indian mind, unfelt and unsuspected by Europeans. They lived in the woods and streams, on the mountains and under the sea – everywhere the aboriginal imagination conceived them. Brought to life in myth and ritual, the spirits charged their human accomplices with the elemental powers of the world. The Europeans had no such ghostly allies; they were Christians, not animists. Savage nature was the adversary, and religion was their fortress. They lived on the coast in a state of voluntary exile, sustained by the lifelines of mail, radio, children sent out to school, magazines, books and visitors.

Alien ground for the European was homeland for the natives. The difference is apparent upriver from the Halliday ranch. The Indian village is a pretty place of gardens and clipped lawns, new houses and a burgeoning crop of kids. Across the river, the logging camp consists of a few acres of oil-soaked mud, trailers and a boneyard for dead machines. The white people who come here park their lives at the airport before they fly in to do their shift. It's a place to be endured, not lived in.

Ernest and Lily Halliday would not have understood how anyone could live this way. Nor would they understand either why their hard-won farm is being turned back to the wild. I thought of them at dusk, as nighthawks plunged down a green sky above the fields that would soon be under water. Alan Halliday told me the dyke was to be cut within the next week. Twice in the past century, flood waters had topped the dyke and lain on the fields for a few days. This time when the river flowed in, it would be coming to stay.

A surfeit of rainforest and seascape had given me an appetite for meadowland and open space to stretch my legs. And so I stayed on for another day at Kingcome, tramping the flats with birdbook and binoculars. In the evening I drifted downstream, planning to sleep on a float that was tied to shore in the inlet, where log booms awaited the towboats. The tide would be out in the morning and the riverbank too muddy for loading the canoe.

Near the mouth of the river I climbed up onto the bank. The westerly had been blowing all day, and the inlet was flecked with whitecaps, except at the base of the cliffs straight off the river where I could see rollers but no breaking waves. The float was out of sight around the point; I expected (and there was my mistake) that it would be in a lee.

At the dropoff into deep water, the canoe rode easily over the first waves. Keeping close to shore, I soon found myself swept along at a great clip by the river current, which was concentrated by some set of the tide against the cliff. I paddled harder, gaining speed and driving the canoe down the waves like a roller coaster. It was a terrific ride – until I rounded the bend and plunged headlong into a wild sea that nearly sent me to the bottom. The waves stood on end, without pattern or direction, flinging water straight up from their crests. The canoe corkscrewed sickeningly, pitching and wallowing so violently that I feared I'd be knocked sideways and dumped. I thrust the paddle deep in the water and jammed it against the gunwale as a stabilizer. The canoe steadied and I hung on, wondering what to do next.

The current had made a sharp bend away from shore, carrying me out into even rougher water. I turned and started paddling again, but the canoe was still drawn backwards. When I tried angling towards the cliffs, meeting the current obliquely, waves slopped over the gunwale behind the spray cover, forcing me to turn back into the current. I needed the help of the motor, but to start it I had to let go of the paddle, which was the only thing keeping me upright. It was a ticklish business to tilt down the motor, snatch up the paddle as the canoe yawed on a wave, wind on the starter cord, grab the paddle again, and finally turn myself around in the seat to pull on the cord. For once the motor started at the first yank, and the canoe wallowed dead-slow around the bend to the float. But, alas, the float was awash and likely to smash the canoe if I came alongside. Just beyond it, a log boom was tied to shore, awash like the float on the outside. On the inside a crack had opened between the boom and the cliffs. The entrance was blocked by two cables secured to an iron ring anchored in the rock. Every so often as the boom shifted, they sagged momentarily to the water. I shut off the motor, waited my chance and, when the cables dipped, drove the canoe ahead. With a dry rasp of steel under the hull, the canoe glided into flat calm water.

I slept that night on the boom, bedding down on a pallet of thin boards which I carried in the bottom of the canoe. My dreams were orchestrated with tortured groans and shrieks from the logs and the dungeon clank of boomchains. In the darkest pit of the night I woke and heard only muttering from the logs; the tide had turned and the waves were down. (Later I learned that the confused sea is caused by a summertime conjunction of tide, river current and westerly swells, well known to locals.) At first light I woke again to the sound of a distant engine; a yacht or fishboat, I thought, and rolled over to go back to sleep. A minute or two later the bellow of a diesel and a sharp thump on the boom jerked me awake.

"Sleeping late this morning, are we?" someone shouted, much too hearty for such an hour. It was the skipper of a steel tug, *Kaymar*, nosing up against the outside of the boom. A deckhand with a pikepole skipped off across the logs to unhook the cables to shore. "Stay aboard," the captain hollered, "we'll give you a lift all the way to Vancouver."

I hopped about on the logs, pulling on pants and socks and feeling very much the fool. The boom was loose and swinging out into the inlet by the time I slipped the canoe into the water. The tug paid out cable and settled down to a week of tedium, or longer if the weather didn't co-operate. As the logs began to move, I paddled in their wake, toying with the idea of climbing aboard. I remembered lazy Huck Finn afternoons as a kid, riding the booms down Georgia Strait. We would jam our salmon rods in the auger holes of the boomsticks and leave them to fish on their own, while we swam and lay in the sun, sleek and carefree as seals.

But now I was too old, too purposeful, too impatient, too whatever ... I had lost the capacity to fool away the day. Starting the motor, I passed the boom and then the tug creeping along at knot-and-a-half top speed.

8

In the summer months when the westerlies blow, the coastal inlets are like a drunk who assaults you and then appears the next morning, all smiles and repentance. So it was with Kingcome, beginning the new day sunny and calm, without a trace of the waves that tried to dunk me the night before. Lining up on Galway Point, ten miles ahead, I hooked the tiller onto the motor to steer with my knees and fell into a paddle stroke I could maintain for the four or five hours it would take to travel the length of the inlet. The wind would be blowing again by noon or earlier, and I intended to be off the water.

The summertime westerlies rule the inlets with an authority that commands respect, even from fair-sized boats. In the steep-walled inlets like Knight and Bute, which cut deep into the coast mountains, the afternoon winds build a formidable sea, particularly against an ebb tide. Fortunately, their comings and goings are highly predictable.

Typically, on a summer morning in the inlets, there is a cool, still time between the frantic birdsong of dawn and the coming of the wind. The sunlight descends slowly into the gorge between the mountains, pushing a shadow skyline down the western wall and out onto the water. As the rock bluffs warm and dew dries on the grassy flats, spider's silk and wisps of seed cotton rise and drift east on the first small breeze of the day. Cat's paws full of sunsparkle wander aimlessly over the water, then spread and join. Quickly now, ripples align in waves and set off, capped already with white, on their march to the head of the inlet.

These are convection winds which invariably begin at the heads of the inlets, where the updrafts are strongest, and back their way *down* to the mouth, even though the direction of the wind is constantly *up* the inlet. In a big fjord where the breeze starts at about ten o'clock, the wind will not reach the mouth until nearly noon. By mid-afternoon the convection wind is drowned under a torrent of air moving onto the coast from a ridge of high pressure lying offshore in fair weather. When these "push" winds combine with the "pull" of convection over the land, westerly gales fill the inlets with spindrift and the din of rushing air. For the canoeist it's time to get off the water – if possible. In inlets such as Bute, where the mountains plunge almost vertically into the sea, one can go on for miles without finding a place to haul out. Running before the wind you are in for a fast ride and a high good time – until the waves become so big the canoe begins to surf. Loaded bow-heavy or even level, you risk broaching; stern-heavy, the whitecaps will bury you from behind. Paddling down-inlet, into the wind, you can still make headway by paddling right against the shore, where the friction of rock and trees slows the air. But at about twenty knots the quiet zone is swept away and paddling becomes futile. If you haven't found a haul-out, the best you can do is to get ashore behind some point or projection and stream the canoe downwind on a line. Most days, the westerly will drop before sunset and you will have your release.

At dusk the cooling mountain air drops and fans over the water, a mere breeze except at the mouths of some glacial creeks, where frigid air screeches down the ravines like a blast from the Greenland ice cap.

94

This is the summertime pattern, regular and predictable for weeks on end, until autumn nears and the westerlies abate. By September, the best month of the year for the canoeist, there are days when the winds never get started, and the inlets are unruffled all through the golden afternoons. And in wintertime, when the high country is cold and the sun too weak to draw in the air, there comes a time of stillness and hard blue skies, and the coast is somehow more beautiful than at any other season.

At the mouth of Kingcome I turned left through a crack behind the high dome of Gregory Island and into Shawl Bay, a circuit of coves and islands opening to the northwest towards Sutlej Channel. I had been here a dozen years earlier and remembered it fondly for its quintessential floatcamp. The Didriksens lived here – Alf and Aashild and their three children, together with Alf's elderly parents – in a neat red-and-white house, tucked into a snug cove. A bunkhouse, machine shop and boatshed floated next door and two A-frame logging rafts, the source of the family livelihood, towered over the the water.

The Didriksens appeared to live enviable lives. They were self-employed, paid no rent or property taxes, had Shawl Bay virtually to themselves (Alf's two sisters were their only neighbours), and taught their kids at home by correspondence courses. With boats at the door and freedom to come and go as they pleased, they were independent – or so it seemed. But even then there was a portent of things to come: a roving prawn boat from the city had recently blanketed their bay with traps and when it moved on, the Didriksens could catch nothing. They were indignant; they had always taken all the prawns they could eat right in front of the house.

For a moment after I turned into the bay, I thought I had come to the wrong place. Many floats and yachts, a store and a large new house were scattered around the perimeter. The Didriksen's house, the machine shop, bunkhouse, the A-frames – everything was gone. Shawl Bay was so changed I couldn't even be sure where they had been. Eventually, I found Alf Didriksen in a little shack on some rickety floats where he now spends the summer. He looked his sixty-five years, walking and talking even more slowly than when I'd seen him last. Otherwise, he was unchanged: tall and gangling, with eyes of palest blue.

"When you were here back in the seventies," he told me, "we were pretty near washed up, even if we didn't know it." When he talks, Alf chops the air with big hands, stiffened by wooden handles and obstinate machinery. "We thought we were going to get more timber and go back to logging, but the big companies had it all and we never got a stick."

(In the 1970s the provincial government consolidated cutting rights to most of the coastal timber under a few big companies. The Didriksens got only a small quota and had to sell even that to meet their expenses.)

"We'd send a boom down to Vancouver and, if the market went sour, it would sit in the Fraser River for a year before it sold. Once we had a big boom in the river for three years and by the time someone bought it, the interest on the towing and the other charges came to more than the logs were worth. We did all that work for nothing."

The end when it came was swift: in 1978 Alf towed the red-and-white house to Vancouver Island and moved it onto a lot in Port McNeill. Aashild went to work cooking and cleaning at the hospital.

"After all those years of working we had nothing but my old age pension and a little army pension that they're always trying to take away from me."

Alf held onto his bit of waterfront in Shawl Bay, though it is now a dubious asset. He is sandwiched between floats on either side, and the government has slapped a $1000-a-year charge on his land. Boat berthing rentals pay some of the bill, though not all. Alf is too soft-hearted for business; when people promise to pay but never do, he lets them stay anyway.

We sat outside in the slow twilight while Alf's daughter, Nora Mae, barbecued salmon and he talked about the coast that once was.

"There used to be people in every little bay around here and everyone went to the dances. Dad would knock off work at noon and we'd all get on the boat and run down to Echo Bay or Simoom Sound. The dances went on all night and some of the young fellas kept them going all day Sunday, but I was never up to that. Too hard going back to work on Monday.

"All this country could be resettled again if they'd open the woods to A-frames and boat loggers. A lot of the timber is in small pockets that can only be logged that way. It would be easier on the country, too. This power logging is tearing hell out of it."

Alf's logging and dancing days are done because of a heart condition. He tinkers with an old double-ender boat and goes fishing, but without much enthusiasm. "The cod holes are cleaned out," he said, "the yacht people have got prawn traps everywhere and, for some reason I don't understand, there aren't any salmon. I've only caught three all summer."

Alf is bored at Shawl Bay, though he prefers it to being bored at Port McNeill, where he spends the winter. He talked quietly in the arcane language of his trade about bull blocks and barber chairs, jill pokes and steam pots and the huge, dangerously leaning fir he never had the nerve to fell. His son-in-law, a pulp mill worker and strong union man, sat nearby, looking bored. He said little until Alf remarked that wages were one of the many soaring costs that forced him out of business. For the son-in-law, this was a call to battle.

"You don't know what you're talkin' about," he said. "You've never been in a union in your life and look where it got you. You worked for peanuts and now you want everybody else to put up with the same kind of crap. Don't go tellin' me wages are too high."

Alf tried to explain that he was neither anti-union nor against good wages; it was just that he couldn't make ends meet. But the son-in-law would have none of it. We ate our salmon in awkward silence, and I slipped away early, mumbling excuses about a long day.

At first light I paddled away from Alf's float, taking care not to rap the gunwale and wake his family. I needn't have bothered; a salmon fisherman started his outboard motor near the head of the bay and four others fired up in rapid succession. They tore past at top speed, putting up a wash that slopped against the floats and set the boats to thumping.

Southeast of Shawl Bay the land falls back from an open expanse of water where six passages converge like the spokes of a crumpled wheel. Penphrase Passage, through which I had come, enters from the north. To the west and southwest, Fife Sound and Cramer Passage curve towards Queen Charlotte Strait. Southeast, Viner Sound dead-ends in Gilford Island, and to the east, Tribune Channel slices a mile-wide chasm through the mountains to Knight Inlet. Simoom Sound, the one-time floatcamp capital of the coast, now abandoned, leads north and then west to within a few overland steps of Shawl Bay. From the open water at the hub of the wheel, the panorama is dominated by Deep Sea Bluff, vaulting sheer from a hundred fathoms at the entrance to Tribune Channel.

A mile to the south, the Burdwood Islands huddled so closely together they appeared at a distance to be a single mass of land. Not until I was almost upon them did they resolve into separate knobs of timber and ash-grey granite. There was said to be a sand beach here with a good campsite, but I had learned to be skeptical of such reports; boaters rarely notice things that matter most to the camper, like how much of the beach, if any, stands above high tide or whether the ground is rough or overgrown.

For an hour I threaded serpentine passages over grottoes of green and red anemonies and pockets of finely ground shell, alive with purple crabs no bigger than dimes. But there was no sign of a beach. With the last islands in the group just ahead, I had all but given up when I passed an island, rock-bound like a dozen before it, and chanced to look over my shoulder. Nestled in an east-facing cove, a slope of shell sand no bigger than a tennis court shone white in the morning sun.

Occasionally, if we are lucky, we happen upon islands of the imagination that welcome us like old friends from the moment we step ashore. The island in the Burdwoods – call it Burdwood Cove, for want of any name on the chart – was such a place. I walked up to the driftlogs and looked back. The tide was well out, drawing the shallows down to palest Burma jade over the shell bottom. Half filling the cove and joined to the beach at low water was a cone-shaped islet, tufted with grass and a clump of firs. On the right the beach tapered to an isthmus of pure shell and a larger island of flat granite sheets and stunted cedars. To the east a procession of islets stepped off the distance towards Tribune Channel. There was fire-wood, shelter from all winds, level ground in an evergreen grove, a fine view – everything the ideal island should have, except fresh water. I was, to judge by the depth of the clamshell middens, only the latest in a long succession of people who had found the place to their liking. The beach was composed almost entirely of shell, the bulk of it carried ashore by human hands and washed down from the midden through the centuries by the slow, insistent sea.

Burdwood Cove was a quiet place – I neither saw nor heard another boat – except for the curses of a band of pugnacious crows that came morning and night, a hundred strong, to pester a pair of bald eagles on a neighbouring island. In the afternoon, when the tide was flooding over the clam beds, a pair of greater yellowlegs swept into the cove and landed with a flurry of reedy cries. They fed in the shallows, neatly pointing their toes downward with each wading step, so that their feet lanced into the water without a ripple. Later a chocolate brown mink ran over the driftwood, ducked behind the log where I sat, and popped up at the end of the beach. It paused for a second to look back, then rattled swiftly down the isthmus of shell and melded without a sound into the water. There is something frantic and driven about mink, as if they are compelled to run on and on to survive, much as sharks must swim every moment of their lives just to breathe. They have none of the ambling or play of their otter cousins. Mink are all urgency, and glittering black eyes, forever searching.

At sundown the shadows of the higher islands stalked down the

99

line of points and islets to the east, snuffing them out, one by one. The thrushes and robins fell silent at dusk; with the nesting season long past, summer was winding down. Only the Mew gulls called, far out in Tribune Channel. At dark a wind blew from the west, soughing through the trees on the high ground behind the camp. I heaped driftwood on the fire and lay watching the sparks eddy up through the boughs to mingle with the stars. The beat of waves on the outside of the shell isthmus took me back forty years to a sleeping porch on a lake in New Brunswick. I remembered the enchantment of that sound in the night, and the whistle of wind in the screens that always accompanied it.

This was the journey of my expectations – a snug camp, firelight, solitude and the sounds of the night. And yet it was not enough. As I confided to my notebook: "After three weeks on the water, much of the time alone, I'm hungry for companionship. Not for help; I'm sure enough of my competence. What I miss most is conversation and especially humour. With no one to make jokes to, my sense of the ridiculous is drying up. Even the splendours of Burdwood Cove seem incomplete without someone to share them with. Alone, I'm content enough for a day or two, but ready to move on, to see other faces and hear other voices. I suppose I am, after all, a social animal."

Travelling alone was giving me a different slant on the solitary life of coast people. What I had always romanticized as splendid isolation must, in fact, have been a lonely and limited existence. The Didriksens, for instance, must at times have felt marooned in Shawl Bay when nearly every neighbour had moved away. Their kids probably loathed correspondence courses and pined for an ordinary school and friends. But I had seen none of that when I went there in the 1970s. From my city-bound perspective they lived a grand and independent life.

In the morning as I loaded the canoe, fog rain laid a tracery of rings on the water. Paddling around the island of stunted cedars, I looked back with regret to the white beach. I would have many a poor camp before I saw its like again.

★ ★ ★

Across Hornet Passage to the south of the Burdwoods, Gilford Island fills the horizon from east to west. Its sixty-mile circumference embraces a mix of country: high-shouldered and steep-to above Tribune Channel on the north and east, low and indented by bays and lagoons on the south and west. I planned to skirt the latter shore, stopping first at the community of Echo Bay, an hour or two ahead, and then detouring through an archipelago to the west.

Following up the peevish keening of a young bald eagle from the Gilford shore, I made out the nest of not one but two fledglings high in the fork of an old-growth cedar. The larger bird flapped and lifted above the edge of the nest like a kid on a trampoline, while its much smaller sibling hunched with its head held low, mewing hungrily. The parents had gone off hunting, quite likely to the Burdwoods. With their young so nearly fledged they would be foraging farther afield, spending entire days away from their brood. Any kill they brought back would be dumped unceremoniously in the nest, leaving the offspring to feed themselves.

After young bald eagles have learned to fly, they hang about the nest, waiting for the daily food drop. Over the next few weeks the parents gradually lose interest, bringing food less and less often and finally abandoning their brood altogether. The young stay on, sometimes for many days, calling piteously until hunger drives them to hunt for themselves. More than half of them never make it on their own, starving to death in their first year.

The Gilford shoreline on the way to Echo Bay was attractively cleft by coves and peppered with islands. A few houses were spaced here, each a little domain with its float and boatsheds and patch of garden; fragments, they seemed, of a lifestyle that once prevailed widely on the coast. In a pinched cove I spotted what appeared to be a floating church. A white cross jutted crookedly from a squat clapboard steeple atop a hip-roofed structure which looked for all the world like a barn. No one answered my knock at the cottage next door. Around the back, a yacht from Tacoma, Washington, was tied to another float. A tall, grizzled man with bleary eyeglasses and hairy jug ears was fiddling with some fishing rods on deck. His name was Bill Pipes.

I asked about the church. It was built, he said, by a logger for his fundamentalist sect, though it had recently become nondenominational to appeal to a larger constituency.

"We're short of money and there's no pastor now. But families are starting to come in from Echo Bay and all around. We tie up here because we like to go to the services. You should come on Sunday."

Regretfully, I explained that I was just passing through and wouldn't be able to make it. He invited me in and his wife, a tall, laconic woman brought us coffee. I asked how the fishing had been.

"Terrible, just terrible. All five people on this boat have licences and we were out all yesterday morning and we didn't get a damned thing."

Fishing is serious business with the yacht people. Few come north without canning machines or freezers, and their proudest boast is that they paid for the trip with the fish they take home. They tow runabouts to fish from and many carry smaller boats on deck. When the salmon are biting well, the support craft are kept busy throughout the day until all on the mother ship have taken their limit. If salmon fishing is off, they turn to cod or halibut or work their prawn and crab traps. Production is what matters, and success is measured in cases of cans, or pounds in the freezer.

"Maybe they've been fished too hard," I suggested. "A lot of the runs are in pretty poor shape."

"No, that's not it," Pipes said. "Now, I don't want to say nothin' bad about anybody, but the trouble is you Canadians aren't putting anything into it. Your fishermen up here don't pay anything voluntarily towards the hatcheries."

I pointed out that licence fees are supposed to fund the hatcheries.

"Well, it's just my opinion," he said, "but it seems to me the Americans are taking better care of the salmon. In Alaska a lot of the hatcheries are paid for by the fishermen."

"How much public support are the hatcheries getting in Washington State since the Bolt decision?" I asked.*

"That's got to be worked out yet," Pipes said. "I don't want to say nothin' bad about anybody, but the Indians have gone too far. They want all their rights as Americans and their rights as Indians, too. They're always in the press about their culture, but they've got no culture left; they can't be Indian any more than I can be Dutch. We've got freedom of the press down there in America – anyone can say what they want. It seems to me those who don't do anything always have a lot to say and those who do the work, you never hear from. And the Indians up here are even worse."

Abruptly, he trained his sights on a new grievance. "There's another thing you Canadians have got to do something about and that's these damned killer whales. A bunch of them came right by the cove here just the other day. It's just my opinion, but it seems to me they're pretty damned destructive. And the seals, you're going to have to do something about them, too. There are way too many of them and they're eating all the fish. The fishing is terrible."

Pipes raised his voice a notch. "You Canadians have got to start doing something for the tourist. We come up here and all we do is spend money. I don't want to say nothin' bad about anybody, but look what they're charging over here at Echo Bay for gas – three, four times what we pay. And now they raise the fishing licences to thirty-five dollars! That's terrible, terrible!"

I told him that I saw an American weighing in a forty-pound salmon at Sullivan Bay. "That seems like pretty good value to me."

He ignored me. "You'll see. The fishing is terrible. I've been coming up here for years and I've never seen it so bad. Just terrible."

As I left, Bill Pipes had some advice: "This is a great country

---

*In a landmark 1974 decision based on Indian treaties, U.S. District Court Judge George Bolt awarded half of some major Washington salmon runs to Indian bands. The Indians had offered to settle for twenty percent before they were forced into court by the State.

you've got here, all these natural resources, but – and this is just my opinion – you Canadians are going to have to develop this country or somebody is going to take control of it."

I was tempted to point out that foreign control of Canadian resources and the export of profits, mainly to the United States, has been bleeding Canada white for years. But I didn't want to say nothin' bad about anybody. And, in truth, we have no one to blame but ourselves.

9

The "bay" in Echo Bay is a bit grand for a cove only 200 yards wide and perhaps twice as long. Nonetheless, the setting is attractive, opening to the northwest from behind a round island that half-fills the entrance. On the left near its head a gravelly beach curves around a shady grove of maples, an old brown community hall and a one-room school. This much of Echo Bay I recognized from a visit here a dozen years earlier, but the rest, like Shawl Bay, was much changed. On the right near the entrance the floats around the store and fuel dock were spreading like weeds. The old pub on the rise above the wharf was now dwarfed by a new lodge. And the view across the bay to the opposite shore was rapidly filling with shacky floathouses and waterlogged rafts collecting junk.

I climbed the long flight of stairs between the pub and the lodge and passed over the height of land to a cliff-top cabin which turns its back on Echo Bay and looks west down Cramer Passage. There I found Alexandra Morton working in her vegetable garden. A New Englander, she is in her thirties, with brown hair pulled back a bit severely. I had come to talk with her about her work on killer whales.

Alex Morton arrived in Echo Bay in 1984 with her husband, Robin, a cinematographer who did some of the first underwater filming of killer whales in the wild. She was the sound technician of the team, recording the calls of the whales with hydrophones. The

Mortons had been working together since the late 1970s in Johnstone Strait, twenty miles to the south, where killer whales are more accessible than anywhere else in the world. But they were forced to move on when the strait became so crowded with whale watchers that they could no longer film or record without interference.

It was the Morton's ambition to make their living from films and stills of the whales. By trial and error they perfected underwater techniques, slowly collecting the footage and sounds they would need to make their first film. Meantime, they supported themselves and their young son by chartering their sixty-five-foot boat for coastal tours. Finally, in 1986 they got the break they had been waiting for. *National Geographic* agreed to make a film on their work, using their footage and recordings as the core of the program. In September, just three days before the *Geographic* film crew was due to arrive, Robin drowned in a freak diving accident.

"We'd paid our dues and we were just getting it together," Alex told me. We were sitting in the cabin, surrounded by Robin's photographs, among them a breeching whale, stopped at its apogee in splendid black and silver against a deep shadow background. "Robin was so happy. It was beautiful the day before – we were amongst the whales all day. We anchored in the kelp and all through the night we heard them blowing around us. The next morning, Robin put on his wet suit just like he had hundreds of times before. And then he was dead."

Alex decided to stay in Echo Bay, continuing her research into whale vocalizations and earning a living, if possible, from freelance writing and still photography. She sold the charter boat and began, with some trepidation, hunting for whales alone in an outboard runabout.

As we talked, a radiophone crackled annoyingly from its place on the wall. At last, I asked Alex if she wanted it on. "It's always on, except at night," she said. "I've got notices posted in stores and marinas asking people to call me if they see any whales. It works pretty well in the summer but in the wintertime there aren't so many boats out there and I'm more likely to find the whales myself." Alone among the dozens of researchers who study the killer whales, Alex Morton is on the water year-round, specializing in a little-known branch of the killer whale population called the transients.

The existence of the transients was one of a number of revolutionary discoveries about killer whales made in the 1970s by Dr. Michael Bigg, a fisheries department scientist. Using photographs of dorsal fins and distinguishing body marks, he compiled a registry that individually identifies every killer whale on the British Columbia coast. His study revealed that generations of killer whales spend their entire lives in matrilineal family groups, known as pods, under the leadership of the oldest female. No other animal stays all its life with its family. In addition, he found that killer whales on the British Columbia coast fall into two distinct populations that never mix: a race of resident whales, which spend part of the year in certain known areas, and transients, whose movements are unpredictable. The more numerous residents are primarily fish eaters and quite vocal, whereas the transients hunt seals and sea lions and are silent much of the time, likely so as not to warn off their prey. The two groups display physical differences – most conspicuously in the shape of their dorsal fins – that suggest a long genetic separation between them. Transients and residents will pass one another without a sign of recognition.

The identification system opened the way for further revelations. By linking tape-recorded killer whale calls to individual whales, another fisheries scientist, Dr. John Ford, discovered that each family or pod of resident whales has its own dialect, which is distinct from every other pod on the coast. He reproduced all the dialects in the form of sonograms and assembled them in a catalogue, so that it is now possible to identify any resident pod solely from a tape recording. Much of this research was made possible by easy access to resident whales that camp in Johnstone Strait from June to September, feeding on salmon. The transients, which no one but Alex Morton has made a sustained effort to study, are a much more elusive subject.

"They usually travel right in against the shore, where they're more likely to catch seals and sea lions," Alex said. "That makes them really hard to see, especially in the winter when there's frost or snow along the water's edge. The vapour of their blowing blends right into the background. Sometimes I've gone a month without seeing a whale."

But her persistence is paying off. In her first winter working by herself, she witnessed a remarkable hunting foray by eleven transients. "I was lucky to spot them because it was raining like hell and blowing. Just before they got to a big bay, they stopped to take on copious quantities of air. They just lay there on the surface, breathing and breathing and then they dove."

Alex ran the boat to the center of the bay, lowered her hydrophone over the side and waited with her stopwatch in hand, timing the dive. After more than ten minutes, the whales surfaced in the head of the bay.

"It was an eruption – a line of white water going straight up in the air and whales flinging their tails and slapping them down and others breeching and coming down on their backs. I wish I'd seen it from the air because I think they were in a circle. They had three sea lions hemmed in and they were demobilizing them, jumping down on top of them and flinging them in the air with their flukes. Sea lions are big strong animals and I guess the whales were wary of being bitten. They stun them before they try to kill them.

"After about forty minutes the water went quiet and there were just fins on the surface and gulls circling overhead. They were eating the sea lions – or two of them. A third one was drifting off to one side, dazed and just lying there on the surface. I was recording all this time, though there wasn't much sound from the whales until they killed the sea lions. Then they really turned up the volume.

"But this is what really fascinates me: all the time they were in that long dive, they were absolutely silent – not a single call or echolocation click. So how did they locate their prey under water without sonar? Obviously, they knew that the sea lions were there before they dove. Otherwise, why did they take on all that extra air? And they travelled without a sound for at least half a mile before they came up – right under the sea lions. I can only guess that they detected their prey with sonar before they dove and then zeroed in on them with an incredibly accurate navigation system. It boggles the mind!"

Alex agreed to take me along if she went out after whales, though I would have to stay nearby and be ready to leave in minutes if she got a call. That meant camping in Echo Bay. Reluctantly, I pitched my tarp under the maples near the community hall and settled in to wait; if no whales turned up within two days, I would move on. I passed the time reading, catching up on my journal and answering endless questions from the yacht people. A despondent kayaker hung about the camp long past the limits of our conversation. Locals warned me not to leave anything of value unattended, so that I fretted about my gear when I went to the store or up to the pub for a beer.

Like many such places on the coast, Echo Bay sells a bit of its soul each summer. The yachting crowd brings in money – little of which ever gets past the store or the gas pump – and there are lively times on the floats with Scotch and bouillabaisse. The floating crafts shop has many visitors and a lesser number of sales, and the local lady artist sells a few paintings. But by the middle of August, people tire of the uproar. The woman behind the counter in the store is tired, snapping sometimes at the regular customers, though still smiling gamely for the tourists. (I didn't make the grade as a tourist.) By September the novelty of visitors wears thin and everyone is relieved when the last of the boats heads south and peace returns to the bay.

It was not yet eight o'clock when I rapped on Alex Morton's door to tell her that I was leaving that morning; there didn't seem to be any killer whales in the area. She yelled for me to come in, and I found her scrambling together recording gear and cameras and urging her son, Jarret, to get his rubber boots on.

"A yacht just called – there are whales in Fyfe Sound," she said, handing me an armload of things to carry to the boat. "Damn, I've got to get gas, too."

A quarter-hour later we were flying at twenty-five knots down narrow Indian Passage. As we swung into Fyfe Sound we saw the whales ahead, travelling tight against the north side of Eden Island. A yacht and a runabout were jogging behind them, keeping a respectful distance. Out in the middle of the sound, two very fast speedboats were streaking towards the whales.

"Oh Jesus," Alex shouted over the noise of the motor, "there's going to be a free-for-all here. That's the trouble with the radio – someone calls and everyone knows."

The whales – two cows, a calf, a juvenile bull and an adult displaying a fin like a six-foot scimitar – were travelling in a tight pod, led by one of the females. Alex ran well ahead of them and shut off the motor. Moving fast, she lowered a hydrophone into the water, clapped on earphones and started her tape recorder. She focussed binoculars on the approaching whales and flipped rapidly through a looseleaf binder of identification photos, hoping to find a match.

The whales were travelling in short dives on a track that would bring them past within fifty yards of the hydrophone, close enough to get a recording to identify their dialect. As they drew near, I could hear whistles and squeals coming from Alex's earphones. She was listening hard, straining to pick out the sounds from the background of boat noise. "Wow, this is something!" she cried, "I don't know this dialect."

The pod was nearly opposite us when one of the high-powered speedboats raced up from behind and almost onto the flukes of the whales. Three young men leaned over the windshield, snapping pictures. Underwater, the throb of their engine obliterated every other sound. Tearing off her headphones, Alex yelled: "What do you guys think this is, a goddamned zoo?" If they heard her, they paid no attention and kept right on taking pictures. She waved them away from the pod. "Go fishing guys, go on. Bugger off and get that big halibut."

By this time the whales and the boat were leaving us behind. Alex pulled in the hydrophone and started the motor, speeding up gradually so as not to race the outboard and add to the annoyance of the whales.

"This is the kind of crap you expect in Johnstone Strait," she said, "and it pisses me off to see it happening up here."

None of this touched Jarret, who had been sitting content in the front seat, munching cookies and listening to *Wind in the Willows* on his own headset. He'd seen it all before – the whales and the confrontations. Twice we ran ahead of the pod and Alex set up to record and twice the speedboat blotted out the calls of the whales. And then she got a break; the pod split to pass on opposite sides of an islet at the mouth of Fyfe Sound, taking the speedboat away in pursuit of the bulls. Alex followed the two cows and the calf out into Queen Charlotte Strait, recording and photographing their dorsal fins for identification. But the wind was rising, and before long, the boat was pounding into heavy chop. "We might as well go back," she announced. "I'm not hearing anything but water noise."

In the shelter of an island at the mouth of Fyfe Sound, Alex played back her recording. To my ears it seemed a hopeless muddle of sloshing and thumping, engine noise and, distantly, the squeals and moans of the whales.

"It's pretty bad," Alex agreed, "but I think there are enough clear bits so I can pick out the dialect. It's completely new to me, so I'm going to have to rely on my pictures to identify the pod."

Some day Alex hopes to learn much more from her recordings. "Quite simply, I'm trying to understand their language. Many people have tried to correlate whale sounds with behaviour – feeding, resting, encounters between pods – that sort of thing. I've devoted a lot of time to this myself and I can find no connection between behaviour and any particular sound. I think it's a dead end. If we tried to understand human language that way, we'd fail too. When we're in distress or eating or gathering food or whatever, we use all kinds of different words. I wonder if the key is something altogether different, like the speed with which the sounds are produced, or the spaces between them. Maybe the same calls have different meanings at high and low pitches, like Chinese. Or perhaps its not language at all, as we understand language. We've got to loosen up our heads and come at it in an altogether different way."

Alex Morton's approach is easily dismissed as romantic and

unrealistic, and she knows her work is open to criticism for its lack of focus. "You're supposed to be out here with a specific question: how long two-year-old killer whales spend away from their mothers. That sort of thing. You get really nice numbers; its very clean, but that's all it tells you."

Lacking an advanced degree or standing in the scientific community, Alex's great fear is that her work will not be accepted. "My life would be a failure if I do eventually understand some things of importance about the whales and nobody believes me. So I'm trying to build a very strong scientific base, which means keeping precise records and producing solid articles on the physical things I'm learning here."

Field work like Alex Morton's – however unfocussed – is becoming an endangered species in a world of science that deprecates natural history in favour of narrowly specialized applied research and mathematical modelling. In the long run the greatest value of her work may be simply that she's out there on the water, watching and listening, at every season of the year.

Outside Echo Bay I turned west and plunged into The Tangles, a maze of islands and passages confounding the waters between Fyfe and Blackfish sounds. This was archetypal canoe country, and I was ready for it. After weeks of blisters and aching muscles, the lard was melting from my belly, my hands and arms were hardened, and I could paddle for hours without tiring. I had gained the freedom of the country.

The Tangles was bewildering: a dozen high islands a mile or so across and hundreds of smaller ones, strung along passages coiled in such confusion I wondered at times if I were travelling in circles. I had the place all to myself; reefs and shoal water mined the archipelago, confining all but the smallest boats to a few broad channels. Only one family lived here, close to Echo Bay. I struck straight west, dragging the canoe through a drying chink between Mars and Tracey islands into Monday Anchorage, and on through nearly landlocked Sunday Harbour to the edge of Queen Charlotte Strait. A heavy swell rolled in from the west, burnishing the twenty miles to Vancouver Island silver in the afternoon sun. The myriad islands to the southeast merged in the distance into a line of cliffs, shining white over the wind-darkened sea.

Across Arrow Passage on the edge of the labyrinth off Bonwick Island, a great many gulls – Bonaparte's, mew and glaucous-winged – were feeding noisily in the kelp. With binoculars I could see the fins of some kind of fish milling in the center of each screeching cluster of birds. I paddled closer, intending to fish; if the birds were feeding on herring, salmon might be cruising beneath the school. Just outside the kelp a fin cut the surface, showing the unmistakable line of a shark's tail. Others thrust up and within seconds dozens were crowded together. They were Pacific dogfish, small sharks that grow to about four feet.

Taking their cue from the fins, gulls descended on the spot, whirling and stabbing at some feed just beneath the surface. I had the binoculars pressed to my eyes, trying to see what they were eating, when I felt something bumping the canoe. Thinking I had drifted against the kelp, I paid no attention. But when the bump-bump-bump became more insistent, I looked over the side, and my stomach clenched. Beneath me was an undulating mass of thousands upon thousands of sharks, densely packed from the surface for as far down as I could see into the depths. Swimming with sinuous, hypnotic grace, they glided over and under and around one another, never touching and never stopping. They possessed a sinister kind of beauty: their bodies velvety dove grey with fins and tails edged in dusky chalk, and backs longitudinally stippled by parallel rows of white stars. I resisted an urge to reach out and stroke their flanks; spines stood up behind their dorsal and adipose fins, and the dogfish's teeth, I knew, could slice a fish as cleanly as a scalpel. Even the touch of their sandpaper skin provokes a shiver like the screech of steel on glass.

I pushed ahead into the feeding mass, sending the gulls wheeling overhead. The water was a mauve soup of slender, inch-long organisms, swimming in short bursts just beneath the surface. In the brim of my hat, which I used to scoop a few out, they appeared insubstantial as water, except for a scarlet thread of internal organs and a pair of pinpoint black eyes. They were krill, a species of planktonic crustaceans.

The dogfish fed all around me, swimming back and forth through the mauve cloud with their mouths open, for all the world like baleen whales.

The Tangles is not camping country. After three hours without seeing a single place to go ashore, I turned back to Monday Anchorage and onward through Misty Passage to Insect Island, the site of an old Indian village Alf Didriksen had marked on the chart. It was to be the eeriest camp I would have on this journey.

Even as I waded ashore, I felt unwelcome. The cove was insufferably hot, tilted to trap the afternoon sun and shut out the breeze. The shell beach was very steep and crowded from behind by a twenty-foot bank. At high tide I had to retreat to the woods to find room to sleep. There was neither water nor driftwood for a fire. Yet none of these things could account for a dark malevolence that seemed to hover about the place, especially in the forest above the beach, where a populous village once stood. A deep midden, roughly terraced for at least a dozen large houses, paralleled the bank for a hundred yards. The site had once been open to sun and wind; but now closely grown cedars shut out the sky and most of the light. Dead limbs cascaded like lianas down the trunks and snaked over a forest floor so deep in needles that nothing green could grow. In the evening when the fog blew in from Queen Charlotte Sound, moisture dripped from the trees and the sound of the sea was hushed to a whisper. No bird sang.

I have felt a presence or atmosphere of some kind in other abandoned Indian villages on the coast, especially in old Haida villages on the Queen Charlotte Islands. It's as if you are being

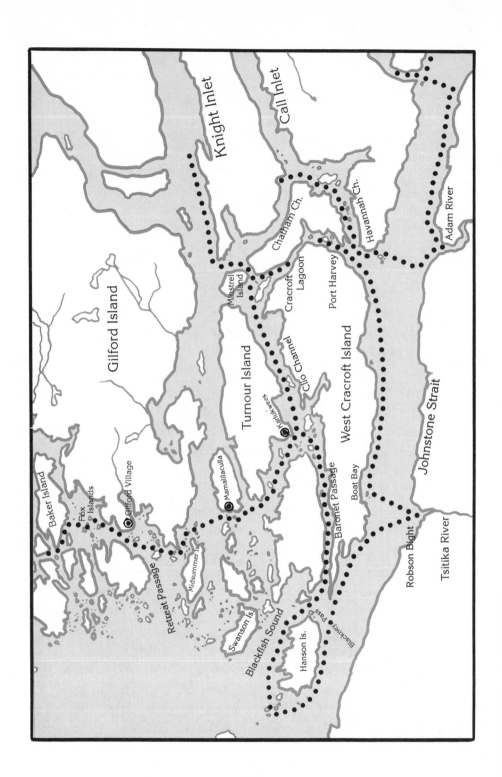

watched by something – or someone – beyond the fallen totems and rotting house posts, back in the shadows under the trees. The feeling is neither hostile nor benign, yet you know for a certainty that you are an intruder on alien ground. For years I dismissed all this as romantic nonsense until I discovered that many people experience the same thing. The natives themselves say they feel the presence of their ancestors in the villages, and they routinely speak of the spiritual power of whole valleys and mountains.

There were no watchers in the shadows on Insect Island. Rather, the old village seemed to be steeped in an atmosphere of violence or despair, as if a residue persisted from some bloody fight or nineteenth-century epidemic which scythed the people down. After dark I walked under the cedars and tried to will the feeling away as fantasy, or the shadow of my own mood. But the presence stood its ground and followed me to the edge of the trees when I went back to my beach fire.

For reasons I can't now imagine, I stayed on for another day and night in the gloom of Insect Island. The weather conspired with the gods or ghosts, or whatever they were, to keep the cove muffled in fog. The day passed almost without sight or sound of another creature. Once I listened for long minutes to the breathing of some animal – always three sharp expirations and then silence – and eventually glimpsed the humped back and rounded dorsal fin of a harbour porpoise. As I left in a drenching fog rain, a red-throated loon circled in front of the beach, calling plaintively. It swam off into the fog, and I heard it call again, a sad small cry for such a large bird.

10

Two miles south of Insect Island, I launched into fog from the tip of Baker Island across open water towards the Fox Group, and almost immediately lost sight of land. With no wind or ripple on the water to judge direction by, and my five-and-dime store compass buried at the bottom on the gear box, I kept on by dead reckoning, glancing often behind the canoe to keep its track straight. After ten minutes, kelp showed on the water and then a suggestion of rock and trees, which I took to be one of the Fox islands, though I had no idea which one. I paddled around it and crossed to another, groping from island to island until they ended in more open water. Guessing at a course, I set off again. At length an island loomed ahead where I expected a bay. Befuddled, I puzzled over the chart, wiping fog rain from the plastic cover and turning it this way and that. With only a fragment of an island for reference, it might as well have been a map of the moon.

There seemed only one thing to do: turn to what I took to be east, away from any possible straying into Queen Charlotte Strait, where I would be well and truly lost. If my reckoning was correct, I would strike Gilford Island.

After an interminable crossing, land took shape on either side of the bow, as if I were heading into a channel, which was not on the chart. I soon saw my mistake; what I had taken for a passage was merely the gap between an island and a point on the Gilford shore. Turning south, I followed a slit of beach beneath the fog until a wharf reared out of the murk and then smudges of turquoise and blue, the houses of the Indian village of Gilford. The only signs of life were a naked lightbulb in a gauzy corona and a ghostly dog that looked down from the wharf. Gilford was fast asleep.

One summer in the late 1850s the Kwakiutl people of Gilford, or Gwayadams as the village was then known, met to trade with Indians from Bella Coola, 200 miles to the north. A woman from Gilford stole a hamatsa (cannibal dance) whistle of great symbolic value from a high-born Bella Coola couple. Although the theft was a capital offense, the Bella Coolas did not retaliate at the time. Revenge came the following winter in the form of a raiding party which swept down from the north in war canoes and attacked Gwayadams by night. All sixteen buildings were razed and most of the men, women and children killed. Except for a few people taken as slaves, only seven men and four women survived.

A few days later thirty-six canoes from other Kwakiutl villages set out in pursuit of the Bella Coolas. But they were too late. In Rivers Inlet they met a group of Heiltsuk (a northern Kwakiutl tribe from Bella Bella) who told them that the Bella Coolas had reached their home village and barricaded their houses. Then, in the impulsive fashion of coastal warfare, the Kwakiutl attacked the Heiltsuk and killed them all, for reasons that history does not record.

Gwayadams was abandoned for many years after the raid. But over time its clam beds and attractive location outweighed its tragic past, and people began to move back. It was a winter village, inhabited mainly from November to March by natives from Hope Island, farther north, and by people from the inlets who moved here to escape the cold winds from the interior. In the spring they left again for oolichan fishing at the head of Knight Inlet or Kingcome Inlet, then moved on to their summer villages and fishing camps.* After the turn of the century the seasonal pattern gradually broke down until Gilford, as it became known, was a year-round village. At the end of World War II, some military buildings were moved from Vancouver Island to provide housing, and people stayed on, despite pressure from the Indian Affairs Department to abandon the village. Today, Gilford is holding its own with about twenty families.

South of Gilford the sea crinkled to washboard and the wind came close behind, driving grey-green chop in from Queen Charlotte

---

* The oolichan, a small anadromous fish, was the source of an oil which was once an indispensable condiment in the native diet. It is extracted after allowing the fish to putrify, imbuing the oil with an overpowering and tenacious odour. Although it is often called oolichan grease, it has the consistency of heavy engine oil.

Strait. Fine rain stung my face, and my breath streamed in a plume over my shoulder. Fog scudded just overhead. Ducking out of the wind behind Seabreeze Island, I stuffed my hands under my jacket to warm. The waterway I had been travelling was Retreat Passage, named perhaps for the flight of the Bella Coolas after the raid. Within two miles of where I drifted, they would have entered Queen Charlotte Strait, turned north and set off on a run of more than seventy miles to the next sheltered passage in Fitz Hugh Sound. Although no record of the trip survives, it must have been miserable, especially for the captives, who would have been made to lie in the bilges, likely with the severed heads of friends and relatives, which were customarily taken home as trophies. They travelled at the time of winter gales and surf so heavy that landing would have been impossible for most of the way. History records only one captive who returned to tell of the experience, a ten-year-old boy who remained with the Bella Coolas until 1908. He was sixty years old when he finally returned to Gwayadams.

The canoeist on this coast paddles in the thousand-year wake of some of the finest canoes and canoemen the world has known. The charts abound with names such as Canoe Pass, Canoe Islets, Canoe Cove, and the countless shoal and kelp-strewn passages are made to order for canoes. Few white men have been privileged to travel in the great sea-going dugouts, and even fewer left an account of their experiences. None was exposed to greater perils or wrote about them better than Henry William Collison, the first missionary in the Queen Charlotte Islands.

Collison was posted to Masset by the Church Missionary Society in 1876. Before his stint had ended he was to make seventeen canoe crossings between the islands and Fort Simpson on the mainland, near the present-day city of Prince Rupert. On three of those voyages, Collison recounted in his memoirs, "we were well-nigh lost." The route lay across Hecate Strait, notorious for steep seas and tides that stream like a river, opening fierce rips around Rose Spit, at the northeast corner of the Charlottes. The shortest crossing was forty miles, almost due north to the islands at the tip of the Alaska Panhandle, followed by a long roundabout of island-hopping, east and south to Fort Simpson. The shorter but more exposed route was sixty miles straight across to the mainland. The return trip was made doubly dangerous by the Indians' commerce in canoes.

The Haidas capitalized on the islands' enormous western red cedars to do a profitable trade in canoes with mainland tribes who were not so blessed with suitable timber. They carved the canoes in winter and early spring and paddled them to the Nass River in late March to trade with the Nishka for oolichan oil. (There are no oolichans on the Charlottes.) To get back to the islands, the Haidas took old canoes in exchange for their new ones. The trade-ins were rotten derelicts, always on their last legs; otherwise their owners would not have given them up. If a canoe was in especially bad shape, the Haidas nailed cedar branches inside the hull as makeshift ribs. But many were still ill-found for the waters of Hecate Strait.

In March 1877 Collison prepared to make his first crossing from Masset to the mainland with his wife and child. "All along the shore in front of the camp the canoes lay ready for launching," he wrote. "All were perfect in outline and beautiful in construction." After days of waiting for favourable weather, more than thirty canoes set out, some of them fifty-footers, six-and-a-half feet across the beam. Before embarking, Collison knelt on the beach, commending his family to the care of the Almighty. The Haidas took more tangible precautions, exchanging their children and other relatives to bind the party together in common interest.

With a fair wind, they raised their small triangular sails on stubby, unstayed masts, two and sometimes three to a canoe. (Sails were unknown before contact with Europeans and never were well adapted to the coast canoes, except for running before the wind.) More than twenty miles from Masset and well out into Hecate Strait, Chief Edenshaw in the leading canoe saw a portent of bad weather – a small cloud moving rapidly from the northeast – and immediately took the party ashore near Rose Spit. The next morning the wind was fair, though strong from the northwest and running a heavy surf. In launching, one of the canoes was caught sideways by a wave and smashed to pieces. Its occupants lost everything except the clothes on their backs. "They were left standing on the shore in dire distress," Collison wrote, "and nothing remained for them but to walk back again thirty miles to the nearest camp."

The crossing to Fort Simpson was anticlimatic: fourteen hours of hard paddling, and a few squalls that slopped seas over the gunwales and kept a slave busy bailing. "We reached the outer islands long past midnight," Collison reported, "all weary, exhausted and wet. Fortunately, the children had fallen asleep, which rendered them unconscious of their misery."

A year or two later Collison made a return trip to the Charlottes from the Nass. Although he secured a place for himself in the large, sound canoe of Chief Edenshaw, most of the others were travelling in derelict trade-ins, heavily loaded with oolichan grease sealed in cedar boxes. The party gathered in a small harbour near Cape Chacon at the southern end of Prince of Wales Island. And there they stayed for two weeks, waiting out the storms that blew day after day. Their food supplies ran out and they were reduced to scrounging for mussels at low tide. Collison prayed and proselytized and taught his captive audience songs of praise. When they set out at last, the signs were not good; Collison's aneroid had fallen in the night, and dark clouds were banked on the horizon.

At first they made good time with the wind on their starboard beam. Then, halfway across Hecate Strait, the canoes were caught by a sudden squall from the Pacific. As Collison tells it: "The sea arose and great waves crested with foam threatened continually to swamp our frail craft. As the large boxes of fish grease broke loose from their fastenings, they were tossed about until their lids were loosened and fell off. Then every wave that struck us caused the grease to splash forth over everything. I was soaked with it from head to foot."

Collison stripped to his underwear and put on a life jacket, which Chief Edenshaw pointed out would only prolong his misery if the canoe capsized, as they could never reach shore.

"Just then Cowhoe [Edenshaw's son] arose in the canoe and called upon us to assist him in casting the grease boxes, with what grease remained in them, overboard. A huge wave struck us at that time and he was well-nigh gone, but by clinging to the thwart he was saved. We were all opposed to casting the grease overboard, as it not only ballasted the canoe, but also the grease, as it washed overboard smoothed the waves and prevented them from breaking over us in full force. Every wave threatened to engulf us and, as we could see only a few yards ahead, we feared we might be running towards Rose Spit." They ploughed on "with but two feet of sail to the wind," bailing sea water and congealed grease.

After three hours the storm passed to the east and they found themselves nearly on course. Miraculously, none of the trade-in canoes had split or foundered (a frequent occurrence), although all aboard had lost their precious oolichan oil and jettisoned many other possessions to lighten the load. Much as he admired the seamanship of the Haida, Collison gave them to understand that they owed their survival to the Great Steersman in the sky, not to any skill or courage of their own.

The fog was lifting and shredding on the high bluffs of Midsummer Island, which belied the sylvan promise of its name with beachless shores and slopes mangy with old logging. At the edge of Knight Inlet I stopped for a hard look at the open water ahead. The tide raced through the islets around me, spreading a broad fan of slick water into the inlet. Farther out a swell rolled inland, bordered by a thin line of white, which the binoculars showed to be a tide rip: a meeting of fast and slower-moving water opening a tear in the surface. And way across near the far side, wind blew dark along the shore.

Starting the engine, I crossed the smooth water and rode into the swell, which was being stretched and flattened by the flood tide running in the same direction. It was the rip tide that concerned me.

As it came closer, I slowed to an idle and stood up in the canoe, hoping to determine how big it really was. But I could catch only glimpses of white between the waves. Opening the throttle, I shoved the paddle deep and braced for a wrench when the canoe cut through the line of opposed currents. It bounced over some broken water and cut through the line of white with hardly a nudge from the turbulence. The rip was a chimera, all fuss and foam.

The end of the ebb and beginning of the flood tide were meeting in a wavering line, no wider than a sidewalk, stretching as far as I could see up and down the inlet. Little dishpan whirlpools spun along its edges. But there was more there than met the eye. In crossing the rip, the canoe had skimmed over the real turmoil beneath the surface. A deep-draught vessel would have been spun off course and heeled over by the contending currents. Sizeable boats have been capsized by tide rips and especially by tidal overfalls, which are really just rips turned on edge so that one layer of water slides over another. For the first and last time on this trip, I could feel a bit smug about my canoe; for crossing tide rips, at least, it was superior to the fanciest yacht.

The Indians knew these tidal streams with the sort of intimacy that Eskimos bring to the many kinds and conditions of snow. Even so, there were accidents and drownings. Just across Queen Charlotte Strait from where I crossed the rip, forty Kwakiutls perished in front of Fort Rupert in 1870. Their canoe apparently capsized at night, though the scanty record reveals nothing of the cause. Clearly, it was something extraordinary – a faulty hull or a sudden storm – because every coastal Indian was trained almost from infancy in the techniques of handling canoes in heavy weather.

Big waves were crossed at a diagonal rather than straight-on to avoid leaving part of the hull unsupported, which could cause it to split. In very rough seas inflated bladders or sealskin floats were tied to the sides as stabilizers. If a breaker threatened to curl over the gunwale, paddles were used to cut horizontally through the crest to weaken it. Taking a comber on the beam, all the paddlers on the weather side would pull the water towards them with a single powerful stroke, lifting the side of the canoe and tucking the wave underneath. Running before a heavy following sea, the canoe might be paddled backwards to face the high, flared bow into the waves. The steersman was in charge of all these manoeuvers, shouting his commands from the stern and guiding the canoe with a paddle half again the size of the others.

Landing in surf demanded timing and co-ordination between the steersman and his crew. Particularly dangerous were the shallow entrances to rivers and channels open to the sea, especially when ebb tides or stream currents piled into the swells. In places like Nitinat, on the west coast of Vancouver Island, the only access to the village lay through such a gut. In the 1860s Gilbert Malcolm Sproat rode through the surf in one of the big canoes. He wrote:

> Their mode of landing on a beach shows skill and coolness. Approaching warily, the steersman of the canoe decides when to dash for the shore; sometimes quickly countermanding the movement, by strenuous exertion the canoe is paddled back. Twenty minutes may thus pass while another chance is awaited. At length the time comes; the men give a strong stroke and rise to their feet as the canoe darts over the first roller; now there is no returning: the second roller is just passed when the bow paddler leaps out and pulls the canoe through the broken water. It is a question of moments, yet few accidents happen.

Although a dunking in the breakers would probably end with a smashed canoe and lost possessions, the occupants stood a good chance of being cast up on the beach. Foundering or capsizing at sea was more serious; the water was too cold to survive a long drift clinging to the canoe, or a swim of any distance to shore. Techniques were evolved for righting a canoe and bailing it out, or if the sea were too rough, for paddling the swamped hull. It must have been cold and tedious work, though preferrable to drowning or being dashed against the cliffs in an attempt to swim ashore.

★ ★ ★

The dark streak I had seen across the inlet proved, indeed, to be wind, a chill breath from Queen Charlotte Strait, thick with drizzle from the fog which had dropped again, almost to the water. The windline was almost as abrupt as the tide rip; one minute the canoe was in rippled water and the next I was banging into chop and taking spray over the side. I groped for a time along the shore, trying to sort out the half-dozen different channels between the islands to the south of Knight Inlet. At last I turned into Eliot Passage and, thankfully, out of the wind. On the left a pier stilt-walked on barnacled pilings out from the Village Island shore and ended in the air. Its float and ramp had been gone for years. The dock once led to Mamalilaculla, an abandoned Kwakiutl village screened from view around the point.

The village's front yard proved to be a watery plain of mucky sand, eelgrass and treeless islets that looked like stranded whales. Cutting inside a more substantial island that bordered the flats, I ran aground and got out of the canoe to slog back and forth, trying to get warm. If I stopped even for a moment, my rubber boots sank to the ankles in the mud. Forlorn in the blowing fog, Mamalilaculla had subsided into bush that swarmed up to the gable ends of the few houses still standing. The village was abandoned in the 1950s, after generations in decline.

I was standing, hock-deep, in the village larder. Where I saw only mud and scowling wind on the tidepools, the people of Mamalilaculla beheld an inexhaustible supply of clams and cockles. Their centuries of feasting had built a ribbon of shell sand in front of the village. Many hundreds of people must have lived here once; the bushy mounds of former house sites undulated above the curve of beach far beyond the collapsing buildings.

A bald eagle had been watching the advancing tide from a dead tree on the high island. Now it launched into a flat glide and, raking its talons through the shallows of a tidepool, hooked up a small flounder. Landing on a reef, it began to tear the fish apart. Immediately, a dark juvenile eagle landed nearby, just out of pecking range. And there it stayed, mewing hungrily but coming no closer until the adult (likely one of its parents) had eaten the fish down to the last morsel.

Supplying a populous coastal village like Mamalilaculla with food, firewood and building materials was a formidable undertaking in a country where travel ashore is so difficult. Thus canoes became the cornerstone of the Indian economy. They ranged from delicate women's models for long-shore food gathering, to hulking freighters of sixty feet or more, capable of carrying many tons. In between came a variety of sizes and designs for hunting, fishing, whaling and war.

The annual round of food gathering required the entire population of many villages to be waterborne at least twice a year, moving between summer fishing and berrying sites, autumn salmon streams and back to their winter villages. Seagoing canoes were put together for these moves in pairs, catamaran-style, and decked with hewn planks borrowed from house roofs. Shelters were constructed and cooking fires laid on a pad of split green hemlock or alder, covered with gravel. People lived on board for days, travelling the inlets in leisurely procession and anchoring at night. The smaller canoes acted as tenders, ferrying wood and water from shore and keeping the mother ship supplied with ling cod, red snapper and black bass from well-known fishing spots along the way.

This Huck Finn style of travel was probably more the norm than the disciplined paddling that so impressed early observers such as British naval officer John Meares, who was met near Cape Flattery by 400 Makah circling his ship and singing in unison. Farther north in Nootka Sound, on the west coast of Vancouver Island, he was greeted by 600 chanting warriors in twenty canoes. He wrote:

The chorus was in unison and strictly correct as to time and tone . . . everyone beat time against the gunwale of the boat with their paddles; and at the end of every verse or stanza, they pointed with extended arms to the north and the south, gradually sinking their voices in such a solemn manner, as to produce an effect not often attained by the orchestras in our quarter of the globe.

Meares, of course, was treated to a performance, not a workaday paddle chant. Those chants were much less elaborate, sung for keeping time and perhaps simply for pleasure. It makes an attractive picture: paddles dipping and lifting as one, elegant canoes cleaving the green inlet and voices drifting over the water. And at times, no doubt, that's how it was. But if there was no hurry (and there usually wasn't), the natives were given to a much more casual manner of travel. The paddlers stroked in little spurts of a minute or so and then rested, sometimes all together, sometimes in rotation, spelling one another. There was a lot of talking and joking and stopping to smoke their pipes. They went ashore every night, quitting early if they came to a good camping spot, hauling out all the canoes to prevent them from becoming waterlogged. Only a very big, heavily loaded canoe would be left anchored overnight.

Canoemen took exceedingly good care of their craft. Landings were made on sand or gravel beaches, if possible, and the canoes were carried or rolled ashore on cylinders of wood and covered with mats to keep the sun from drying and cracking the wood. The hull was frequently rubbed down with grass or bark to clean off marine growths, and periodically charred and oiled to maintain a smooth, hard surface. And to give them an odour pleasing to sea beings, both real and supernatural, canoes were switched with spruce boughs.

A seagoing canoe was a costly and prized personal possession. Many were given names like Open Sea, Dancing Canoe, Red Cod, Copper-thwart, Twisted Canoe and Lazy Canoe. They were the work of shipwrights commissioned for the job, artists really more than carpenters because a canoe was a piece of carved sculpture, executed largely by eye, without aid of plans or patterns. The technology of canoemaking was fully developed before contact and it changed little with the arrival of European tools, unlike other Indian manufactures such as totem poles, which grew rapidly in size,

126

number and decorative opulence when fast-cutting blades became available.

Steel tools were in use on the coast long before Europeans arrived, though they were scarce and not particularly favoured over blades of nephrite (a hard stone of fine texture, similar to jade), shell, beaver incisors, horn and bone. The source of pre-contact iron, none of which was smelted on the north Pacific, is something of a mystery. One theory maintains that it originated in some Iron Age center in Siberia and was traded hand-to-hand across the Bering Strait and down the west coast of North America. Or the iron may have come ashore on Asiatic vessels swept away in storms and carried across the Pacific by the Japanese current. At least five such wrecks washed ashore in the historical period, two with surviving Japanese fishermen who were enslaved by the Indians and later ransomed by the Hudson's Bay Company.

Confirmation for the drift iron theory was unearthed on Washington's Olympic Peninsula in the 1970s when archaeologists discovered a Makah village, named Ozette, which had been buried by a mudslide sometime around 1650, entombing several of the inhabitants. The mud sealed the site so effectively that a treasure trove of artifacts was preserved, including the rusted remains of small iron tools. Laboratory analysis showed the metal to be Japanese, from the medieval period.

Canoemaking enjoyed a brief renaissance in the last quarter of the nineteenth century and the first decade of the twentieth, because of the demand for small canoes in the Bering Sea fur seal hunt. But it came to an end when overhunting foreclosed commercial sealing in 1911. In the years following World War I, boats with gasoline engines rapidly supplanted canoes of all types. The last seagoing canoe from the hands of master carvers was made in 1937 at Masset in the Queen Charlottes by brothers Robert and Alfred Davidson for a museum somewhere in the eastern U.S. No records survive to tell who the buyer was and no one in Masset has heard of it since. Robert Davidson's grandson and namesake, artist Robert Davidson, has tried without success to track the canoe down. He suspects it was sold to a collector or museum in Germany and destroyed during World War II.

The recent revival of canoemaking has produced craft of uneven quality, undoubtedly because the carvers are at least a generation removed from the old skills and sensibilities. With time, their skills can be polished, though there is no remedy for the chief obstacle facing the modern carvers: the near impossibility of finding quality red cedar trees of canoe size.

11

Heading south, the wind was under my tail, driving the canoe down Beware Passage, past Beware Cove and Caution Rock (names prompted by some desperate episode or merely hazards to navigation?) to another abandoned village at Karlukwees. Here the tideflat is replaced by a steeply tilted gravel beach, and the village is smaller. Otherwise, it's a carbon copy of Mamalilaculla: blank windows staring out of sagging houses drowning in crabapple and salmonberry bushes.

Outside Karlukwees and around the point on the left, I turned east down Clio Channel towards Minstrel Island. The day had worked its summer magic: not two hours since I was freezing on a mudflat in a dismal fog rain, the westerly was puffing softly and cloud patterns drifted over the ridges. I lay back and nodded along at three or four knots, one knot by paddle and the rest a gift of wind and tide. A one-trailer gyppo camp slipped past on the left, then Bones Bay on the right, without a trace of the great shambling salmon cannery that stood there a half-dozen years ago. The history robbers had been at it again, stripping the country of its past.

Minstrel Island loomed ahead, a squat stone plug, blocking the end of Clio Channel. A passage on the left opened onto Knight Inlet and a narrower waterway called The Blow Hole rounded Minstrel on the right, leading on into Knight via Chatham Channel. The tide ran fast in The Blow Hole, sweeping the canoe through streaming kelp and nearly onto a reef in mid-channel. I swung left, narrowly missing boulders the size of refrigerators close to the Minstrel shore, and veered back into deeper water.

Tradition has it that Minstrel was named for a black minstrel show that performed there in the early years of the century. It seems an unlikely place for a touring troup at any time. And yet the chart corroborates the story; Sambo Point and Negro Rock are nearby. And, of course, Bones Bay.

For a moment I didn't recognize the village at Minstrel. Its only landmark, an old three-storey clapboard hotel, was gone. Where it had stood, a bulldozer was pushing the last scraps of lumber into a fire. Without its hotel, Minstrel didn't amount to much: a house or two on the right, a row of shacks over the water on the left and a store at the head of the wharf, recently tarted up with an addition and fresh paint. Some new floats had been built for the summertime yachts, though they seemed only to add to the air of impermanence.

Eleven years ago when I was here, Minstrel was already moribund and its beer parlour, once the rowdiest on the coast, was locked. The old folks who lived in the back of the hotel made me tea, and I plied them with questions about Minstrel's salad days in the 1940s and '50s, when loggers from more than fifty gyppo camps came here to pick up their mail and take on a load of beer at the hotel. (The Post Office opened in 1909 and still operates.) But all of that seemed too long ago to matter any more, and they talked instead about friends who were dead or dying.

In 1908 the London Times ran a story from "A Correspondent" quoting a logger's description of life in the Minstrel hotel when men were making a heady nine dollars a day in the camps:

The bar was a-roaring day and night. Billy had a band of bully boys tending bar for him: about sixteen strong they were and there was always some of them sober enough to work the cash register – right around the clock. Gee, them was great times! If a man liked he could keep drunk right along and never cost him a cent. I seed some of the finest kinds of fights, too, in this very barroom – four or five a night. There was always a card game going on, $10 or $20 the bet and I seen a fellow go up to $900 on a single jackpot. In the morning you would see the boys scattered all over the rocks and down on the beach – just like a lot of dead flies when you've emptied out a jug of stale milk.

Some of it was true, including the part he didn't tell about the drunks who drowned on the way back to their floatcamps and the cases of "logger's smallpox" – men who had their faces stomped in by caulked boots. I had stayed one night in the old hotel. There was no rustic charm, no sense of history; just pubic hair on the soap and the sad smell of long-closed rooms.

The history robbers had claimed this place, too, and perhaps it wasn't such a bad idea.

Bucking the tide I retraced my route through The Blow Hole and turned left through a reef-strewn passage to Cracroft Inlet. "Inlet" overstates the case; Cracroft is only a few hundred yards across, tapering within a mile to a crack in the forest. And yet it had no feeling of confinement; the land to the west and south lifted softly to distant hills, and the lagoon, as people hereabouts prefer to call it, was filled with sun and wind.

Finding the head of the lagoon too beset with thickets to make a camp, I turned back to a dock I had passed on the way in. Its sign read: CRACROFT MARINE SERVICES and, what I was really looking for, SHOWER. A long string of floats, many of them waterlogged and tilted askew, paralleled the shore, with fuel pumps and a shed in the center. Only one yacht was berthed in all this sprawling establishment. The people on board directed me to a house up on the bank to inquire about the shower.

From the rickety pier I looked down onto the tracks of a marine ways which ascended the beach to a boat works. Dismembered machinery, lumber and sundry junk spilled out of the building and into the blackberry bushes. Old fuel tanks were mired like rusty elephants in the underbrush. From the head of the wharf the path looped steeply past a tin shed, pulsating to the thud of a diesel generator, and around to the rear of the two-storey house, which was four-square and ugly. The view, however, across the lagoon to the west and out between the islands into Clio Channel, was magnificent.

The woman who came to the door took my breath away. Olive-skinned, tall and gracile as a reed in the wind, she was Eurasian, the daughter (she told me later) of a Dutch father and Javanese mother. Her name was Maria Laan.

"The shower is down in the fuel shed. Jan will show you where." She had a trace of Dutch accent, muted by the echo of another language I couldn't identify. "If you'd like a loaf of bread, come up when you're done. I'm just putting it in the oven."

Jan was Maria's husband. I found him working on an outboard engine on the far end of the floats. Bearded, grizzled and bespectacled, he looked ten or fifteen years older than Maria. His accent was heavy and unmistakably Dutch.

"There's no hot water but if you want to wait around I'll turn it on when I'm finished here."

I said I was in no hurry. Little did I suspect that I would be stuck in Cracroft Lagoon for the next two days.

I slept – or tried to sleep – that night in Jan's boatshed, with the canoe loaded and ready to leave before daylight to beat the wind in Knight Inlet. The yacht people had a party on the float and the drunks howled late, led by a woman with a voice that could dent a tank. After midnight a gale sprang up from the northwest, driving the revellers inside. The wind rattled the tin walls of the shed, snapped the yacht flags and beat up waves that wrung shrieks and moans from the floats like the cries of some vast wounded animal. At three-thirty, with the gale still building, I cancelled the alarm; there would be no travelling on the water this day.

I'd been living a charmed life; this was the first real storm in more than a month since the fish packer dropped me off Seymour Inlet. All through the morning, while the wind bayed over the ridge behind the house, I sat in the kitchen, drinking tea and talking with Maria.

They had emigrated from Holland eight years before with two children and the promise of a good job for Jan in Vancouver. At home he had done well as a mechanical technician building containment vessels for nuclear reactors. Although there was no such work in Vancouver, he found other employment for three years. And then the economy went into recession and the jobs dried up.

"At first he tried hard, looking farther and farther from home, but there was no work for someone with his qualifications." A weariness crept into Maria's voice when she remembered it. "After a year or two, he got discouraged and quit trying. He usually didn't get up until noon and he couldn't get started at anything until late afternoon. After a couple of hours he'd quit. I got so depressed."

This went on for five years; Jan sinking deeper in despair, the family scraping by on welfare and Maria feeding them all – there were now four children – on $250 a month. Then she saw a For Sale advertisement in the newspaper for a resort at a place called Cracroft. "I had no idea where it was. I thought it must be in the States. Jan wasn't interested but he phoned anyway and we were surprised; the price seemed to be within reach. We've since decided that it was probably because no one else wanted it."

In April they flew to Cracroft to see the "resort." Maria could laugh now at their naiveté. "Oh, the country was so beautiful, but everything else was awful. The house was filthy with soot from the oil stove. There was trash scattered all over the place, and Jan found that most of the machinery was broken. And it was raining, just pouring, with a dreadful cold wind. If it was only me, I probably wouldn't have taken it. But we had to do something to get Jan going again."

They borrowed money for a small down payment and took on a heavy mortgage. It was already mid-June, just weeks from the yachting season. They shipped their things from the city by barge, and their neighbours in the lagoon and at Minstrel came to help them move in. "They were wonderful," Maria said, "everyone was there." She showed me a snapshot of a human chain ascending the wharf, burdened like coolies.

Jan got the marine ways working by the time the first yachts arrived in early July. But there was no hope of reopening the store this year, nor time to repair the floats or begin the assault on the mountains of junk. The yachts came in twos and threes, bringing a trickle of money from berthage, fuel sales and repair jobs on the ways. Business was slow; the resort had been run down for many years and once-loyal clients had gone elsewhere. Where the lawns and orchard had once been, Jan and Maria found only a path hacked through the jungle and fruit trees subsiding into the brush. The generators for electricity were broken down and the water system needed repairs. The cedar foundations under the house were rotting. "When the wind blows," Maria said, "it shakes so badly I'm afraid it's going to fall over."

The kids at least were oblivious to all this. They had been lifted out of suburbia and set down in heaven. Life was suddenly rowboats, fishing, animals and rambles in the woods. From time to time as we talked they burst into the house for bread and brown sugar, breathless and shouting all at once. The girl and two of the boys have their mother's olive skin and dark eyes; the youngest boy is fair with eyes of cool grey, like his father's.

Jan came in and sat with us at the table. He talked about repairing fishboats and tugs to bring in money in the off-season. Maria said they planned to restore the gardens and make a place where boaters could come ashore to stretch their legs. Perhaps there would be barbecue pits and, eventually, a guest cabin or two. They intended to reopen the store next year and Maria would make handicrafts and grow vegetables for sale. As they chattered excitedly about their plans, I wondered if they were aware of the people who had lived in this same lagoon long before they were born. The first settlers had no airplanes, radiophone, electricity, perhaps not even mail or a motorboat. But they had no mortgage either, and they were not dependent for their living on the whim of wealthy yachtsmen. They logged, fished, beachcombed, trapped – anything that would provide a meal or turn a dollar. Although nothing paid very well, several things together paid well enough. Versatility was the key to survival, and it still is for someone who proposes to live in a place like Cracroft Lagoon. Jan's predecessor at Cracroft beachcombed for logs with a boat that was still tied at the dock. I wondered if Jan intended to use it next winter.

"No, I've got too much to do around here," he said. "I'm going to build up the marine service again. There should be plenty of fishboats that want to go up on the ways."

I couldn't imagine where the business would come from. When the yachting crowd had gone south for the winter, the local waters would be all but deserted. The loggers and fishermen who once brought their boats to Cracroft had moved away years ago.

The nights were getting longer. Outside Jan's boathouse at 4:30 stars winked through rents in the fog, and there was still no light in the eastern sky. The canoe was drenched in dew, an indication that the wind had been down for most of the night. Prospects looked good for a try at Knight Inlet.

I paddled silently past the yachts of the slumbering tycoons and out into the lagoon on the path of the moon. Away from its reflection, the water was featureless matte black and the islands dull silver. A croak sounded from shore and then the swish of a blue heron's wings in the dark.

The motor was damp. I yanked at the cord for a quarter-hour before it started, berating myself for forgetting a spray-can of ether which would have jolted it to life in an instant. In The Blow Hole the canoe dragged against the tide, and the propellor fouled twice in unseen kelp. By the time I passed Minstrel, an apricot dawn was climbing over the ridges across Chatham Channel. Around a bluff beyond the village, the entrance to Knight Inlet opened a mile ahead, plugged with fog, blowing inland. Beneath the rolling bank was a dark line which I took to be the far side of the inlet. Through binoculars, the land proved to be water – long, grey rollers, melding in the distance into more fog.

I was looking into one of the worst wind tunnels on the coast. From its mouth at the bottom of Queen Charlotte Strait, Knight stretches east thirty-five miles without a bend to Glendale Cove. On the south shore between Minstrel and Glendale only one cove makes a break in the rock walls. The chart shows names like Shelterless Point, Stormy Bluff and Rough Point.

Rounding Littleton Point into the inlet, I seemed to be turning upstream into a river. One of the biggest tides of the year rushed out to sea, streaming current waves from every point and dragging the kelp beneath the surface. Running against the ebb was a crazy quilt of waves piled up by yesterday's storm, which must have kept blowing in the inlet long after it died in Cracroft Lagoon. The shoreline dropped away so sheer that the tide ran fast right in to the toe of the cliffs, leaving no backeddies or helpful lanes of slower water. With the motor wide open, the wall inched past, just beyond my paddle. Before long a wind began to blow up-inlet, standing waves against the tide and slopping water into the canoe behind the spray cover. After an hour of heavy going, a moment of mature reflection seemed in order.

I shut off the motor and removed my ear covers. An eerie sound hung overhead in the fog, like the roar of the sea in a conch shell, yet deeper and darker. It was the growling of great energies in contention, tide meeting waves and wind, muffled by fog and distorted by cliffs. With my eyes fixed on the waves in front of the canoe, I hadn't noticed how wildly the trees were tossing, or seen the strings of moss trailing like airport windsocks. Bailing with a big sponge, I dithered about what to do. If it got much rougher, I would have to go ashore, which was not an inviting prospect. The rock fell away so steeply that I couldn't expect to find more than a toehold on a ledge. The canoe and all the gear would have to be rammed up into the bush at high tide. Camping in such a place would be like a rock climber sleeping

135

in his ropes. I'd be better off waiting for weather in Cracroft Lagoon than in some rathole in the inlet. I turned back.

Not half a mile inside Chatham Channel, the first bars of sun were slanting down from the eastern ridges, gilding the bluffs on Minstrel Island. Far ahead at the entrance to The Blow Hole, a tideline winked gold like a necklace cast on the water.

There was no telling when Knight Inlet might let me pass, and the thought of waiting around did not appeal. I got out the chart to look for alternatives. The obstacle in Knight was the straight gut between Minstrel and Glendale Cove. East of Glendale, the inlet bends north and snakes another thirty miles to the head, confounding the winds with its contortions. If I could get to Glendale, the rest would be a snap. I had been there once before in the 1970s, travelling overland by road from a logging camp in Jackson Bay on Topaze Inlet, an hour's drive to the south. The logging camp was still there, so why not do the same thing again? Surely I could hire someone to haul me and my outfit across in a pickup.

Decision made, I caught a boost from the tide through The Blow Hole and turned into Clio Channel. On Turnour Island I fried eggs from the Minstrel store and made sandwiches with Maria's bread. Across the channel mist curled up from the ridges on the first updrafts of the day.

At its western end Clio Channel loses itself in a cluster of islands and emerges as Baronet Passage, which continues west another six miles to Johnstone Strait. The islands here are flatter and more hospitable than the humped granite outcrops in The Tangles. In aboriginal times they were heavily used; the intricate passages wound past so many beaches and clam beds and old Indian encampments that I stopped marking them on the chart.

Baronet Passage is rarely more than a few hundred yards across and, had the tide not been so far out, would have seemed more like a river than an arm of the sea. Pink coraline algae and purple and orange sea stars encrusted the boulders near low water. Kelp sprawled in limp piles along the shore, glistening with a rainbow sheen, like oil on water. At Walden Island, the channel split and the tidal stream gathered speed; I clawed up a hill of water, barely beating the current. At the top, where the chute ran fastest, two otters came riding down on their backs, like kids on a waterslide. Near the western end of the passage, the canoe slipped under a tongue of fog from Johnstone Strait and I went on at the center of a pearly orb.

Beyond the skinny finger of Cracroft Point, the last of the ebb in Johnstone Strait nudged the canoe northward into Blackney Pass. A flock of northern phalaropes whirred out of the fog and landed dead ahead, spinning and stabbing at some miniscule feed on the surface. They looked like wading birds, long-legged and needle-billed with unwebbed feet; and yet they spend much of their lives far out to sea. Fearless, they fluttered like lovely white moths over the bow of the canoe.

Often, I stopped paddling to listen for the killer whales that move through Blackney Pass almost daily in the summer months. And eventually I heard them, blowing somewhere out in the fog to the north on Blackfish Sound.* For a long time I drifted, hoping they might pass within sight. But they sounded and I didn't hear them again.

12

Late in the afternoon lightning crackled over the mountains on Vancouver Island, strobe lighting patches of late summer snow beneath the peaks. A rain squall poured its travelling waterfall down the Tsitika River valley and caught me trying to outrun it along the shore of West Cracroft Island. I landed in a deluge on a little hook of gravel and threw up a lean-to, finishing just as the sun broke through and set the drift logs to steaming. But my efforts were not in vain; within ten minutes, the downpour began again.

---

* Until the 1950s killer whales were generally called blackfish on the B.C. coast.

It was a choice camp, looking southeast down Johnstone Strait, though I wondered how much of it would be left above water at high tide in the middle of the night. The line of tide wrack left by last night's high was perilously close to the drift pile heaped up by winter storms. And tonight's tide would be even higher. I puzzled over the tide tables, sighted and measured and, after a lot of dithering, decided to stay. After all, it was only water; if I were flooded out I could move elsewhere tomorrow.

I built the obligatory two fires for rainy weather, a bonfire for heat, directly in front of the lean-to, and a small cooking fire at the corner, within easy reach of the Scotch and the grub box. I fried lingcod, watching the aquamarine flesh turn white, and dined like a lord, basking in the warmth that came through the curtain of rain.

As the day dipped, the rain eased off to drifting mist, and a great white queen from Scandinavia swept up the strait with all four decks ablaze in light. I was camped on the north-south freeway of the Pacific coast, the route of cruise ships, tugs, trollers, trawlers, freighters, container ships, kayaks – perhaps 10,000 boats a year. By day, they were nearly lost in the immensity of the strait. Only after dark, when I saw scattered pinpricks of light, did I have any sense of the traffic.

Several times in the night I woke to the beat of waves after a ship went by, and once the wash came hissing over the hot rocks where the fire had been. As the tide advanced until it lapped the poles at the front of the lean-to, I scrunched into the very back against the logs and prayed that no ship would pass. When I woke again, the tide was dropping and a lavender dawn was climbing up the eastern sky.

Perhaps it was the blowing of the killer whales that roused me; the first thing I heard was a far-off swoosh of air. The sounds grew louder, and three whales came into view around a point to the east, travelling on a line that would bring them close to the camp. As I rummaged for shoes and a camera, one of the whales – a bull with a six-foot dorsal fin – veered away from shore, while the other two, a female and a half-grown calf, angled in towards the beach directly in front of me. They stopped at the outer edge of a band of kelp and dove

138

in water scarcely deep enough to cover their up-ended flukes. For a time they rooted at the base of the kelp, then surfaced briefly and dove again in the same spot, heads down and flukes beating just beneath the surface.

After they were submerged I ran down to the water's edge with the camera. When the whales came up they were so close that I could have tossed a pebble onto their backs. They lay quietly for a moment, breathing deeply, then dove in unison. The roiled water calmed, and I thought I had frightened them off. (The rattle of stones under my feet would have carried well under water.) Just as I started back up the beach, the kelp bed erupted as if a depth charge had gone off. The surface heaved, flinging kelp and spray into the air. Thrashing flukes churned the water white. Dorsal fins thrust up and plunged again into the foam. Suddenly, both whales popped to the surface, blew sharply and dove. The heaving subsided, bubbles rose slowly and the kelp drifted back into place.

When the whales next blew, they were well out into the strait and travelling fast on the track of the bull. So what was all that about, I wondered? Were they after a fish hiding under the kelp? An octopus, perhaps? I was none the wiser.

Although killer whales range over every ocean of the world, almost all the research in the wild takes place within sight of the point where I was camped. Nowhere else are killer whales so accessible and so habituated to people as the ones that take up residence in Johnstone Strait from June to September to feed on migrating salmon. Researchers from Canadian and American universities flock here every summer, pitching their tents and observation posts along the bluffs.

That afternoon I sat on the cliffs and watched a procession of more than thirty whales passing the estuary of the Tsitika River, across the strait. They were strung out in small groups, swimming at three or four knots in their travelling gait of shallow dives and frequent blowing. The mist of their spouts drifted on the wind, silver against the shadow of Vancouver Island. Four boats followed them – two inflatables, a whalewatching tour boat and a fast runabout that buzzed from pod to pod, crowding the whales. As they crossed the strait and passed close in front of me, a young male leapt three times in rapid succession, crashing down in geysers of spray. Cheers came from the tour boat; the tourists were getting their fifty bucks worth.

Most of the whales had gone by when I noticed two females and a juvenile approaching rapidly along the near shore. They were travelling parallel to one another, perhaps ten yards apart, on an erratic course that must have been designed to sonar-scan the water in front of them for fish. Every so often one them dashed away from the others in pursuit of some prey, most likely salmon. They launched themselves with an astonishing burst of acceleration known as "porpoising," driving their streamlined bodies high in the water and down in a smooth arc. Usually that was the end of it and the whale surfaced quietly after a minute or so some distance away. But there were other chases right at the surface; the whale tearing a white swath through the water, striking left and right on the track of the fish, and catching or losing it in a swirl of flukes and fins.

Abruptly, the three whales broke off the hunt and headed west on the track of the other pods. They travelled in perfect synchronization, the two females surfacing, blowing and diving in unison, with the juvenile a quarter turn behind them, as if they were locked together on the rim of a great wheel. Some scientists believe killer whales travel this way to take advantage of pressure waves, just as geese fly the path of least resistance in a V.

At sundown, when only a only a few small pods were left in the strait, a cruise ship slowed and idled for a while behind a solitary bull. The whale circled slowly, spouting golden plumes, as if performing for the passengers who lined the upper deck.

Killer whales weren't always so admired by the public. Less than thirty years ago the fisheries department attempted to machine gun them at the southern end of Johnstone Strait to prevent them from feeding occasionally on salmon in the sportsfishing grounds near the town of Campbell River. The gun was mounted on the cliffs in Seymour Narrows north of the town and manned by an army gunner. But the whales never came within range or they slipped past under cover of darkness. After a while the gun was taken down, and the whales went elsewhere to feed, likely because the salmon at Campbell River were decimated by overfishing.

Today, shooting at killer whales is against Canadian law, and the law is, for the most part, obeyed. Many commercial fishermen who shot whales on sight at the time of the Campbell River incident are now among their most ardent defenders. There are exceptions, of course, and whales occasionally turn up with bullet holes in their dorsal fins. But there is no longer any equivalent in British Columbia to the situation in Alaska where, only a few years ago, black cod fishermen shot nearly half the members of a pod taking fish from their lines. Eight of the whales died of their wounds.

At the upper end of Johnstone Strait, Blackney Pass leads between Hanson and Harbledown islands into Blackfish Sound and on to Queen Charlotte Strait. This is Main Street for killer whales moving between the strait and waters to the north. From a laboratory on Hanson Island, a New Zealander named Paul Spong has been observing their comings and goings for nearly two decades. This man, perhaps more than anyone else, turned the world on to whales.

His laboratory – Orcalab, Paul calls it* – is what first catches your eye. It's an observation post, all glass across the front and down one side, leaning over the water on stilts at the end of a rocky promontory. A boardwalk from the lab leads through the trees to a house looking down into a cove of translucent green. The design is Late Hippie: a semicircular front room of many windows and skylights,

---

*From *Orcinus Orca*, the killer whale's scientific name.

weathered cedar shakes and a loft like a fat bell tower with more skylights.

I paddled into the cove on a hot afternoon, uncertain of my reception. Paul is besieged with summertime visitors and likes to be forewarned when you come to call. Despite many attempts, I'd been unable to contact him by radiophone. Three children were wading in the shallows, and I recognized Paul's blonde wife, Helena, among a group of people on the rocks. She called Paul out from a shed behind the house and he came down to meet me, tanned and fit in shorts and bare feet. He spoke softly, the New Zealand accent muted and pleasant. This was not the harried figure of public controversy I had come to know from newspaper photographs.

Paul Spong stepped into the public spotlight in 1969. He had been hired two years earlier, fresh out of the University of California with a Ph.D. in physiological psychology, to do brain research at the University of B.C. Part of his time was to be spent studying the visual acuity of Skana, a young female killer whale recently acquired by the Vancouver Public Aquarium. For a while the work went ahead as expected, with Skana pushing the correct levers and getting her half-herring reward. She was scoring close to 100 percent on the tests and Paul was able to establish that her sight was roughly equal to that of a cat. Then, overnight, Skana went into what Paul was later to call "spontaneous reversal." She simply refused to carry on with the project. It's not uncommon for animals to withdraw their co-operation when they tire of scientific experiments, but Skana went far beyond that. She gave the exact wrong answer eighty-three times in a row, something without precedent in the annals of behavioural science. By the laws of probability, there was no possibility of accident. Skana was making a deliberate statement: she was quitting.

Paul was shattered. His statistics were a shambles and the project was a write-off. Finally, a bit uncomfortably, he accepted what seemed to be the only possible conclusion: Skana possessed intelligence far beyond anything he had suspected. Setting aside his research, he began spending time with Skana, feeling his way towards some common level of communication. He talked and sang to her, swam with her, played his flute and brought recordings to observe her response to everything from Ravi Shankar to the Beatles. Over many months he became convinced that Skana and Tung Jen, the Aquarium's other killer whale, suffered severely from the breaking of bonds with their families in the wild. He saw them as prisoners in an acoustic hall of mirrors, being driven insane by the reflections of their own calls from the concrete walls.

Paul summarized his findings in a 1969 lecture at the University of B.C. "My respect for this animal has sometimes verged on awe," he said. "*Orcinus Orca* is an incredibly powerful and capable creature, exquisitely self-controlled and aware of the world around it, a being possessed with a zest for life and a healthy sense of humour and, moreover, a remarkable fondness for and interest in humans."

Sense of humour? Fondness for humans? Many of Paul's university colleagues were rolling their eyes to the ceiling; this was hardly the language of scientific detachment. He ended with an appeal for the whales to be returned to the wild. The aquarium directors were unconvinced, and he was fired.

In 1970 Paul Spong discovered the unusual summertime concentrations of killer whales in Johnstone Strait. He made a start on the Hanson Island observation post and began spending his summers there. But he was increasingly drawn away by the campaign against commercial whaling that was to make him an internationally known figure.

In the late 1960s and early '70s, the International Whaling Commission was turning a deaf ear to the growing outcry against whaling. A more direct and dramatic form of protest was needed. Paul, together with Vancouver journalist Bob Hunter, conceived the idea of following the whaling fleets at sea and running inflatable boats between the harpoon ships and the whales. But when they presented the plan to the Vancouver-based Greenpeace Foundation, the embryonic organization was focussed exclusively on opposing nuclear weapons testing and had no interest in whales.

Greenpeace was cool to Paul's idea. Reluctantly, he proposed a solution: he would undertake to finance a protest voyage himself if

Greenpeace would allow him to attach its name to a fund-raising whale show he was producing. The result was the First Annual Greenpeace Christmas Whale Show, a celebration of cetaceans in film, music and words, attended by nearly 3000 people in Vancouver in 1973. He took the Whale Show to Japan, touching off a heated national debate between whaling interests and conservationists. In rapid succession came a two-page spread in *Time*, talk show appearances on network television and a big press conference at – of all places – the Vancouver Aquarium. The rest is history: the Greenpeace confrontations with whalers at sea and the moratorium on commercial whaling.

In the evening I walked the logs to the house from my camp at the head of the cove. Paul was outside, tinkering with a portable generator. We were venturing into the *terra incognita* of the carburetor when Helena shouted from the house: "Orcas, orcas." Paul downed tools and ran, as if he'd never before seen a killer whale. Helena was already out on the lab deck, focussing a spotting scope on three fins turning from Blackfish Sound into Blackney Pass. She had heard the whales' calls, picked up by a hydrophone and relayed to a speaker in the house.

"It's Nicole's pod," she yelled, so that Paul could hear her inside the lab. "That's her out in front about twenty yards." Nicole was one of several pod matriarchs that have been given names, in addition to their number in the killer whale registry.

Paul punched the start button on a tape recorder and turned knobs on a bank of sound equipment to tune in the whales' vocalizations. Faint whistles and squeaks trickled from the lab speakers, interspersed with echolocation clicks like bursts of machine gun fire. He listened on headphones, recording verbal notes at the same time on another channel, all the while jotting rapid observations on speed, direction, grouping, weather and tide.

The whales were directly in front of the lab now. Just as their calls were becoming distinct, the thudding of an engine began to intrude. "Oh Christ, not now," Paul moaned, taking off his headphones. An Alaskan fish packer plowed into view around the point, heading south and rapidly overtaking the whales. Engine noise swelled in the speakers until the whales were drowned out.

"This is what we've done to them," Paul shouted over the racket. "They're acoustical animals and have been for millions of years. It's their world down there and now they have to live with this!"

Turning down the volume, he unrolled a chart. "It's interesting, these guys have been up here all day in Queen Charlotte Strait. All this time another pod has been down in Johnstone Strait. These two groups spend a lot of time together. They'll probably meet in Blackney Pass, almost as if they planned it." Paul calls the strait the Longhouse. "Whenever orcas are about to enter the Longhouse, they call. I guess they're saying something like, 'Hello there, anyone home, we're such and so' and they identify themselves. If there are whales in the strait, they usually answer."

Paul has five hydrophones located in the core area of whale activity between Robson Bight (the bay off the mouth of the Tsitika River in Johnstone Strait) and Blackfish Sound, each with a remote radio transmitter to beam the signal back to Orcalab. The hydrophones are all on separate radio frequencies so that by switching between them, Paul can determine the approximate location and the direction of whales even when they are out of sight and miles from the lab. Wherever he goes, Paul takes a portable receiver with him to monitor the signals – in the house, the boat, down on the beach, even in the bedroom at night.

"In a way, I'm putting my head in the ocean," he said. "We don't want to participate in the harassment of whales, so we devised this system of remote radio stations. We can identify who's there, who's hanging out with whom, where they go – these sorts of basic questions. Of course, the picture is really filled in visually by other people out in the strait, doing what we say we don't want to do. But if we persist, I believe we can do this work without anyone having to go near the whales."

145

The whales had disappeared around the point to the south, into the range of another hydrophone in Blackney Pass. As the drone of the boat engine faded and dropped out, they passed through the Long-house door, sending forth a chorus of whistles and clicks. Immediately, a pod answered, faint and far off from somewhere down the strait.

"Those must be the A5s and A6s," Helena said. "They were in Robson Bight when the *Gikumi* [a whalewatching tour boat] saw them this afternoon."

Paul is not at all sure what he will learn from the data he is collecting. "At the very least we'll get a long-term picture of the status of orcas in this area – their numbers, seasonal movements, and so forth. Beyond that, it's hard to say. We see such tiny fragments of their lives."

By way of illustration, he told me about a recent incident that had left him baffled. He was filming with a television crew when a female whale broke away from her pod and dashed through the kelp at the base of some cliffs. For several minutes she rooted just beneath the surface, as if trying to reach something in a crevice in the rock.

"When we came closer to see what she was doing, she backed off and rejoined her pod. In the crack where she was thrusting her head, we found a thirty-pound salmon, stone dead. Yet, there was not a sign of injury on its body." Paul cleaned the fish and found nothing to indicate why it died. "No disease, no internal damage, nothing. But the whale must have had something to do with the salmon being where it was, and I suspect it also caused its death. But how? Hydraulic pressure? Stress? A sound pulse? This is what I mean by fragments; this little bit of information suggests a huge area of the orca's life we know absolutely nothing about."

It has been shown experimentally that dolphins can produce sounds loud enough to kill fish. The same capacity is suspected but unproven in killer whales. A few weeks later, one of the student researchers found an even larger salmon under identical circumstances.

146

At three the next morning Paul woke me where I was sleeping under the trees behind the house. "The whales are coming," he called softly. "I thought you might like to watch them pass." He had heard their calls in his sleep on the speaker in the bedroom.

Stumbling half-dressed along the walkway to the lab, I heard the whales blowing off the mouth of the cove. But with the night as dark as the bottom of a mine, I saw nothing. Other whales blew and sounded out in the middle of the passage, and then there was only the silky lapping of water under the lab. After what seemed a long time, a whistle sounded from the speaker mounted over the deck and another more distant whale answered with the identical call. Other voices joined in, graded in perspective from close and loud to the faintest whisper. As they passed the hydrophone across Blackfish Sound on Swanson Island, the voices came together in a kind of dialogue or part singing, rocking back and forth like echoes in some vast vaulted space. The effect was unearthly and beautiful.

Surely, I thought, there is more to this than mere communication. The sounds themselves are so alien to us, might not their purpose be equally beyond conception? Something entirely outside our experience; perhaps a kind of tactile music that plays upon the undersea physics of sound to set the bodies of the whales throbbing like goblets of crystal.

One by one the voices dropped out, leaving only a few sporadic calls, fading as the whales moved on into Queen Charlotte Strait. The concert or conference, or whatever it had been, was over.

When I left the lab, Paul was hunched over the counter, making his meticulous notes by flashlight.

★ ★ ★

At breakfast I asked Paul what he made of the vocalizations of killer whales. Scientists are deeply divided on the matter. Some accept the whale's acoustical capacities and its big brain as evidence of intelligence equal or superior to ours. Others point out that, relative to body size, the whale's brain is no larger than that of many other animals, and its calls, they maintain, are mere noise, meaningless as the mooing of cows.

Paul looked out across the cove for a long minute, mild hazel eyes masking an intense concentration. "The point I began with in this whole exercise and the point I remain with is that whales possess immense, complex brains, and I don't believe that biological evolution produces an instrument like that without function or purpose. I firmly hold to the view that there must be something going on."

"What do you mean 'going on?' Their calls?"

"I can't imagine that their calls are only for identification. Why would they keep on saying, 'I'm here, I'm here, I'm here.' I don't think that would be useful and I don't think they're that stupid. So there may be some other use to the calls beyond information transfer. But I don't know what that is and I can't imagine how we'll ever find out. It's beyond me.

"I know one thing, though: from an evolutionary point of view, whales are successful and we are almost inevitably doomed to failure. On our present course I can't see how we can succeed, yet they have. They've been here for millions of years; where we have had a flash in time, they've had a clear day.

"Public attitudes *have* changed, but we still have an exploitative mentality. We are still being users when we snatch whales out of the oceans and put them in tanks. We are still being users when we take thousands of people out on the water and chase gray whales up and down the the coast of California, or humpbacks off New England. I'm not very critical of these things because they've been very helpful in terms of people's growth with respect to whales. But I don't think that's where we want to be. Where we want to be is where we understand that whales have rights – the right to life and freedom of existence, freedom from capture, harassment, imprisonment and freedom from death at our hands."

When the resident killer whales pull out of Johnstone Strait it's as if they've dropped off the edge of the world. One day they are familiar as house pets, named and numbered, indentified by sight and sound and tracked all through their daily round. And the next, they are off on a winter odyssey about which we know almost nothing. There are occasional sightings, sometimes hundreds of miles from Johnstone Strait, and then weeks and months that are simply blank.

It's a lean time for the whale watcher. The students head south, and the local tour boats are tied up for the winter. Paul Spong's focus shifts from studying whales to defending them, and he goes on the road, sometimes for months, lecturing, demonstrating, protesting in any way he can against commercial whaling and live capture of whales for aquariums.

Paul is particularly critical of the live capture trade in killer whales. "The public has the idea that it's benign. But if you look at the statistics, live capture is a death sentence, just as surely as commercial whaling."

More than sixty killer whales were taken alive on the coasts of British Columbia and Washington between 1965 and 1979 and another twelve died in botched attempts at capture. Of the fifty-nine that went to aquariums, only three or four are alive at this writing. In the wild they would have lived for up to seventy years. After the capture trade was stopped on the Pacific coast, another thirty or so killer whales were taken from waters around Iceland. It's not known how many of them survive.

The capture of killer whales is not outlawed, as the public has come to believe. In Washington and Alaska, live capture is blocked only by jurisdictional disputes between state and federal governments. Killer whales can still be taken in British Columbia under permit from the fisheries department. Despite public opposition, the department authorized the capture of beluga whales in the summer of 1990. It might yet permit killer whale captures on the British Columbia coast if the Vancouver Aquarium should lose its whales and be unable to replace them elsewhere. After all, it is the whale show that keeps the turnstiles clicking.

Before I left, Paul took me into the woods back of the cove to see a giant cedar tree. The splayed and fluted bole, four yards or more in diameter, rises from a carpet of moss, thrusting up through green shade, high into the sun above the forest canopy. We stood in silence, subdued somehow by its monumental presence, and then Paul said, "We need trees like this, need their timelessness to take the measure of our little lives."

Paul has waged a long and futile battle to prevent the logging of Hanson Island. Sometime within the next few years loggers will strip the slopes behind his cove, including the creek ravine from which he draws his water. Exposed to the sun, it will almost certainly go dry in the summer. The house and Orcalab and a narrow belt of trees will be marooned in a moonscape.

"They're going to destroy our life here," he said. "I don't see how we can carry on."

It was drizzling when I drifted on the flood tide through Blackney Passage and into Johnstone Strait. Columns of smoke stood straight above the research camps along the bluffs of West Cracroft Island. The students left the shelter of their tents and plastic lean-tos and came down to invite me up for tea.

We sat under the dripping shelters and they told me about their work. They were from Oregon and California, Alberta and urban British Columbia, bright and determined young men and women who were here to gather the statistical minutae that would earn them a university degree. As they talked, their research projects seemed narrow and bloodless, and I felt none of the mystery and wonder of whales that animates Paul Spong. But perhaps it was the mood of the day; there were no whales in the strait and, with their research subjects gone elsewhere, the students felt thwarted and bored.

In the biggest of the whale watchers' camps at Boat Bay, Jeff Jacobsen, a red-head with a perpetual sunburn, sat close to the fire overlooking the strait. He's from Humboldt State College in California. "You get a narrow, myopic view by focussing on one little group of orcas," he said, "but if you are going to do your thesis on an animal like this that you don't even see most of the time, you've got to restrict your subject or you'll never get enough information together. One student is doing her whole master's degree on the energetics of babysitting – how the female offspring care for the younger calves in the pods."

What effect is all this attention having on the whales, I wondered?

"In the past five years there hasn't been a day when the whales haven't been followed almost constantly." Jacobsen spoke from the perspective of eleven consecutive summers with the whales. "The disturbance keeps them in a higher state of arousal; you can measure that vocally, and they aren't able to rest as much as they used to."

Occasionally, all the members of a pod will line up abreast and make very slow, shallow dives or lie almost still on the surface, moving and breathing as a single animal, in perfect synchronization. They will hold this pattern for an hour or more, apparently in a state close to sleep. Once common in the strait, these resting lines, as they're called, have not been seen for at least five years.

That night I camped again on the gravel hook across from the Tsitika River. As the stars came out, a line of phosphorescence glowed in the ripples lapping the shore. I slipped the canoe into the water and paddled out through open lanes in the kelp. The sea beneath me was luminous with green fire, as if the world had turned over and the canoe was gliding across the cosmic night. Spiral nebulae spun from the paddle and meteors glowed in the slipstream from the bow. Swimming through watery space, every fish and moving thing trailed a wake of phosphorous. And deep down in the kelp forest, stars smouldered in the waving fronds.

I tried to imagine killer whales rushing through a fiery sea on such a night. What, if anything, did it mean to them? Did they experience delight? A sense of wonder? Fear? Or something else beyond our knowing?

There was a clue perhaps in something Paul Spong had told me. On an autumn night a few years ago, the northern lights, which are rarely seen on the coast, lit up the sky over Blackfish Sound. Killer whales came down from the north – a big pod or several together – and set the sea to ringing with a concert of calls more wild and grand than anything he had ever heard.

Was it a paean to the shimmering heavens? Or something more prosaic, like a conversation about the weather? Or the state of the fishing? Or just a noisy fight in the family?

We'll never know and perhaps it's just as well. A little mystery is a healthy thing.

13

In 1864 artist Frederick Whymper stopped at one of the Gulf Islands in Georgia Strait on his way from Bute Inlet to Victoria. His party was careless with their campfire and the sparks

> set light to some dry grasses which, in their turn communicated the flame to the underbrush and in a little while the forest itself, covering the whole of the island, formed one immense conflagration . . . . the last we saw of it was a cloud of smoke on the horizon some hours afterwards as we skimmed away with a favouring breeze. These forest fires are often grand sights and burn for weeks.

There is no knowing which of the Gulf Islands went up in smoke, though we can be pretty certain that the "grand" sight was fueled by some of the finest Douglas fir in the world. Logging had not yet reached beyond the environs of the few towns in Whymper's time, and all but the smallest Gulf Islands were covered by towering forests of old-growth trees.

Little more than a century after Whymper made his trip, every island in Georgia Strait has been logged two and three times over. All around the strait, virtually every square yard of timberland up to 3000 feet above sea level has been cut, and on the east coast of Vancouver Island, where the finest stands of Douglas fir once grew, every watershed save one has been stripped. The lone survivor is the valley of the Tsitika River, across Johnstone Strait from my camp.

In the cool of the early morning I paddled towards the Tsitika, watching the rising sun flood the valley and fire the golden grass along its estuary. From tidewater to ridgetops, the forest was a slope of seamless green, unbroken by road or burn or even the natural break of a rock bluff. Inland, the valley climbed and lost itself between mountain spurs that press from either side. For the next seven miles the river ascended a succession of rapids and falls, then forked into tributary creeks, fed by lakes and chains of lush water-meadows.

Although I could see none of the upper river from the strait, I knew it from a trip there in the early 1970s. I had flown into the headwaters with a film crew and a government wildlife biologist to make a television program that would state the case for preserving the valley. There was hope then that the entire watershed could be saved from logging.

We went in early May, flying north in a Beaver floatplane. All up the east coast of Vancouver Island the rivers were in spate with snowmelt and silt washed down from the logged hillsides. But when we landed in the Tsitika, the winter's snow was melting gradually in the cool of the forests, and the river was clear. The meadow creeks flowed slowly under grassy banks, skirting ponds where skunk cabbages were thrusting, sulphur and apple green, through the black mud. In the timber above the meadows, we found the hard spring snow cut like a cattleyard with tracks of elk and deer which had fed through the lean months of late winter on lichens that dropped from the trees.

We made a melancholy camp in the perpetual twilight of virgin timber. The cameraman, a health food freak, pined for his sprouts and wheat germ. The writer was stricken with acrophobia and froze on the mountain. And the biologist was prickly and morose. When it rained, as it did much of the time, we filmed the obligatory water-beaded spiderwebs and mist along the mountainsides, then sat under the tarp in front of a steaming fire.

The Tsitika was to be logged by MacMillan Bloedel, the biggest of the multinational timber companies operating in the province. (Two other companies held cutting rights in the valley but had no imminent logging plans.) It planned to truck logs down the valley and boom them near the mouth of the river, a process which had devastated every other estuary on the east coast of Vancouver Island. As far as MacMillan Bloedel was concerned, the way was clear; it had rights to the timber under provincial licence and it owned land for its log dump at the river mouth. But it was not to be.

In the early 1970s fisheries scientist Ian MacAskie discovered that killer whales come to the pebble beaches adjacent to the Tsitika estuary to rub themselves, much as bears scratch their backs on favourite trees. The public was treated to underwater video pictures of the whales swimming on their backs and sides, scraping themselves on the bottom. The behaviour had never been seen elsewhere; the role of the beaches was apparently unique. If MacMillan Bloedel went ahead, noise and pollution were all but certain to drive the whales away.

The controversy spread from the beaches to the entire Tsitika watershed. Scientists and wildlife groups argued that aesthetically and as a baseline for future research, an undisturbed Tsitika was worth more to the province than any conceivable return from its timber. The government waffled for a year or two and then caved in to the demands of the loggers. But there was a condition: MacMillan Bloedel would have to abandon its plans for a log dump on the estuary and truck its logs out through the headwaters of the valley. The pebble beaches and river mouth were to be protected by two ecological reserves, one on land and another in the adjacent waters.

154

The marine reserve fell under the jurisdiction of the federal government, which acted quickly, closing Robson Bight, the bay where the Tsitika enters Johnstone Strait, to industrial activity. But the provincial government weaseled for a decade before giving up enough timber for a narrow reserve parallel to the beach.

The government's actions only aggravated the controversy, which grew in intensity through the 1980s, culminating in ugly confrontations in the fall of 1990 between loggers and environmentalists. Under public pressure, logging plans have been modified, though the changes are more public relations than real concessions. Cutting has been spaced out over a longer time frame to reduce the area of naked slash on view. And forty percent of the watershed is to be set aside for parks and wildlife. On closer inspection, most of this area turns out to be swamp, alpines or slopes too unstable to log, leaving less than ten percent of the valley's old-growth forests protected.

The hillsides facing onto Johnstone Strait will be logged over a period of years in smaller than normal patches. But these will be clearcuts nonetheless, with burned-over slash, washed-out roads and eroded watercourses. Such will be the backdrop for the grand procession of killer whales, witnessed by visitors from all over the world.

At the outer edge of the Tsitika's alluvial fan, the bottom rises abruptly from depths of more than a thousand feet to a shelf of gravel, clamshell and eelgrass. Drifting with the tide I passed over a winking cloud of herring minnows and white jellyfish big as salad plates. Flounders darted away from the canoe, melding so perfectly into the background that I could see only their shadows scooting over the bottom. In the trench cut by the river, a trout or Dolly Varden char flashed bronze in the amber water.

With the tide half out and the river too shallow to paddle, I tied a line to the back thwart and tracked up the riffles, walking the bank and pulling the canoe at an angle to keep it out in the stream. As the

155

ground became higher and dryer, salt-tolerant sedge and rockweed gave way to silverweed, meadow barley and hairgrass as high as my chest. The grass stretched east for a quarter mile, nodding in the morning wind, like a strip of virgin prairie set down between the mountains and the sea. Chocolate brown fox sparrows sang the clear, liquid song of the estuaries.

The Tsitika emerged from the forest in a confusion of fallen trees and abandoned channels, overgrown with alder. Around the first bend the forest canopy closed overhead and the river purled through dappled shade. It was a small stream, scarcely thirty feet across, much contorted by logs and the roots of standing trees, creating deep pools and dark caverns under the banks. Its bed was gravel, with drifts of sand in the pools and moist crescents of clay at the edge of still water, glinting with fool's gold. The cool air smelled musty with skunk cabbage and damp earth. On a gravel bar broken twigs and sprigs of red elderberries – the leavings of a bear's meal – were caught in the trickle between the stones.

Occasionally, as I walked upstream, I heard a thrush singing off in the woods, or the drumming of water falling in a hollow under the roots. Even a few steps away from the bank, the rustle of the stream was lost in the silence of great cedars, hemlocks and Sitka spruce. High overhead, in the forest canopy, ruby-crowned kinglets were peeping faintly.

Like most coastal streams, the Tsitika is awkward to walk because of the underbrush and fallen timber. Crossing and recrossing on logs over the water, I stopped often to watch fish darting up to snatch insects off the surface. They were bright, nimble fish of four to five inches – coho and chinook salmon and steelhead and cutthroat trout – holding over for a year or two before they migrated to sea. In slower water closer to the bank, two-inch fry – this year's brood – kept their distance from the cannibal trout.

It is the measured, self-regulating equilibrium of a natural stream that clearcut logging destroys. When the water storage of the forest is gone, flash floods sweep away or by-pass many of the obstructions

156

in the river, and with them go the pools and best holding water for fish. Spawning gravels plug up with silt. Others are left high and dry as the stream fills in old channels and cuts new ones. In hot, rainless summers the flow slows to a trickle and a great many of the young fish starve to death because there is not enough water to bring down food.

A mile inland from the beach, where its gradient rises sharply, the Tsitika becomes a mountain stream, broken by nearly continuous rapids and falls. As logging progresses in the headwaters (about ten percent has already been clearcut) the river will become increasingly subject to flash floods. Logs that now check the rapids will be bowled down the slope and stranded in jams where the stream levels out. The strip of ecological reserve land will not protect the estuary from the rampaging river; gravel, silt, bark and smashed wood will spread over the flats and work their way along the shore towards the rubbing beaches. None of these effects of logging are conjectural; they have occurred in scores of other watersheds. All that remains in doubt is whether the killer whales will continue to use the rubbing beaches.

Frustrated by clutching underbrush along the stream, I turned aside and climbed through the timber, leaving the elderberry, salmonberry and thorny devil's club behind on the wet alluvial flats. Huckleberry and sword ferns stayed on, joined now by gangly hemlock seedlings, rooted often as not in rotten logs.

The term virgin timber brings to mind groves of towering monarchs, all much of a size, with open ground beneath, where one can walk freely, as if through a game park. Although there are such forests, particularly where a single generation of trees has grown up after a fire, old-growth timber is usually a mix of species and ages, and the ground is littered with dead trees in all stages of decay. The Tsitika is this kind of forest. Red cedar, western hemlock and Douglas fir predominate at low elevations, with Sitka spruce on the wettest ground near the river mouth. Higher in the valley, the fir

157

dwindles, yellow cedar replaces red cedar, and western hemlock gives way to mountain hemlock and true firs. Except for a few bell-bottomed red cedars, eight or ten feet in diameter, there are no trees on the scale of the giants in the Queen Charlottes or the west coast of Vancouver Island. It is an impressive forest nonetheless; trees six feet at the butt are common, with straight, slow-tapering trunks, clean of branches for 100 feet or more above the ground. There are many snags (standing dead trees). The cedar snags endure for years, needle tips jutting through the canopy, until rot at the base brings them down full length. Hemlock and fir decay more quickly, rotting from the top down, until only the thickest part of the trunk is left to fall as one piece.

Trees do not die of old age. Unlike the human body, whose parts eventually wear out, a tree is infinitely self-renewing. In theory, it could live forever, if disease or parasites did not intervene. As a tree nears old age, the growth rate slows and it loses vigour until it is no longer able to resist the invasion of the organisms that will eventually kill it. Disease is therefore the principal agent of health in the forest, weeding out the weaker young trees and bringing down old trees that are past their prime.

This of course is not the view of the forest industry. Foresters describe the Tsitika's type of old-growth forest as "decadent," and their policy in British Columbia is to cut the virgin forests as rapidly as possible, replacing them with plantations of young, fast-growing trees. But a natural forest is a primeval entity of unimaginable complexity which cannot be replaced by simplistic monoculture. All the so-called decadent elements of the old-growth forest – snags, rotting logs, lichens, fungi, insects, disease – are indispensable sources of fertility and renewal.

In the first generation or two, a plantation may grow well on the residual assets of the old-growth forest. A six-foot fir log, for example, will return its energies to the ecosystem over 400 years of slow disintegration. But the coastal rainforest depends on a continuing supply of recycled wood. At least ninety percent of its sustenance comes from the few inches of humus that lie over the barren mineral soil. Eventually, without rotting wood, fertility dwindles and the weakened trees lose their resistance to insects and disease. As the natural system breaks down, ever more pesticides, herbicides and fertilizers are needed to achieve the same results. Finally, after three or four generations, the forest collapses under such stress. Disease becomes epidemic, insects can no longer be controlled, soil breaks down and the trees grow poorly or die outright. It has happened in China, Western Europe (even before the effects of acid rain) and elsewhere.

But events two or three centuries in the future don't concern the government or forest companies of British Columbia. Old-growth forests like the Tsitika are simply an asset to be liquidated for short-term profit.

A half-mile from the river, I stopped to rest on a knoll in a grove of cedars and hemlocks. High overhead a breeze moved through the forest canopy, animating patterns of sunlight playing on the great trunks and over the forest floor. Inland, a flicker hammered on a resonant cedar snag.

When the Tsitika's virgin stands are cut, the valley's wildlife will be affected in ways we are only beginning to understand. Deer, for example, will thrive at first on the abundant forage that grows on new logging slash. But as more of the old-growth forest is cut, the deer will face starvation in winters of heavy snowfall. Gone will be the protein-rich lichens found only in virgin timber.* Gone, as well, will be the broad crowns of the old-growth forest which intercept eighty percent of the snowfall. Snow accumulations on the logging slash will be five times as deep as they were in the timber, burying food supplies

---

*The forest service and the companies have made much of the fact that cutting has been deferred on some critical winter range. However, all of it will be logged eventually, and when it is gone, the new forests of the Tsitika will be far too young to grow the lichens that now carry deer and elk through the winter.

vital to the deer. Then, as the young plantation forest rises, its denseness will prevent the growth of browse. Deer numbers in the Sayward Provincial Forest on Vancouver Island, planted from 1939 to 1942, were found to be only twenty to thirty percent of populations on unlogged land. By far the most productive regime for deer, elk and many other species is a mix of logging in small strips or patches, separated by blocks of virgin timber.

The wind was freshening now, rippling over the grass on the estuary. I stood there for a long time, drinking it in, certain that I was seeing the unspoiled Tsitika for the last time. In the headwaters logging had already scythed down the forest where I had seen the deer and elk tracks in the snow.

The old-growth forests will be extinct when they are cut. Although old-growth is biologically renewable, given another thousand years, the plantations will all be harvested before they are a century old. The small patches of virgin timber that have been set aside as museum exhibits will succumb to fire or disease or forest succession. (Douglas fir is eventually replaced on the coast by cedar and hemlock.) Then, when our artificial forests break down, as they inevitably will, we will have no prototype to turn back to. Nature's blueprint, drawn over thousands of years, will be lost.

Crossing Johnstone Strait in the trough of the westerly swell, I turned and rode the waves to the east along the shore of West Cracroft Island. The land was low and logged right down to the shore, in defiance of forest service policies requiring a leave-strip of trees at the water's edge to enhance the view.

Too often as I traversed this pillaged country, I caught myself working up a pointless rage. It was not logging itself that got under my skin – there is nothing inherently harmful about harvesting timber – but rather the trees stolen from leave-strips along streams and beaches, salmon creeks choked with debris and silt, mountainsides washed down to bedrock, and the trail of industrial garbage that loggers leave wherever they go. Some of this vandalism is ideological, the anti-environmentalist policy of a right-wing forest service that insists on logging slopes too steep to hold their soil, or destroying sites of life-or-death value to wildlife. Much of it is sheer greed: the huge clear-cuts; the high-grading that takes only the best logs, and the theft of trees that should never be cut. But a lot of the worst devastation has no apparent cause or purpose.

I wondered sometimes whether violence plays a part. The entire history of logging on the coast is one of violence against the land and reciprocal violence endured by loggers. So great is the toll of death and destruction that logging has often been described as a kind of warfare in which the workers are expendable shock troops. Between 1900 and 1980 more than 4000 men died in the woods of British Columbia and many times that number were maimed. They were crushed under rolling logs, skewered on splintered trees, decapitated by whipping cables, flattened beneath falling snags, split by axes and saws, pulped under toppled machines, drowned, burned, suffocated and killed in a hundred other ghastly ways.

In its day, steam made a special contribution to the carnage. The steam donkey gave the logger what he liked to call "almighty power." It was instant power, much quicker and more dangerous than any internal combustion engine; when the donkey puncher opened the throttle, steel ropes twanged like fiddle strings and logs jumped as if they were alive. When there was a hangup, cables an inch-and-a-half thick could break like string and huge cast-iron pulleys shattered and flew like shrapnel. Steam boilers exploded, splaying their tubes like blasted spaghetti, scalding the engineer and riddling bystanders with rivets as deadly as machine gun bullets.

In the early years, "unavoidable accident" was the standard excuse for all manner of avoidable safety lapses. When someone was killed it was his own fault, according to the standards of the day. There was no training of any kind and few of the camps cared if a man was green, careless or clueless. "The boss felt them," it was said, "and if they were warm, they were hired." Many died in their first hours on the

161

job because they had no idea where the danger was coming from. Many more knew their way around, yet succumbed to the deadly machismo that glamourized risk-taking in the bush.

The companies did their part, too, especially the highball camps where even the most woods-wise men were imperilled by the frantic rush to keep the daily log count high. The worst of them became known as death camps. One, the Hanson camp on Sonora Island, was said to have claimed the lives of twenty-two men, whose names were inscribed on an "Honour Roll" in the company office, each with a gold star.* Death was so commonplace in some camps that work did not stop when a man was killed. The body was simply moved out of the way and packed back to the camp at the end of the shift.

Although the death camps are long gone, logging in British Columbia remains by far the most dangerous occupation in Canada. In fact, the number of fatalities has been rising in recent years (seventy-one in 1988-89) because of the proliferation of non-union contractors whose workers are not protected by union safety standards.

As I paddled beneath the clearcuts and grunting machines, moving like yellow elephants along the skyline, I puzzled over the cause of so much pointless carnage. Was it violence in man that begat such unremitting violence against the land? The more I thought about it the more it seemed too facile, too ready an excuse. Ignorance and indifference seemed closer to the truth. And perhaps a last hurrah for Paul Bunyan and his blue ox, Babe.

---

*Recounted by Eric Flesher, in *Timber: The Log of a Western Logger*, unpublished manuscript, Special Collections, University of B.C. Library.

14

Turning away from Johnstone Strait, I skirted the high bluffs of West Cracroft Island and went on into Port Harvey. There the hills drew back from the head of an island-dotted inlet, making way for an expanse of salt marsh and tidal channels, royal blue between the bleached grass.

Before World War I Port Harvey, known then as Cracroft, was one of those go-ahead places supposedly destined for big things. It boasted a post office, store, hotel and church, and the Union Steamships made a scheduled stop here. But the land proved to be too wet or sandy to farm, the timber played out, and Port Harvey no longer had any reason to exist. The church and hotel were towed away to hardier communities and the metropolis was no more.

Three new families have moved into Port Harvey in recent years: a logger and a tugboat man, both retired, and a salmon fisherman. Finding no one at home at the fisherman's floathouse, I went on to the logger's place, set on a knoll of lawns, flowers and fruit trees, like a spread in a homes and gardens magazine. When I was still some distance from the float, the owner hurried down from the house, calling out: "Is there something I can do for you?" in a tone that said unmistakably: "I'm not about to do anything for you."

I explained myself as he stood looking down at me in the canoe, a big man, still hard-bodied in his sixties. He didn't intend to let me set foot on shore. "Why don't you go talk to my neighbour?" he suggested. Even though the neighbour's property was several hundred yards along the shore, I could see the large signs: PRIVATE PROPERTY – KEEP OFF. "Oh, that's for the yachts," he said. "They come in here as if they owned the place. They tie up and bring their dogs ashore and let them shit all over the place. When I tell them this isn't a public float, they give me a big argument. Some of them are a real pain in the ass."

As I pushed off he said, "I'd ask you up to the house, but we're just leaving to go to Minstrel. Where are you going to camp? I'll come by this evening." I pointed out a beach across the inlet, though I knew he wouldn't come. I had no quarrel with his wish to be left alone, though I'd rather he'd said so plainly.

From an island in mid-inlet a brood of half-grown red-breasted mergansers slipped into the water and milled about, undecided which way to go. When they bolted in a waddling line behind the lone female, I counted twenty-one young. How many eggs went into the making of such a flock? Scores certainly, and perhaps a hundred or more. Flightless and utterly devoid of cover for two months on an open seacoast, the chicks must suffer an enormous attrition. Eagles, mink, otters, killer whales and even lingcod pick them off. As the broods diminish they combine, sometimes under the care of a single female, sometimes several. Is it companionship or the immunity of numbers that brings them together?

I camped in a haze of mosquitoes on a field of parched grass and lichen-shrouded apple trees. At sundown I sat out on the point in the breeze to escape the bugs, grawing green apples and watching the salt marsh turn to orange and indigo. Pretty as it was, Port Harvey proved to be a Cinderella kind of place; after midnight the tide went out and transformed the lovely inlet into acres of mud. Morning found the water a half-mile from the grass flats and still retreating. Forewarned by shallows beneath the canoe, I had camped as close as possible to deep water and beached the canoe even farther down the inlet, where the bottom drops away more steeply. But I had no idea the tide would run out so far.

I dawdled over breakfast, gauging the progress of the water by a stick poking out of the mud far out on the flats. Low tide was at nine, according to the tide tables, but that was in Alert Bay, thirty miles away. It would be later here. At nine the stick was at the water's edge. By nine-thirty it was high and dry and the tide was still falling. At this rate it would be afternoon before I was waterborne.

My patience at an end, I dragged the canoe down into an empty tidechannel and lugged gear for an hour, slogging back and forth through the mud. When the last box was in, I sat in the shade, swatting horseflies, like Noah awaiting the flood. At eleven a tongue of water advanced into the channel, and I pulled the canoe free.

There is much to be said in favour of canoeing on lakes.

Outside Port Harvey I came upon a river otter swimming very slowly towards the shore of East Cracroft Island. Approaching quietly from behind, I closed to within a few canoe lengths before it noticed me and dove. But it stayed submerged for only a few yards, marking its course with a trail of bubbles. When it came up for air, I saw that the otter had a big dogfish clamped in its jaws. The shark – which was at least as long as its captor – was caught across the back so that the otter was pushing it sideways through the water. It was still very much alive, lashing its tail and arching its body around the otter's head.

I hung back, hoping to see the outcome of the struggle. The otter kept on, diving less and less often and breathing with a laboured rasping. Close to shore, it dove again. I waited, expecting the otter to drag the dogfish up onto the rocks to kill it. A minute passed, then five, and still there was no sign of otter or shark. Finally, I searched along the rock for some crevice where the otter might have hidden, but could find nothing to account for its disappearance. And so I went on. Later, far ahead, I caught one fleeting glimpse of the otter's arched back and bowed tail as it dove.

East of Port Harvey, Chatham Channel branches to the left and Call Inlet to the right, forming a broad Y. Facing south from the crutch of the Y is a blunt 700-foot promontory. Fluted cliffs wall its west side, dropping sheer to a grove of alders and a shady creek which trickles into the corner of a cove. Overlooking the cove is a blocky two-storey house of blushing pink and red, surrounded by gardens and lawns. To its left a cavernous boat repair works stands over the water on pilings, and to the right, beside the creek, a log skidway rises from the water into the black maw of a shingle mill.

It was mid-afternoon and very hot when I paddled into the cove. From the water I could see no sign of life about the house. Then an outboard motor started somewhere over by the creek; a small motor, idling. An old man appeared from the midst of a loose boom of cedar logs, kneeling on some sort of boat that was so low in the water he barely showed above the logs. He unhooked a chain, putted slowly out of the boom with a log in tow, and closed the opening. His boat consisted of two short logs, with some planks thrown across and an ancient six hp Johnson clamped to the back. The logs were water-logged, leaving almost no freeboard.

The outboard gasped out a lot of blue smoke and stopped often. Repeatedly, the old man yanked it back to life and maneuvered the log, by fits and starts, to the base of the skidway, where the motor shuddered and died, as if it knew its work was done. Leaning stiffly on his pike pole, he looked at the canoe.

"You must have to pick your weather, travellin' in one of those things."

"Yes, but it's pretty seaworthy," I assured him. "You must have travelled in a canoe."

"Yes, I did. And I fell overboard, too." He spoke with a lilting cadence, as if he found everything amusing. His name was Merril Hadley. He and his wife Edie had lived here for nearly fifty years, becoming known as the archetypal coast people, survivors who stayed on when nearly everyone else was moving into town.

Merril threw a length of cable across the log and fished in the water with the pike pole, expertly hooking the end and pulling it up, encircling the log. He passed the cable through a loop and drew it tight.

"There, isn't that lovely," he said.

"You look like you've done that before."

"Once or twice, but at eighty, I'm gettin' awfully slow." He was a flat-bellied six-footer with rosy cheeks, deep-blue eyes, a sharp

166

nose and a full head of snowy hair under a greasy peaked cap of the kind that working men rather than baseball players wear. Climbing the skidway to drag down a cable from the winch in the mill, he slipped and narrowly missed falling ten feet to the beach. "Dammit, when you get old, you get clumsy as hell, too."

The mill was a cave of cool shade, sweet with the scent of red cedar. Bundles of shingles were stacked in neat rows on the ground floor. Above, on the loft that opened onto the skidway, blocks of cedar, cut to length and trimmed, awaited the nearby saws. Merril was rummaging through drawers of bolts for a shackle to join the cable from the log to the winch. I asked if he ran the mill alone; normally it takes a gang of men to operate a shingle mill. "Yep, I'm the whole outfit," he chuckled. "The missus used to help me, but she quit one day in no uncertain terms. Bundling shingles gets to be pretty boring."

Poking along the wall where bolts and steel dogs were tucked between the studs, he pulled out a shackle. "There's that son of a bitch right there." He peered closely at it, then put it back. "No, that's a different son of a bitch." At last he found what he was looking for and climbed the ladder to the loft, talking steadily. "My sons and I used to log together and when we broke up, they didn't want any part of the mill. It's whatever you care for; a shingle machine always thrilled me, but it didn't do anything for them."

I noted that Merril had all his fingers, a rarity among shingle sawyers, who work between two horrific circular saws three to four feet in diameter. "Well, not quite all," he said, holding up four fingers. The tips of three of them were missing and the fourth was severed higher up, near the base of the nail. "I cut that one off the first year I had the mill, in 1936. I got pretty careful right after that."

Shackling the cables together, he climbed down the ladder to start a diesel the size of a sportscar which powers the mill. First, he had to hand-start an auxiliary motor. "I call this one the banger," he said, turning the crank. It fired twice then started with a roar that was physically painful, belching smoke from a hole in the exhaust manifold. Merril held a scrap of metal over the opening – which had no effect at all – while he started the diesel and, mercifully, shut off the

167

auxiliary. Using his palms and keeping his fingers well clear, he fed a belt onto a whirling drum; the machinery lumbered into motion and the entire building began to dance to its rhythm. The mill was a time-trip back to the days when entire factories ran on man-eating belts driven from a central power source.

Up on the loft Merril climbed onto the top of the skidway and tugged a rope to start the winch. The cable twanged tight and the log began to move. "I get up here so I can see the log when she starts up," he shouted. "Sometimes they jump over the side." With the log well into the skidway, he climbed down onto the loft floor and started the winch again. As the back end of the log came out of the water, its full weight dragged and the rusty, half-inch cable made ominous crunching noises on the drum of the winch. The diesel was putting out only a fraction of its power, and the winch was geared so low that its pulling strength was hardly tested. Something had to give. The log squealed to a stop and the cable parted with a bang, whipping across the top of the skidway where Merril was standing moments before.

"Now look at that son of a bitch," he said, picking up the splayed end. "It was that damned rotten loop. Old and worn out, just like me." He peered down the skidway at the log. "Anyway, that's good enough for now; the tide won't get her there."

Down on the ground floor he explained how the shingles were sorted into three different grades and bundled separately. The number ones – clear cedar with no knots – went to Vancouver on a freight boat. "It's at least ten days before the money comes back," Merril said, "and the price usually changes. Always down, never up."

He hauled the other shingles, number twos and utility grades, across Johnstone Strait on his converted troller, *Edie H.*, and trucked them down Vancouver Island. In fact, there was a load on the boat already, which he and Edie planned to take to the island early in the morning.

"I'd ask you to stay, except we still got an awful lot to do."

"Carry on and I'll just tag along," I suggested. "Can I give you a hand?"

"Oh, I couldn't do that," Merril said, "it wouldn't be hospitable." But he insisted that I come to the house for coffee.

We sat at the kitchen table, looking across the tidal race in Chatham Channel. Edie – Merril calls her Eed – brought cookies and coffee, and the two of them reminisced about the boom years when Minstrel Island was the liveliest logging town on the coast.

"Oh, I remember the fights," Merril said, wistfully, "there were the loveliest fights at Minstrel."

"What I remember is the kids going to school at Minstrel," Edie said, "five miles there and back alone in their own boat. That's what turned me grey."

But it was the future that preoccupied them. Edie believed it was time to leave. "We're not going be able to carry on here forever and I think we should move to Vancouver Island while we're still young enough to get set up there."

Merril was dead set against it. "It takes years to get a place this far and I'd be broken-hearted if I had to leave it all behind. There'll be no shingle mill for me on Vancouver Island. If I have to quit work, it would be just like pullin' the coffin lid over my head."

Unfortunately, they were probably both right.

A summer snowstorm of fireweed silk was blowing in Chatham Channel when I crossed. Billions of gossamer tufts streamed out of the west, glinting like ice crystals and rising on the warm air until they were lost in the sky.

I camped on a gravel beach on East Cracroft Island, across from Hadley Cove, as it is now called. When the evening shadows had climbed the promontory behind the Hadleys' house, a light came on in their kitchen. I wondered if their life here was as idyllic as it seemed, or had it been monotonous and overburdened with physical work? Certainly, it was not all clear sailing – they'd lost a son in an accident and only a few years ago their house burned to the ground, leaving them with nothing but the nightclothes they fled in. Still, after more than fifty years together, they laughed easily and, it seemed, harboured few regrets.

The tide crept under my fire at dark and snuffed it out with a slow, steamy sigh. As the water came on, I moved the camp back to the edge of the trees, laying my pallet of boards across the driftlogs for a bed. I woke in the night as if someone had nudged me in my sleep. At the very top of the tide, the sea was gently rocking the logs under my pallet.

15

The rising sun bowled down the alley of Call Inlet straight into the camp. One minute I was shivering in the dawn under my dew-soaked blankets and the next I was sweating. With the tide still three-quarters high, the blinding light glanced from the water almost at my feet. The bush was too thick to afford a retreat, and raising the tarp would have provided only the stifling shade of a greenhouse. My choices were clear: I could stay and be parboiled or move on to cooler places. Regretting the lazy morning in camp I had promised myself, I loaded the canoe and pushed off.

Crossing to some islands in the middle of the passage, I paddled in their shadow towards Johnstone Strait. More and more in recent days I found myself retreating from the sun. Although I was thrice peeled and tanned, the weeks of glitter were getting to my eyes; they ached at times and teared as if I had hay fever. The glancing morning sun was the worst, boring under my straw hat and behind reflecting sun-glasses that my wife said made me look like a pimp.

I went slowly, gliding often to listen. Over on the Cracroft shore, tiny ant people moved about the net pens of a salmon farm, their voices carrying thin across the water. Three ravens passed, swooping and clacking. Thrushes and robins scattered their calls among the islands, and occasionally a woodpecker drummed. As the sun climbed they all fell silent, and a blue grouse on the ridge south of Havannah Channel began the desultory hooting it would keep up all through the heat of the day.

On the point outside Port Harvey, a black bear sniffed for crabs at the water's edge, nose-to-nose with its own reflection. It looked up as I paddled close, peering into the sun with small, weak eyes and swinging its head to test the air. Catching no scent, it went back to its sniffing, as if I weren't there.

From the western end of Havannah Channel, I could see fog ahead, drifted like dirty snow up the flanks of Vancouver Island. On the near side of Johnstone Strait, the Broken Islands formed and faded in the shifting edge of the bank. I stopped by the outermost island to take a bearing for the Adam River, three miles across the strait and a mile to the east. Judging by the chart and the lay of the land behind me, I could not go far wrong if I kept the sun – or what I could see of it – on my left shoulder. But it was not the fog that concerned me so much as the heavy boat traffic. This part of the strait is deep and wide enough for a vessel with radar to run fast in the fog with little risk. The risk would be all mine: on radar the canoe would be indistinguishable from a bit of driftwood. I could be run down or swamped by the bow wave of a freighter and no one on board would ever see me.

Out in the strait the tide would be ebbing at three knots, fast enough to sweep me half-way back to the Tsitika if I tried to cross by paddle alone. With the motor I'd cover the distance in half an hour, but at the cost of drowning out the sound of other boats. Not that it mattered; even if I heard something, paddling would do little to evade a cruise ship or freighter barrelling along at fifteen knots.

Even now I could hear engine noise, far off and muffled; a tug and boom, perhaps, or some other craft going dead slow. But there was no point drifting here; a person could grow old waiting for Johnstone Strait to be free of boats. Starting the motor, I aligned myself with the sun and plunged into the fogbank. The light dipped to grey dusk, shrinking the visible circle of water to a few yards. Then the sun, my lodestar, grew faint and vanished entirely, and I steered by the trace

171

of a ripple, which I hoped was still coming from the west, as it had been at the island. At times even the ripple disappeared, leaving me to navigate by-guess-and-by-God. All the while I kept a sharp lookout for boats, glancing left and right every few seconds, as though it were possible to see more than a few yards.

After about twenty minutes, which I figured was most of the way across, the motor slowed and died in a flurry of farts. The symptoms were familiar: carbon had clogged the spark plug. Turning to tilt up the motor to clean it, I pulled off my ear protectors and froze in my seat: the air was throbbing with diesel engines, very close. I snatched up the paddle, expecting to see a freighter loom out of the fog, pushing a great white wave ahead of her bow. Almost in the same instant, there was another sound: the clank of aluminum and the hollow *plonk* of the plungers that seine fishermen use to frighten salmon into their nets. Then I remembered: it was Monday; a two-day salmon fishery had opened in Johnstone Strait at six the night before. Scores of seiners would be concentrated along the Vancouver Island shore and hundreds of gillnetters scattered in the strait. This was the engine noise I had heard from the Broken Islands; the sounds had all been far off because the mainland side of the strait was closed to fishing.

The fog was lifting, leaking watery light under the edge of the bank. A gillnetter passed in silhouette, suspended eerily in the mist, as if it sailed at the lip of the world. A line of white floats appeared and then a seine boat, towing one end of the net in a long circle around to its other end, held fast to an aluminum skiff. The ends were joined and the purse rope winched tight, closing the bottom of the net like a giant bag. The drum in the seiner's stern began turning, reeling in black web until only the toe of the net was left in the water. Fewer than a dozen small salmon thrashed at the surface. Disgusted, the crew jerked them over the sternroller with a turn of the drum.

I paddled alongside to buy a fish for my supper. "Here, take it," a deckhand said, handing me down a nickle-bright pink salmon of about four pounds. "They're worth bugger-all to us."

Bugger-all was about $1.25 a fish, compared with $20 or more for a sockeye. Pinks are the smallest and least-prized of the five Pacific species because the flesh is pale and turns soft within a day or two after they are caught. Fresh from the water, they're fine eating.

The deckhand's complaint was echoed by the seiner's captain, Stan Hunt, a Kwakiutl from Alert Bay. "There was a good showing of sockeye last night, but they seem to have gone through. One guy got a whole school in his first set just the other side of Robson Bight. They say the crew share is more than ten thousand. This morning, nobody's getting much but pinks." By crew share he meant $10,000 for every man on the boat, plus much more for the captain and the owners.

The fog was drawing back from Vancouver Island, snagging mist in the ravines. The warming air plucked it out in ragged strings and bore them spiralling up through shaggy crowns of the firs. Scores of boats were in sight now, gillnetters drifting at the end of corklines set athwart the strait, and seiners pursing up or setting. Many more seiners were anchored, killing time until the flood tide, when they would tie one end of their net to shore and stretch a deadly curtain 860 feet long and nearly 100 feet deep across the path of salmon swimming south with the current. For twenty minutes (the legal limit), they would hold the net open before casting loose and pursing up. The best tie-off points are well-known and reserved by seiners that anchor nearby. According to the conventions of the fishery, the first boat makes the first set, and so on down the line. The seiner that made the $10,000-per-man haul had been waiting for a week at the head of the line.

The few seiners that bothered fishing the ebb tide didn't seem very serious about it. The crew of the *Patricia Louise*, all Indians from Bella Bella, sat on deck drinking coffee.

"We don't expect to do any good here," said a young crewman with a wispy mustache, who couldn't have been more than sixteen. "We just came down yesterday from Rupert. We knew there'd be a shitload of boats but we'll still get two day's fishing, and that's worth two stamps. You need ten to get on pogey." Pogey is the unemployment insurance that sees many a fisherman through the lean winter months.

Paddling through the fleet, I saw no set with more than a few dozen fish. Several came up empty, "water sets" in the parlance of seinermen. Others caught rafted kelp and driftwood which had to be picked out before it wound on the drum and tore the net. The crew of one boat was hanging, purple-faced, upside down over the side, struggling to free a tangle. It was miserable, back-breaking work. The captain stood by the controls, jerking the net in and out and raging, "This is bullshit, absolute bullshit."

There have always been too many boats in this fishery for everyone to make a living. Time after time the fleet has been cut back, only to be replaced by bigger, more efficient boats with even greater catching power. By the early 1960s overfishing and logging damage to salmon streams had brought the fisheries department to a crossroads: it had to either protect the declining natural stocks or augment the supply of fish by artificial means. Conservative biologists argued that the time-tested resilience of the wild salmon offered a safer, if slower, road to recovery. But the department had no stomach for an all-out fight with loggers and fishermen. It opted instead to build more than twenty hatcheries and half a dozen spawning channels over the next two decades. Given enough money and technology, it claimed, man could do what nature could not.

At first the results were encouraging. Production increased through the 1960s and '70s and surged ahead briefly when a batch of new hatcheries came on line in the early 1980s. But then returns of adult salmon began to level off or fall in some cases. The pattern was familiar. In Oregon, a decade earlier, hatchery salmon stocks slumped after a period of early success. Year after year the return of adults from the sea dwindled, despite doubling and quadrupling the output of young salmon from the hatcheries.

The Oregon Syndrome, as it's called, is now firmly established on the British Columbia coast. Many artificially enhanced stocks are dying at sea, and the hatcheries have been labelled "cement dinosaurs." Various theories have been advanced to explain the losses – changes in ocean upwellings, too little feed, a natural cycle of some kind – but none that is provable. There is, however, one critical factor beyond all doubt: seven or eight of every ten young salmon that come out of a hatchery or spawning channel would not have survived under more rigorous conditions in the wild. With natural selection held in check, inferior fish hatch and go to sea, and some of them inevitably return to spawn and pass on their genetic traits. Over several hatchery-raised generations, innate weaknesses accumulate to the point where the fish lose their fitness to survive in the wild.

With its wild stocks extinct, its best rivers dammed and many others polluted, Oregon has no alternative but to face the risks inherent in hatcheries. In British Columbia, where wild salmon still make up the bulk of the fishery, artificial production is a matter of choice. But there may be a term on the options; despite faltering returns, the fisheries department is pushing on with plans to raise artificial production to nearly half the catch in the next decade. The danger is not so much that the hatcheries and spawning channels will fail (already, many do not return their cost), but that they will take the wild stocks down with them. The threat arises from what are known as mixed-stock fisheries. Abundant artificial stocks are often mingled inseparably with less abundant wild salmon. If catch limits are set at safe levels for the artificial stocks, the wild stocks are overfished. And if the catch is cut back to protect the wild runs, the hatchery salmon are underfished.

On the north coast, for example, a mixed stock fishery on sockeye from two hugely productive spawning channels in the Skeena River system has reduced more than eighty wild races of Skeena sockeye to a few thousand or, in some cases, a few hundred fish. Some runs may already be extinct, and attempts to rebuild others through transplants have failed.

Once, in 1985, the fisheries department called the boats off the Skeena in order to protect a few thousand steelhead trout that were mixed with nearly two million surplus sockeye headed for the spawning channels. The steelhead were saved from the nets, though the cost was high. When the salmon arrived at Pinkut Creek and Fulton River on Babine Lake, the spawning channels were full and the gates were shut, leaving the surplus fish to die downstream and along the lakeshore, a total loss to the fishery. Commercial fishermen raised howls of protest, demanding to know – reasonably enough – why millions of dollars were being invested in enhancement projects if the salmon they produce could not be harvested. The fisheries department was deeply embarrassed and it has not repeated the exercise, even though steelhead and other wild stocks are being decimated every summer on the Skeena.

As the wild fish die out, the Skeena, like many other British Columbia streams, becomes more and more dependent on a tottering artificial abundance. The spawning channel salmon, together with one wild stock, now account for eighty-five percent of all the sockeye in the Skeena watershed. Several times in recent years, disease has run rampant through the channels, and with each generation the genetic integrity of the stocks becomes more and more suspect. If they fail, there will be very little of the once-great diversity of the wild to turn back to.

One solution to the problem is to fish salmon in the rivers when the various stocks have separated en route to their home tributaries. That idea doesn't sit well with fishermen because much of the fleet would be redundant. A better way would be to shut down the hatcheries and spawning channels and bring the fishermen and loggers to heel, giving the proven natural stocks a chance to make a comeback. Despite extensive damage, the indispensable resources – spawning rivers and wild races of salmon – are still viable. The missing component, as always, is political will.

It was time to move on; the westerly was kicking up flecks of white that would grow to four-foot waves by mid-afternoon. Under the 4000-foot wall of Vancouver Island, I paddled in shadows that angled down the timbered slopes and out onto the water. Across the strait, the mainland shore rose gradually, stepping away over hills and ridges to the far-off snowfields of the coast mountains. The distance was calibrated in colour: bold forest green in the foreground, fading fold upon fold to palest azure against the sky.

I had just passed two gillnetters, drifting with their nets out, when a solitary bull killer whale spouted ahead. I stopped paddling and watched him come on, travelling a fast, straight line in a series of shallow dives, each followed by three blows. When he was still some way off, the whale went down on a line that would bring him very close. I sat still, projecting friendly vibes and trusting they would be returned. The seconds ticked by and I was looking behind me, thinking the whale had gone past, when his fin sliced up through the waves right beside the canoe. The water bulged and opened around the great, slick body, arching up and over, raising the tip of the dorsal fin well above my head. I felt the inscrutable stare of the bull's black eye. Without a hitch in his stride, he went down, then blew twice more and sounded. With the nets ahead, the whale stayed under and I didn't see him again.

To be so close, even once, to a wild killer whale is to see the captive whale ever after for the broken thing that it is. In the prison of an aquarium tank, its dorsal fin droops and its spirit burns low.

The wind was freshening, driving the canoe on faster than the tide could push it back. Staying close-in to catch the eddies, I came upon the Adam River unexpectly. Around a bluff, much like a dozen before it, the mountains opened suddenly on a broad valley, fronted by grass flats of gold and green and, lower down, the silver thread of the stream picking its way across a cobble beach. The angle of view opened into the near end of the bay, revealing a log dump and sorting grounds severing the grass from the timbered flank of the valley. Beyond the sorting grounds, an island of spruce towered like a four-masted ship over the riverbank.

Anchoring the canoe, I walked up to the grove. Under its spreading limbs, an inviting campsite looked east across the stream and acres of grass. But it was all beyond reach; the canoe was hundreds of yards from the trees and there was too little water to track it up the stream. Shorn of its water storage, the Adam (which is a much bigger stream in its season than the Tsitika) had hardly enough water to wet my feet.

I was squatting by the stream, topping up my water jug, when someone said "hello" close behind me. Startled, I turned to find a tall, burly man with a wild beard approaching with a map in his hand. His kayak was drawn up on the beach.

"I'm heading for Port Townsend, Washington," he said. "Can you tell me where there are any good camping places ahead?"

He was a male nurse from Haynes, Alaska. In less than six weeks he had paddled more than a thousand miles, straight down the Inside Passage, hellbent on making time. I went over his map with him – an ordinary B.C.-Washington road map from a service station – pointing out some of my favourite camping places on Georgia Strait. He drew a line between the few that were close to his route and by-passed the rest.

After only a few minutes he prepared to leave, struggling into a rubber jacket that cinched tight around his neck and wrists. I asked if he didn't find it awfully hot; the afternoon was warm, despite the wind.

"Yeah, some days," he said, pulling on a heavy life vest, "but I don't take any chances." He drifted in the shallows for a moment, fitting a spray cover over the coaming around the cockpit.

Until then I hadn't noticed that someone had scattered a few oysters on the beach, hoping perhaps that they would multiply. "If

I were you I'd take those," he said, "before someone comes and gets them."

He went away fast, straight as a string down Johnstone Strait.

East of the Adam, off Windy Point, the following sea began to lap uncomfortably close to the gunwales. I went on, dodging whitecaps, to the next likely camping spot, a pebble beach in the partial shelter of a point, overgrown by slender jack pines, tossing wildly in the wind.

Towards evening the westerly grew to a gale and the temperature plummeted. The bonfire roared, showering sparks downwind. I banked the cooking fire with fir bark, filleted the salmon and sat back to wait for the bark to turn to embers. My notebook reads:

"A while ago an old black fish packer laboured up the strait, taking water over the wheelhouse. Later, an eagle shot around the point, banked and teetered like a tightrope walker, then set its wings and sheered across the stream of air to the mainland. Now, the strait is swept clean – not a boat or bird in sight. Since the sun went down, I've been watching the blue of the mountains come forward, ridge by ridge, eclipsing the green, right down to the water's edge."

I grilled the salmon with butter, lemon juice, garlic salt and dill, and ate it with Japanese sticky rice, wolfing down the lot before it turned cold in the wind. Heaping driftwood on the fire, I lay back in my blankets, watching waves charge past the light of the fire, breaking on a long diagonal along the beach. Above their crashing, I could hear the gale raging on the mountainside.

The idyll was short-lived. In the afternoon I had done a bit of digging to level the gravel for a place to sleep, stirring up a great many sandfleas in the process. Immediately, they burrowed down into the gravel to escape the light. But now in the dark they came bounding over the blankets onto my face and under the covers. Twice I got up and shook them out of everything down to the groundsheet and

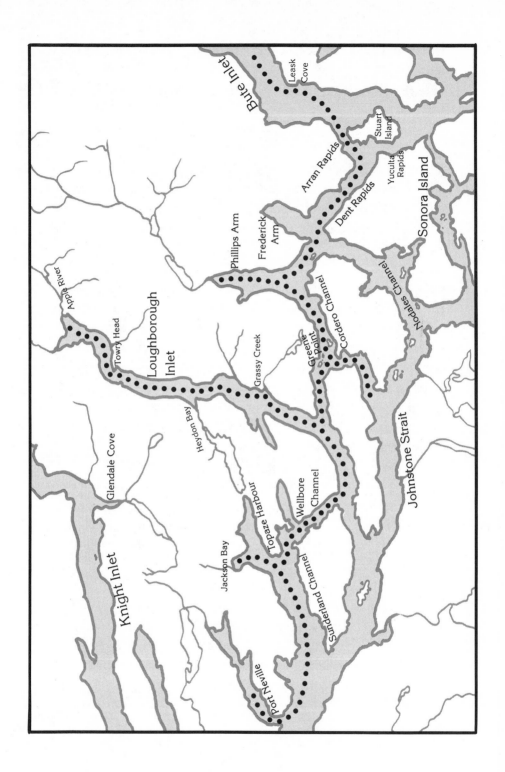

twice they came swarming back. At last, I put up the mosquito net and tucked it under the foam mattress, thwarting the invaders but trapping many of their cohorts inside. One by one, they had to be caught and dispatched before I could sleep.

16

Although its name suggests a town, there is no port in Port Neville; merely an old government dock, a pretty homestead from the 1890s, and a couple of houses owned by people who work elsewhere and live there part-time. The inlet is shallow, reaching inland from the east side of Johnstone Strait, through rolling country, logged long ago and now regrown.

I stayed two days, camped out of the sun on a north-facing point in the shade of a cedar groves. Early on the third morning, with clouds massing over Vancouver Island, I went on south and east into Sunderland Channel, heading for Jackson Bay and the logging camp where I hoped to hitch a ride overland to Knight Inlet.

Six miles inland from Johnstone Strait, Sunderland Channel branches right into Wellbore Channel and left into Topaze Harbour. On the north side of Topaze Harbour the logging camp is strung along the shore of Jackson Bay. Booms with hundreds of gulls on the logs, a log dump, wharf, machine shops, trucks and an assortment of trailers and old houses – a venerable camp of settled demeanour. The leggy trees of an old orchard grow between the cookhouse and bunkhouses, and the trailers along the waterfront sprawled comfortably behind sundecks overlooking lush tideflats.

Garth Dougan runs Jackson Bay. He's balding and boisterous, with a laugh like a thunderclap and a stocky build that had grown stockier in the ten years since I'd seen him last. He was seated at the table in his trailer, talking with some of his men about the future of the camp. For years they had logged on contract for a multinational timber giant. Now a rival contractor was threatening to undercut their bid and move them out of Jackson Bay.

"The son of a bitch cuts every corner in the book," Garth was saying as I came in. "He treats his men like shit and he can't keep a crew for a week. No wonder he logs cheap."

"Hey, that sounds like Dougan Logging," somebody cracked. Hoots of laughter all round; no one seemed to be taking the crisis very seriously.

"Sit down," Garth barked. He grabbed a baseball cap off the counter behind him and tossed it across the table to me. "Here – a souvenir of your visit to beautiful Jackson Bay." The crest on the front read "Dougan Logging" over caulked boots, toes down between a pair of upturned bare feet.

"Well, you're a couple of years too late," he said, when I told him what I'd come for. "I'd be glad to run you over to Knight but one of the bridges got so old and shakey, we bulldozed a barrier across the road."

The bridge was three miles short of Knight Inlet. Although the creek beneath it ran into Glendale Cove on the inlet, there were too many log jams and falls to leave any chance of getting through with the canoe. I was stymied.

Outside Jackson Bay, I sat on the beach in a black funk, pouring over the charts and trying to decide what to do. I measured the distance back to Minstrel Island and up Knight Inlet to Glendale Cove: four days minimum for the round trip, plus six days in the inlet and the rivers at the head. Altogether, it would take nearly two weeks to backtrack and see Knight Inlet and longer if the weather turned sour. It was too much; with August almost over and many miles still to go, I was determined not to turn the trip into a race against the calendar and the fall rains.

The charts offered consolation of a sort. I wanted to see lofty peaks and hanging glaciers, the archetypal inlet country, reaching into the heart of the coast mountains. Knight was that kind of an inlet, but so was Bute, which lay ahead. The chart showed mountains there rising straight out of the water to nearly 9000 feet, well above anything on Knight.

And so I went on, across Sunderland Channel and into the broad approach to Wellbore Channel. There I met the tide, hurrying north at the peak of the ebb. Turning aside into the quiet water of a bay on the right, I followed the shore behind a screen of kelp. Ahead now, the passage was narrowing and I could see white water kicking up above the rapids.

Wellbore, otherwise known as Whirlpool Rapids, was the first of four tidal rapids I would pass through in the next thirty miles. Greene Point came second, then Dent Rapids and, at the mouth of Bute Inlet, the Arran Rapids. All are driven by water ebbing and flooding between the complex of waterways beyond the rapids and Queen Charlotte Sound, far to the north. This is the roundabout route to Georgia Strait, a backdoor through passages pinched between islands and the mainland. The more direct route – the front door – follows the east coast of Vancouver Island.

Although Wellbore gets along at a good clip for all its four miles, true rapids occur only at the north end where the passage is constricted by a bluff protruding from Hardwicke Island. The current there is only about seven knots, but something in the nature of the bottom conformation throws off boils and whirlpools large enough to spin a fishboat end-for-end. Approached from the north, the setting is dramatic. The point on the right rears like the post of a great stone gate, while on the left, the mainland ridges loom high over the rapids. Clouds were snared on the heights as I entered the narrows, casting the slopes and the racing water in somber green. Hundreds of yards before the point, the current next to the shore reversed and began to run upstream, sweeping the canoe along in an immense backeddy. The propellor fouled so persistently in the kelp that I shut off the motor. When I pulled off my ear protectors, the dry voice of the rapids rustled like wind in leaves.

Riding the eddy into the lee of the point, it appeared for a moment that the rapids could be by-passed inside a narrow islet lying just

183

offshore. But the way proved to be blocked by kelp and driftwood stuffed into the passage by the eddy. I backed up and tried the outside. Before I'd gone very far, the eddy gave out at a sheerline of fast water, deflecting off the island. To my left, just beyond reach of the paddle, the lip of a whirlpool tugged at the outer edge of the kelp. It was fixed in a constant position, spinning counterclockwise, at least fifty feet from rim to rim, with white water tumbling into the cone of the vortex. Farther out, beyond the whirlpool, everything else was moving downstream: rips, waves, whirlpools and green boils, cascading water down their sides.

Holding fast to the kelp, I watched until I began to feel disoriented, as if I had been too long on a merry-go-round. Backing down the island, I went ashore and walked to the upper end. The current was piling into the point and tearing around the island at such a rate that the motor could not have bucked it, even if I had managed to squeeze through on the inside.

In mid-afternoon, still an hour before low slack, I started the motor and passed through the narrows, making heavy work of it, even in the slowest water at the edge of the island.

At the end of Chancellor Channel I by-passed Cordero Channel on the right (the route I would later take south) and went on into Loughborough Inlet, steering for the estuary of Grassy Creek on the east side. Ten years before, I had anchored a runabout overnight in the creek channel and slept on the beach. At dusk that evening, big cutthroat trout fed voraciously on fingerling herring all along the foreshore. Any large, silver-bodied fly would have taken them. But that was a filming trip and, true to the work ethic, I had not brought so much as a bent pin for fishing.

Well up into the creek, I went ashore and walked through chest-high dune grass to the beach, hoping to see some sign of the trout. All summer I had been lugging a flyrod around, just for this moment. But there was to be no rise of the trout on this evening; without a pause, the wind that had blown all afternoon in the inlet swung to the west, driving waves straight in on the beach. It was no one's evening for fishing. A kingfisher tried it first, diving several times and pulling up short of the water. And later, an osprey came hunting over the shallows, hovered as if to dive, and sped away on hurried wings around the point beyond the creek.

I pitched the tarp, low side to the wind, on lumpy ground in the tall grass beside the creek. Bears had been here digging for roots in the spring, tearing up the turf as if someone had done a bad job with a garden tractor. For a long time I lay awake, bothered by a pain beneath my shoulder blades that I dismissed as pulled muscle or too much paddling. An hour or two before dawn, the sky cleared and the moon cast a patina of silver over the meadowgrass. Finally, I slept and didn't wake until the sun was cresting the wall of spruce behind the estuary.

At mid-morning I put together my antiquated split cane rod, tied on a green fly with a silver body and set out in search of the trout. I began fishing down the creek, casting across the current so that the sunken fly came round on a long swing. It had been years since I fished, and I felt the stirring of an old passion, long neglected. But I wasn't letting my hopes get too high; with cutthroat, the trick is not so much catching them as finding them.

Cutthroat are mysterious fish, wanderers, whose habits are little studied and poorly understood. Although they are born in the coastal creeks and lakes, they migrate to sea after a year or two and remain there for most of their lives. Fishermen act on the theory that cutthroat spend their saltwater lives close to their home streams, though exactly how close, no one is sure.

Following the dropping tide, I worked down the creek channel and across the front of the flats. Twice I changed flies, first to a grey sculpin imitation, then to a barred pattern, simulating the parr marks on the sides of salmon fry. After an hour, I had yet to touch a fish. The fault, I suspected, lay not with the flies but with the flat calm that made the flyline seem like a rope smacking down on the water. Conceding round one to the trout, I retired for tea.

After an hour, with wind now stirring on the bay, I tried again with the green fly. The tide was lower and better; with a long cast I could reach the drop-off, where the trout were most likely to be. And there I found the first fish, straight off the creekmouth, a skinny twelve-incher that jumped only once and came to my hand without a struggle. I released it and fished on for a quarter hour, without another bite.

I hadn't yet tried the point across the creek because it was an awkward place to fish; overhanging trees left little room for a backcast, and the beach was all boulders, slippery with seaweed. Now I crossed over and saw that the boulders gave way to sand and eelgrass just off shore. My first cast was short, upstream into the tide. As the fly came around on the current, a fish struck solidly, jumped and ran straight away from the beach. Twice again it leapt, then dashed back towards shore. Before I could take the slack out of the line, the trout dove into the eelgrass and fouled the leader. I tightened as much as I dared, then let out slack, hoping the current would free the line. Before I could tighten again, the fish pulled loose and jumped. It made one more long run and spent the last of its strength in short, dogged rushes towards the bottom.

Exhausted, the cutthroat lay on the wet stones at my feet. Its back and tail were serpentine green, fading to white under the belly and throat. Dark jade, almost black, covered the top of the head and speckled the back and tail. Nacreous pink lay over the gill plates and flanks, bordered at the bottom by a shading of lemon yellow. Twin slashes of orange marked the throat, the source of the cutthroat's name. It measured a little more than two handspans, or about nineteen inches. Removing the hook, I worked the fish back and forth, forcing water through its gills until it twitched as if waking, and swam slowly off through the eelgrass.

Over the next two hours, I caught and released more than a dozen cutthroat, all between fourteen and eighteen inches. One I kept for the pot, a smallish fish whose gills were torn by the hook.

I might still be there fishing if the tide had not turned. The bite slowed through low slack and ended altogether when the flood current began to run.

That evening I finally conceded the obvious: I was getting sick. I'd been been feeling lousy all day and trying to ignore it, but now the back pains of last night returned with a vengeance. I recognized the symptoms from a previous bout; it was a virus of some sort that afflicts the pleura. Making ready for a layup of several days, I stacked wood by the fire and set a mouse-proof container of raisins, cheese and bannock within easy reach of my bed. Then I rolled in and slept on and off for much of the next two days. Once or twice I got up to make tea but felt so thwacked that I gave it up and went back to bed.

On the evening of the second day I heated water for a bath of sorts and ate the trout before it went bad. I sat on the driftlogs for a while, watching a squadron of black dragonflies intercept flying ants fluttering down from the forest. They hovered near the ground until the ants came over, then shot straight up to take them from underneath and eat them on the wing. I knew then that I was on the mend; for the first time in two days I was taking an interest in something other than my own misery.

The next morning I had visitors. Rising late, I stumbled bare-assed out from under the tarp for a leak, when I realized that I was on display for a group of people standing near a boat a little way down the beach. They turned out to be Dane Campbell, a prawn fisherman from across the inlet (whom I had met here ten years before), together with his teenaged kids, Arabella and Adam. They had been waiting quietly for me to get up before they came by to say hello.

The kids were interested in camping and canoe travel, so I made them some bannock in the frying pan, explaining how the mix was put together at home, so I only had to add water on the trip. But I found that my supply of mix in the grub box had run out, and I had to dig out a bag that had been stored for six weeks in a fiberglass flotation tank under the front deck of the canoe. Although it smelled strongly of fiberglass resin, I mixed it up without a second thought, certain that the stink would come out with the cooking. The kids ate it all with apparent relish, though I noticed that they laid on a great deal of jam from a jar they had brought as a gift.

Two or three days were to pass before I made bannock from the same bag. The chemical stench was as strong as ever, and it did not come out in the cooking. The taste was unspeakable. I couldn't imagine how Dane's kids were able to choke the stuff down, much less pretend that it was delicious. Only the jam, plus saintly good manners could have made it possible.

Paddling away from Grassy Creek, I could see a log dump and boom and a new clearing on the hill which had been screened from my camp by the high point across the creek. This was no surprise; over the past couple of days, I had heard the sounds of chainsaws and bulldozers. At their home across the inlet, Dane Campbell and his artist wife, Helen, showed me a map of the logging plan, indicating a bridge and clear-cuts on both sides of the creek. I had hoped for something less threatening to the cutthroat.

As we talked on their float, a series of warning whistles for blasting sounded from the logging site. A road was being cut into a rock face above the creek. The whistles stopped and after what seemed a long wait, black smoke mushroomed suddenly over the clearing, followed by the heavy *karuuump* of the blast. Shot rock flew high over the trees and rained down on the estuary, raising geysers of spray in the creek and along the foreshore, where I was camped just an hour before. It was a close call; I had debated about staying another day at Grassy Creek to nurse my sore back.

At the side of his float, Dane pulled the cord to start the Seagull (twisting backwards to do it myself was excruciating), and I headed inland. The Campbells had told me about a prawn fisherman who lived alone at the head of Loughborough, miles from another soul.

188

What sort of man, I wondered, would choose to live in such isolation?

17

Although there are more remote inlets for the dedicated recluse, Loughborough combines isolation with easy access to the amenities of town, a half-hour away by air or a few hours by boat. Only two families and a couple of small loggers inhabit its lower reaches. Farther up, Heydon Bay holds a more substantial logging camp, and from there on, for the next ten miles to the head, the inlet is empty.

The end of Loughborough is made to feel more isolated than it really is by Towry Head, a hog-backed bluff that bulks half-way across the channel from the right-hand shore. As you go by it, the passage bends sharply to the right, so that when you look back, a granite door has rolled across the exit to the world outside. On the inside, Loughborough spreads in a broad Y, with rivers and tidal flats at the ends of the two arms.

Mist lay in the valley of the Stafford River on the left, dividing its lowland forests from a barren peak, far back in the headwaters. To the right the valley of the Apple River was clear, opening a window on massifs more than forty miles away, beyond the head of Bute Inlet. A lofty ridge of timber and rock bluffs filled the expanse of horizon and sky between the two river valleys. On a point at its center, facing the Apple River valley, was a straggle of ramshackle floats and shacks and an old brown bunkhouse, awash in brush on the shore. A double-ender fishboat, dark red and much weathered, was tied at the floats.

The prawn fisherman Glenn Shuart heard the outboard when I was still some distance off and came striding purposefully down the floats. I steeled myself for a cool reception; he looked rough under a week's grey stubble and his face was puffy red, as if he had been on a bender. But I couldn't have been more wrong.

189

When I cut the motor, he called out: "Well, I never thought I'd see a rig like that in here. Come on around to the inside. Your canoe will be out of the wind." He bustled about, moving bumpers to protect the canoe and clearing space for my things on the float. "We can move her to a better spot later on. Here, let me give you a hand. Put your stuff wherever you like. Careful near that edge, the planks are pretty rotten."

In fact, the entire agglomeration of floats was a junk-cluttered booby trap of loose boards and leg-snaring holes. The only solid thing in sight was an aluminum shed, crammed with fishing gear and boat parts that had seen better days.

"Come on up," he said. "I was just going to have lunch."

The floats leading to shore were canted at an angle and sprouting a luxuriant crop of grass. The path to the house had been hacked like a trench through the underbrush. Glenn cleared a hole in the clutter on the kitchen table, put coffee on the stove and took wieners from a cache stacked like kindling in the fridge. He was starved for conversation and hadn't stopped talking since I landed. In no time I had a thumbnail history of his eight years in Loughborough: the decline of the fishing, the coming and going of three women and the past four years of living alone.

The house was a chronicle of his time here. Years of accumulated grime covered older traces of a woman's touch. Three small needle-point embroideries in oval frames had turned bleary with smoke grease on the kitchen wall. The cookware and well-stocked spice rack went well beyond the requirements of Glenn's hotdogs. Dirt had dimmed the colours of an oriental carpet in the living room.

"I'm not much of a housekeeper," he said. "I need a woman, but I haven't found one that will stay."

He took down a framed colour photograph from the wall above the sink. "That's Darlene. She was the first one and the best of them all." In profile, a beautiful childlike face looked out from under a sou'wester rainhat.

"No, it wasn't the isolation. She liked it here and we loved each other, but she had to be entertained all the time. All the women were like that; I'd want to read in the evening or just listen to music and they'd want me to do something with them. I couldn't stand that. I guess it was my own fault they left. I know I'm pretty hard to live with."

Glenn had saved a yellowing photo from a Vancouver newspaper, showing Darlene seated cross-legged on the carpet and himself, looking ages younger, on the arm of the couch at her side. The story extolled the romance of living at the head of a remote inlet. Those were the good years; he had made a daring break with everything he had known and it was working for him.

"I grew up in Hamilton, Ontario, of all places and hitch-hiked to Vancouver when I was twenty. For the next eleven years I had a job, a briefcase and a three-piece suit. I was a salesman for a company that made fine papers and I was damned good at it."

He made more money than he needed, but his life was hollow at the center; he had no family and no compelling interest to keep him in the city. When a chance came to buy an established prawn fishing territory in Loughborough Inlet, with eight months of on-the-job training thrown in, he jumped at it.

"I was probably the most ill-prepared guy who ever came out here. But I was lucky. The people who were here before me were really proficient and they left the territory in good shape. That first year I made as much as five hundred dollars a day and one month I averaged over three hundred dollars for thirty straight days."

Darlene moved in the next year and made a pleasant home of the old bunkhouse. There was little else to occupy her; Glenn didn't want children and she had no place in his fishing, except to go along for the ride. She was bored and pined for the city, and within a year she left. The other two women came and went. Neither stayed very long. Glenn was still bitter about the last one. "She really did it to me. My best friend came up in a sailboat and when he left, she went with him. I thought for a while I was going to break down."

Glenn's isolation is far from total. All through the summer, people come in yachts and planes to buy his prawns. And every three weeks or so, he takes a load of frozen prawns to sell on Vancouver Island.

Beginning in January, when fishing closes for three months, he visits friends in the city, drifting from place to place and moving on whenever he feels his welcome wearing thin. Well before the season reopens, he is back in the inlet.

Inevitably, there are some visitors he'd rather not have. "Nobody out here wants anything to do with the government. But the bloody bureaucrats just can't stand that. They want all the sheep in one enclosure so they can keep control. That's why they stonewall you when you want to move out here. And if you manage it despite them, they never let you alone. Five different government agencies come up here to check on me almost every year.

"The land this house sits on is a special use permit from the Forest Service. They made a trip all the way up here to hassle me because my permit number wasn't posted on the front of the house. Can you imagine that! And every year, without fail, the bloody cops come up here and tramp over the place looking for pot. That started when someone finked on me because I had a few plants growing behind the house. Think what that costs! Is that what we're paying these people to do?"

Glenn's other regular visitors are Jehovah's Witnesses. "They also come every year, a guy in a suit carrying a briefcase, of course, and women with rimless glasses, who look like they could use a transfusion. I always invite them in and we have a good debate. I enjoy the intellectual stimulation, if you can call it that."

Much as I liked Glenn, I needed a respite from his non-stop talking. I excused myself to run up the Apple River for a few hours before the tide got too low.

"Will you come for dinner?" Glenn asked. "I'll see if Cory wants to come over."

Cory, it turned out, was a young woman who had arrived unannounced and flat broke with her logger husband a few weeks before. They had a small boat and a lot of food, but no place to live, and he had no job. Glenn let them move into an old floathouse he had moored farther up the bay. The husband had since found work at a logging camp down the inlet, and Cory was staying on until a job for her turned up in one of the camps.

She came by in a rowboat while Glenn was helping me unload. Painfully, almost obsequiously, Glenn invited her to dinner. He liked having her next door and was wary of scaring her off. She hesitated a moment and then accepted, only, I suspected, because there would be three of us.

The estuary of the Apple River rose almost imperceptibly for more than a mile back from the foreshore, grading from watermeadows, through fields of waist-high grass to clumps of willow and finally a forest of spruce, alders and cottonwood. Evergreen ridges walled the estuary on either side, shouldering abruptly out of the yellow grass. The river flowed deep and slow, forking often into serpentine channels. With cows and milkmaids on the banks, the lower reaches of the Apple could have passed for a Victorian landscape. Inland, high on the valley walls, the pastoral illusion was lost in gorges of splintered granite and summer snow.

A hen mallard erupted from a backchannel in front of the canoe and her quacking raised a shout of red-winged blackbirds into the sky. They were migrants apparently, for they described a ragged arc over the river then climbed towards the east, drawing a wavering bead on a high pass through the mountains.

Upstream in the forest, alders brushed the water, curtaining off caverns of shade along the banks and stippling the bottom with amber sunlight. Drifting leaves wheeled slowly in the breeze from the inlet. After a mile or so of easy paddling against a gentle current, the way was blocked by a logjam left from the logging that ended here in the 1970s. Although there were holes where I could have pulled the canoe through, the river beyond was too shallow to paddle. I drifted downstream, idly casting a fly into deep water behind logs and stumps. Suddenly, the surface bulged over the back of a rapidly swimming fish. Another fin converged on it from behind and two salmon broke water; male humpbacks in their bronze spawning colours, jousting for access to a female. Once I began looking for them, I saw others – twos and threes and, occasionally, a small school – lying near bottom in deep water. They were a meagre lot for a river of the Apple's size; perhaps the bulk of the run had gone on upstream, above the jam. Or maybe there wasn't much of a run; the Apple's salmon are badly depleted, like every stream on this part of the coast.

A transformed Glenn Shuart met me on the float. A bath, a shave and clean clothes had knocked years off his appearance. (He was forty-two.) With his greying hair slicked back and the puffiness gone from his face, he looked healthy and handsome.

Cory, tall, blonde and angular in her early twenties, followed us up to the house, bearing salad and vegetables.

"How about you cook and I'll clean up?" Glenn suggested.

She was not pleased. As an invited guest, she didn't expect to have to prepare her own dinner. "It's your kitchen. I don't know where anything is."

But Glenn had an irresistible argument: "If I fix it, Cory, you're not going to want to eat it. After all, you're the professional cook."

Cory had recently graduated from a school for chefs, though nothing in her training had prepared her for Glenn's greasy stove, dingy pots and salt and pepper shakers that stuck to your fingers. I tried to give her a hand, peeling potatoes and setting the table. Moving about the kitchen, she talked interestingly of natural history, cruising in the Queen Charlottes, oolichan fishing at the head of Knight Inlet and growing up in the Finnish community of Sointula on Malcolm Island. She told me that she would be starting a job next week, cooking at a logging camp down the inlet. This was news to Glenn; a shadow of disappointment fell across his face.

He broke out a few cans of beer he had squirreled away and

selected a tape (The Rolling Stones) from stacks of pop casettes. "I don't play them much any more," he said. "I seem to have lost interest."

Nor does he read as much as he once did; the few dozen books – whodunnits, historical fiction, spy thrillers – had long been gathering dust on the shelves, and the handful of magazines were months or years out of date. I asked what he did here alone in the winter when there wasn't even fishing to occupy him. He told me about the hundreds of Canada geese and the flock of trumpeter swans that winter on the flats. "I like having them around. They're my only companions." But there were weeks on end when Arctic winds screeched out of the two valleys, and it was too cold to go outside. "That's when I hear the wolves howling at night on the flats by the Apple River."

Under the circumstances, Cory produced a very good meal: salad, potatoes, carrots and some steaks from Glenn's freezer. And then, immediately after we'd eaten, she left. Glenn followed her to the door, but she could not be persuaded to stay.

Like many people on the coast, Glenn has a fixed time each day when he listens for calls on the radiophone. That evening a women in Campbell River returned his call; he had been trying to reach her for several days. Of course, she would like to see him when he came to town, but her son might be home visiting and, well . . . it could be awkward. Glenn was scrupulously polite: yes, of course, he understood; he'd call ahead and if it wasn't convenient . . . But her tone was cool and guarded to the end. After all, what future could there be with a man who buries himself at the head of some God-forsaken inlet.

Glenn was downcast and silent for a while after the call. I suggested that, after eight years, maybe he owed himself a break from the inlet. "Yes, you're probably right," he said, "but if I wasn't here, someone would move in on my territory. Every so often a boat comes in here, but as long as my traps are out there, they never stay."

Glenn's prawn fishing territory is a dubious asset, keeping him bound to the inlet, but affording him only a bare existence. The catch declined sharply after the first two years and has remained more or less depressed ever since.

As the evening wore on, Glenn became pessimistic. "Man is nature's one great mistake," he said, introducing a litany of environmental woes. He said he would like to help rejuvenate the salmon runs in the Apple River. "I'll do anything – stream improvement, count fish, anything – just tell me what to do and I'll do it for nothing. I've gone twice into the fisheries office in Campbell River and offered my help. But they're not interested. And, hell, I'm not even a salmon fisherman. The guys who catch all the fish don't lift a finger. Every fisherman who draws unemployment in the off-season – and they all do – should have to do two weeks' stream improvement work before they get their money."

Much as I agreed, I was nodding over the table. Glenn was as eager as ever to talk. As I spread my blankets on the floor, he began telling me about his plans to run traplines up the rivers on either side of the valley in the coming winter. I lay down and my responses dwindled to grunts. But Glenn had lapsed into monologue, talking quietly from his bedroom about fur prices, the depth of the snow in the mountains and other things I don't remember.

Very early, Cory was at the door with a shopping bag full of food for me – potatoes, carrots, cookies, chocolate bars and quarts of home-preserved fruit and pickles. I was in an awful fix: there simply wasn't room in the canoe for twenty pounds of bulky food, but I hadn't the heart to tell her. I thanked her and when she'd gone, gave the heaviest things to Glenn, asking him to hide them until Cory had moved away to her job.

Glenn went cheerfully off to his fishing, and I believed him when he said, "This is the best work I have ever done in my life and I love it every morning when I go out."

I thought about him as I packed up. This coast has a way of breaking people who live alone too long, sucking them down into a vortex of dirt and indifference until the disorder of their lives spreads

196

into their minds. It happens usually in old age; Glenn was still a young and vigorous man. He was bushed, not broken, but I feared for him if he stayed too long here alone. I wished I had told him about an old man I once visited on Nelson Island in Georgia Strait. He had lived alone for years in a gloomy troll's house. Every shelf and table and much of the floor was heaped with thousands upon thousands of sheets of cheap yellow paper, all closely written with what he termed his philosophy of life. He called the place The House of a Million Words, though I could make no sense of what he said they were all about. When I left, he took me out in front of the house, overlooking the strait.

"It's all those electric motors," he told me confidentially. "All over the world, they're leaking magnetism. It comes across the water and hits this point and goes up over the house and through those trees. You can always tell because all the birds stop singing."

They took him away within a year. He was no danger to anyone, except perhaps to himself.

Glenn was piling the last of a line of traps on deck when I paddled alongside. "It's pretty slim pickin's," he said. "But you have to expect that. Spring's the best for prawns and they taper off through the rest of the year."

"I hope that woman turns up."

"Oh, she will. There are women who'd like this kind of life. It's just a matter of finding the right one."

18

All down Loughborough clouds were stacked on the mountains, shading the slopes nearly black, while over the water the sun shone from an open sky, lighting up the green fleece of alders at the creekmouths. In Cordero Channel the soft September westerly puffed at my back, blowing fireweed seed cotton past so slowly that

I could pick the glinting pinwheels out of the air. Ahead, framed in rounded hills enfolding the channel, the naked tooth of Mount Estero thrust 6000 feet into blue haze.

At Greene Point the rapids tumbled noisily over reefs and shredded on an islet in midstream. There was more show than substance here: white water without the boat-spinning whirlpools of Wellbore Rapids, or the power of Dent or Arran ahead. I passed through on the west side, dodging rocks in water so shallow my paddle rattled along the bottom.

Beyond Greene Point, Cordero Channel widens to receive Mayne Passage from the south, then curves to the east and north. Islands ring the meeting of waters – clumps like tea biscuits on the south and east, and flat sheets of pink granite on the north – guarding the entrance to the narrows. Swinging right at the foot of the rapids, I followed the shore of West Thurlow Island to a sand beach and a bank of grass with a few remnant trees of an old orchard. On higher ground in a grove of alders, a house of massive logs was under construction. I tied the canoe at a new dock, next to a timeworn seiner that had been stripped of its fishing gear and converted to a floating home. Dennis and Cathy Langtry were living aboard while they finished building their log house.

Cathy came down from the house to the head of the wharf and invited me up. "Dennis is up back with the tractor getting some soil for the garden," she said. "He'll be down in a minute." She spoke with a New Zealand accent, and her long-boned build reminded me of the rangy athletes her country sends to the Olympics. With her blond hair pulled back in a ponytail, she was strikingly attractive.

I had been forewarned about Dennis. "He's gruff with strangers," Glenn Shuart told me, "but it's just a front. You'll like him." Cathy seemed ill at ease as he came up on the tractor. Dennis was a daunting prospect: a bear of a man with a brick red face, an unruly beard of grey wire, and thick wrists and hands, with fingers like bratwurst. In fisherman's brown tweed pants, suspenders and a baseball cap with the peak hauled down over his eyes, he looked to be in his mid-fifties, nearly twice Cathy's age. He stopped the tractor, but left the engine

198

running, and I gave him my spiel about canoeing the coast and wanting to meet people. "I've always admired this place and wondered who lived here," I added.

"So, what am I supposed to say?"

"This isn't an interview. I thought we might talk later if you have the time."

"I don't care. Stick around if you want."

He drove the tractor ahead and backed it's trailerload of soil up to the edge of the garden. Cathy was furious. "Goddamn him," she said to me, aside, "he always does that when someone new comes around. It's just a defensive thing. Don't go, he'll be fine."

Within a half-hour Dennis was showing me around the place like a long-lost friend. We sat at a picnic table, looking out through the islands to the east down Cordero Channel, while he told me about his work as a contractor building logging bridges all over the coast. He retired early, bought a sailboat and spent five years cruising the South Pacific. In Vanuatu he met Cathy, who was crewing on another sailboat, and she sailed with him through the Orient and back to Canada.

Cathy was waiting for confirmation of an unusual teaching job, flying in to isolated float camps to help kids with their correspondence courses. Her territory was to be the country south of Seymour Inlet, precisely the part of the coast I'd been travelling. Although I told her what I could of the children she'd be teaching, it was the accommodations that worried her. She would be cooped up in the middle of a dozen domestic dramas, sometimes for days on end, if planes or weather didn't co-operate. Three of Cathy's predecessors had quit or been fired, one for diddling the men in the camps. Her supervisor had warned her: "Get in trouble out there and we'll drop you flat."

"Did you ever hear of Gray Hill?" Dennis interjected.

"Yes, but I've never met him. I was hoping I might run into . . ."

"Well, you're about to. He's anchored behind those islands." Dennis pointed to the pink granite slabs across the rapids. "We're invited to dinner with friends at their summer cottage over there and

199

we thought we'd see if the old bugger will come along."

Gray Hill (no one calls him by his first name, Gwyn) was the most fabled sailor on the coast. He had made, I was to discover, thirty cruises to Alaska and nearly as many to the Queen Charlottes in more than fifty years of sailing, always alone.

Late in the afternoon Dennis took us bouncing across the rapids in his runabout to Gray Hill's double-ender yawl, *Cherie*, which was anchored in a pocket of deep water behind the islands. She was a squat thirty-six feet, with a boxy cabin set far back on the deck, and old car tires hanging over her sides as bumpers. Her hull and decks were dingy silver and green, and her sails and rigging black with diesel soot.

Dennis shut off the outboard and rapped a tatoo on *Cherie's* deck with his knuckle. "Gray Hill, you old dog," he roared, "come on out." And aside to Cathy and me, "He's an arrogant old bastard. You have to let him know you mean business, or he'll just ignore you."

There was an answering tatoo from inside the hull and then silence. Dennis shouted again, even louder, "Come out, Gray Hill, we're going to take you to dinner."

This drew a bleat of protest from inside and Gray Hill emerged from the companionway like a light-blinded mole. "Who is it?" he croaked, shading his eyes with his arm. He was a tiny man, with thick glasses held on by surgical tubing around the back of his head. He wore a filthy brown shirt, brown cords and running shoes with the toes curled up like harem slippers. Under white stubble, his face was sharp as a ferret's, and his neck and arms were scaly with old dirt.

"It's Dennis. Come on, we're taking you to dinner."

"No, no, can't possibly come . . . can't see . . . I'm going blind." Gray Hill was incoherent. For long minutes, he leaned against the cabin, head down and eyes closed. At last, he said, "I'm nearly blind," and so faintly we barely heard, "I think I'm dying."

Cathy and I were alarmed. Dennis ignored him. "Come on now, we've got a beer for you and we'll bring you right back here."

Gray Hill perked up instantly. "All right then, just a minute." He ducked into the companionway and was back in no time, with the grease wiped from his hands (he'd been working on the engine) and a Dougan Logging baseball cap clamped down on his head by an elastic under his chin.

At the dock where we landed, Gray Hill shuffled up to the gaps between the floats, unsure where to put his feet. At the ramp he groped for the rail like a man in the dark and, hearing that there was none, allowed me to steer him by the elbow. There was no fakery about any of this; he was nearly blind. How was it possible, I wondered, for this man to find his way around one of the most intricate coasts in the world?

"Nine tenths of eyesight is memory," he said, as if this explained everything. Gray Hill was seated in the living room of the cottage, still wearing his hat. "I know because I've had such a frightful time with my eyesight – nine eye diseases since 1931. I know where everything is on the boat. The worst thing is I can't read, haven't been able to for years."

Soon it became apparent that Gray Hill knew the coast almost as well as the inside of his boat. No matter what place came up in the conversation, he could describe it in sharp detail from the landforms and charts he carried in his head. He did, in fact, navigate mostly by memory, relying on his eyes only for the dim profile of a point or pattern of islands that told him where he was.

"Knight Inlet, now there's an awful place," he said. "Got my boat caught in a tree in Wahshihlas Bay. I anchored and when the tide went down, there I was up in the branches of a great, big cottonwood sunk in the mud. It was dark and pouring rain. I tried a twelve-foot pike pole all round and couldn't find bottom anywhere. The boat began to lean. I was terrified. I took a rope and kept her from rolling over by tying onto a piling in the booming ground."

Gray Hill spoke very quickly in the English accent of someone born to money, if not to the manor. He was secretive about his background, except to say that his father was a Manchester tea importer and he had been sent to a private school in Switzerland. He dropped bits of French and German into the conversation, delivered lectures on the Doppler Effect and Zodiacal light, and was ever-anxious to be first with a fact, like a competitive schoolboy. And he was dismissive of anyone who didn't meet with his approval. "That damned woman is nothing but a little sausage," he said of a well-known writer on the coast. "And her husband was a great bag of socialist hot air." Of another writer whose subject was beachcombing, he said: "The woman is without discrimination. She'll pick up anything on the beach – even string."

Dennis was not satisfied by Gray Hill's cryptic personal history. "Well, what were you planning to do when you came out here?"

"I came to go commercial salmon fishing with a family friend in Courtenay," Gray Hill said. But when pressed for details, he spoke only of canoeing around Victoria harbour until he got his first boat in 1935. Thereafter, Gray Hill withdrew into himself, wandering back through his memories and returning every few minutes with some strange, disjointed question or comment.

"Did you ever meet Eunice Campbell?" he asked at one point. "Her sister was married to a Major Dukes. She ate him in the middle of the Atlantic." And later: "What do you know about the monster of Thurlow Island?"

Cathy: "I'm married to him."

Gray Hill: "It was headless, just came in on the beach, all covered with blood. They phoned the police in Campbell River."

Dennis: "And the cops said, 'Yeah, we get 'em here every Saturday night.'"

When we had finished dinner, Gray Hill downed two shots of neat Scotch and announced, in the tone of someone addressing a servant, "I want to go back to my boat now before it gets dark." He thanked his hostess graciously and started for the door, without a backward glance to see if Dennis was following. Aboard *Cherie*, he announced that he would run up to the liquor store in Blind Channel (two miles west of Dennis' place) in the morning "to get you boys a bottle." Dennis was skeptical: "I'll believe it when I see it; the old bugger's an awful freeloader."

True to his word, Gray Hill slipped out from behind the islands before noon and started *Cherie* into Mayne Passage. A few minutes later I looked up from my notebook to see him heading towards the float. He approached as if he were in dense fog, reversing and creeping ahead for a quarter-hour before he finally brought the boat alongside.

"When I got into the narrows, she wouldn't buck the tide," he explained. "No power. She's not getting fuel. It's that damned filter. I wonder if you'd mind helping me change it?"

Working under the skylights next to the hot engine was like being roasted alive in an oven of soot. The filter was in an awkward spot, wedged between pipes under the floorboards. Gray Hill pointed out a long, wooden tool box – "I call it my child's coffin" – and sat nearby, feeding me a stream of instructions. The filter, when I got it out, was so jammed with sludge it had burst.

"It's plugged solid."

"Well, wouldn't you know it! I had a fellow look at it just a week or two ago. Damned fool. Blind as a bat, he was. Couldn't see a thing."

19

In a cove a mile to the east of Greene Point, a large sign proclaimed RESTAURANT from a rambling building erected on a barge. Doris Kuppers, a short, cheerful woman in her forties, was working on accounts behind the bar in a room of varnished wood, beer steins and pennants, that looked like a bit of Bavaria. Yes, she said, the restaurant was still open, although most of the yachts had gone south and she would soon close for the winter. No, she didn't do light lunches; just full meals, mostly German food. I settled for rye bread and a beer, while she sat at my table and talked.

"There was nothing at all when we came here eight years ago," she said. "We built it all from scratch. It was like emigrating for a second time."

Doris Kuppers arrived from Germany with her husband Reinhardt in 1967 and crossed Canada by train in the dead of winter. "All across the country we saw nothing but ice and snow, until we came down into the Fraser Valley and everything was green. We looked at each other and said, 'This is where we're staying, even if we have to sweep the streets.'"

After twelve years in Vancouver, where Reinhardt worked as an electrician, the transition to Cordero Channel was difficult. "I was used to him being away working. Suddenly, we were cooped up here together, twenty-four hours a day. If something didn't go right, we had only each other to take it out on. That went on for a couple of years. It was very hard."

They stuck it out and slowly built the business, adding guest rooms and space for boaters to hold their parties on the barge. But even today Cordero Lodge, as it's now called, would be on a shaky footing were it not for the Kuppers' German connections. "People flew in from Germany as early as April this year. We're doing pretty well now. I'm sure we'll make it here."

At the time I was there in early September, Doris Kuppers had not been off the barge since the previous November, except for a few trips to the post office in Blind Channel, three miles away. "I'm used to it now, it doesn't bother me any more," she said. "It's like a prison, a pretty prison."

Inland from Greene Point, where Cordero Channel describes a right-angle bend to the southwest, I turned left into Phillips Arm, heading for the Phillips River at the end of the arm. I had seen an aerial photograph of the river, taken sometime in the 1950s, showing the deep pools and spawning beds that had made it a famed producer of trout and chinook salmon. At that time a neat row of red-and-white houses fronted on a sand beach just inside the rivermouth. From the air it looked like a fishing resort but was in fact the prettiest logging camp on the coast.

In 1965 a logging dam on the Phillips River gave way in the fall rains, sending a wall of water careering downstream. The river broke out of its banks and cut a new course to tidewater, leaving miles of the main stream nearly dry and killing the spawn from thousands of salmon. The flood by-passed the logging camp, though buildings from another camp upstream were swept out to sea along with trees, soil and drowned animals, including a number of grizzly bears.

Coasting in on the broad estuary, I could see no aftermath of the carnage. Spruce and fir and softer billows of alder and cottonwood had bandaged the wounds. Three mallard drakes got up from the verge of grass along the foreshore, followed by a score of Canada geese that went honking away to the west, losing themselves in the shadow of the mountain. The logging camp, when it appeared ahead on the left bank of the river, bore scant resemblance to the old photo. Its fastidious owner had died years ago, and now the biggest house was gone and brush had taken over the lawns and garden.

A trapper named Tom was living here. I was quite close before I noticed him kneeling with his back to me on the float, looking down into the water. Although I tapped the paddle on the gunwale to warn him of my coming, he didn't move. At last, within a few yards, I said, "Hello" very quietly. Slowly, as if he'd been roused from a dream, he got to his feet and stared at me. Without so much as a nod, he walked up the ramp and into one of the houses.

By the time I had tied the canoe and followed him, Tom was sitting on the porch. He was shirtless and skinny, with a soft paunch, bloodshot eyes, a nose like a purple road map, and a drooping mustache that he stroked incessantly. He invited me in and offered me a drink from the dregs of a bottle of vodka.

"I don't drink much any more," he said. "Just once every week or so. Unfortunately for you, this is one of my drinking days. Tee-hee-hee." He punctuated everything he said, whether it was meant to be funny or not, with a dreadful falsetto giggle. Unwisely, I accepted a beer and was soon hearing about Tom's divorce. "The old cow got everything: the house, furniture, my tools. All I got was the boat. But it was still a good deal because I shook loose from the old bitch." As

205

I listened to him, I was struck by the contrast between his bitterness and the beauty of the river purling past beyond the open door.

From the wall Tom took down a framed photograph of a young woman in a nurse's uniform and cap. "That's my daughter," he said, with evident pride. "She's a graduate nurse." But it turned out that she was living with her mother, which Tom regretted more than all his lost possessions. I gulped the beer and fled, unmoved by Tom's entreaties that I stay the night. With the tide near high, I intended to ride the crest upriver as far as possible. It was tidal, Tom said, for three miles above the camp.

At high water the lower Phillips is less a river than an arm of the sea, running slow, a hundred yards wide between mud banks, topped by lush grass and trees. (The only sandbank is in front of the camp.) At the head of this reach, where the current began, I started the motor and followed the river in an S bend to the left around a logjam and back to the right in a long swing up the side of a gravel bar. The water was lucid as glass, darkening to green in the pools and black in the holes under the jam. Above the bar the motor laboured up a reach of faster water to a much higher bar that crossed from bank to bank on a long diagonal. The river tumbled down the incline in a chute deep enough to track up but too shallow to come down again, except by lowering the canoe on a line. This was clearly the tidal limit, and I was scarcely a mile from the logging camp.

I anchored and walked over the bar. Upstream, the forest fell back and the blue-green river meandered over a plain of washed gravel and islands of white-barked alder, sharply reminiscent of birch on a northern river. Twin peaks filled the end of the valley, shadow-scoured by fluted ravines. The country beckoned while the river repelled; white water danced down a dozen riffles too shallow to float the canoe.

Dropping downstream I unloaded on the tail of a bar across from the logjam and made camp. Without much hope of success, I cast a fly into the holes under the jam, giving it up after a few minutes. The cutthroat would be out in the estuary at this season; Tom caught them readily from the float on the flood tide. Or so he said.

After an icy swim and a meal of the ineluctable tuna and rice, I walked upstream to cut poles for the lean-to from a fringe of young alders growing by a flood channel behind the bar. Near the trees I came upon a pile of fresh bear scat that would have done credit to an elephant. I wasn't pleased; only a very large black bear or a grizzly could create such an edifice. And grizzlies had been reported by fisheries wardens nearly every fall on the Phillips. I searched for tracks around a pool in the flood channel but found none. Even one clear print would have shown the claws that differentiate grizzly from black bear. The bear had skirted the mud on a bridge of gravel upstream from the channel, or perhaps swum to the bar from across the river.

Thinking grizzly, I stacked the camp boxes three high, with the grub box on the bottom, and enamel plates on top to make a racket if the bear came in the night. And, to put a respectful distance between myself and the bear (assuming it would come for the food, rather than me), I pitched the sleeping tarp twenty yards up the bar. All the while I felt a bit silly; this wasn't springtime when bears are dangerously hungry. There were berries everywhere and perhaps even salmon in the river. Satisfied that I'd done what I could, I threw a few chunks of driftwood on the fire and fell asleep within minutes.

I woke in the night with an uneasy feeling that something was moving nearby. The fire was out and the only sound was the murmur of the river. I lay still for a while, listening, and then began to drift off again. Suddenly, I was wide awake. There *was* a noise, a soft crunch of branches and the faint bump and squeak of wood under pressure, as if something heavy were moving through the bush. Under the tarp I couldn't tell where it was coming from. Nor was there any pattern to the sound; whatever it was moved slowly and stood still for long minutes. At length, I got up with the flashlight; if it was a bear, it's eyes would shine red in the light. A deer's eyes would be blue-green.

The sound, when it came again, was downstream and across the river. Walking quietly to the tail of the bar, I switched on the light. No eyes and no bear. Only the logjam and the trees beyond. I switched off and waited. When the noise came again I turned on the light and saw that it was coming from under the jam. The grizzly I had conjured up was nothing more than the grinding of the logs settling on the falling tide and crushing the branches of a green spruce which had been brought down by the river.

Sheepishly, I went back to bed.

To catch the tide into Bute Inlet I had to be up by four-thirty, an hour before dawn. When the alarm went off it was so light I was sure I had overslept. But when I scrambled out from under the tarp I saw that the premature dawn was created by mist that had formed along the river and lifted just overhead, eerily diffusing the light of the full moon.

I kindled the fire and walked up the bar to get dry wood from a driftpile at the edge of the flood channel. The first branch I pulled broke with a loud crack. Instantly, rapid footfalls sounded behind the screen of alders. Not one but several animals splashed through the pool, rattled lightly over the gravel and ran off, snapping and rustling, through the woods. Deer, I thought; certainly, the steps were too rapid and light for a bear, especially in the water. But there was no click of hooves on the gravel. What then?

I went back to the fire, intending to look for tracks at daylight. But the answer to the riddle came with the first light of dawn. From upriver I heard a short, sharp bark and then the long, quavering howl of a wolf. Immediately, another wolf answered from across the river, and then a third, downriver and farther off. The first voice was a soprano, rising to a high, clear note and trailing away in beautifully intricate modulation. A fourth wolf, perhaps her mate, bayed from the same direction, a deep bass, at least two octaves below the soprano. The others joined in, throwing their combined voices into the mountains to the east, which sent them echoing back, high over the river and on and on across the valley. For the next half-hour I stood out on the bar by the river, utterly transfixed by sounds that surely reach deeper than any other into the primordial roots of our being. It was music from the morning of the world.

When the last howl died away, I walked to the top of the bar, hoping to see the soprano. But the mist was too thick and by the time it began to move, the wolves were gone – or so I thought.

I was kneeling by the fire, cooking breakfast, when what I took to be a dog trotted up onto the bar from the river. It was the size and colour of a Gordon setter, though with longer hair. I stood up and called, "Here, boy," clicking my tongue. Without a sideward glance, it passed within a few steps of the fire and stopped to look back at me from the flood channel. Now there was no mistaking the wolfish ears and the amber fire in its eyes. With a single bound, the wolf cleared the driftpile and was gone.

Downstream, mist coiled up to meet the sun, flooding the valley in pink vapour. The river ran slow and unruffled as far as the logging camp, then dropped into a no-man's-land of mud, logs and upturned stumps, like a scene from the Western Front. This was the aftermath of the flood, which had been cosmetically covered the night before by the tide. I bumped down half the first riffle, then got out and waded, easing the canoe over ridges of gravel and buried logs. Lower down it got worse. Chutes that were ankle deep at the top spread and divided until there was so little water I was dragging the canoe downhill. At times I had to plod ahead through the mud to find the best route. Progress was painfully slow.

I had made careful calculations of travel time in order to catch the slack tide in the Arran Rapids at the mouth of Bute Inlet. Now, with the tide falling, I wondered whether I'd even get out of the Phillips River. I kept on, leading the canoe where there was water and dragging it where there wasn't, until the stream rediscovered its old channel, carved into the seabed, and I could paddle again.

The sun stood well clear of the mountains and the still air was warming fast. Ahead was the longest two-day run of the trip: through two rapids, forty-five miles of inlet and up the Homathko River, one of biggest and most powerful streams on the coast.

I took off my shirt and settled down for a long paddle in aid of the motor.

20

Autumn is a problematic season on the British Columbia coast. Given an even-handed mix of sun and shower, the long, still days may last a month beyond the equinox. But after the first heavy rain, which sometimes comes in early September, slash burning begins. Debris left on thousands of acres of logged land is set afire, blanketing the coast for weeks in a dismal pall of orange smoke. In this year of drought and heat, the fall robbers had been forestalled; a fire started on any logging slash would have run wild into the timber. Week after week the hot and windless days went on.

Keeping to the shade of the eastern ridges, I followed Cordero Channel to the mouth of Frederick Arm and met the ebb tide, piling onto the bluff at Owen Point. The canoe bogged down in the current and crawled across open water to Sonora Island on the south side of Cordero. And there the really fast water began.

In its last five miles before Stuart Island, Cordero Channel carries perhaps twice as much water as it does at Greene Point, thanks to the contribution of Nodales Channel, entering from the south, opposite Frederick Arm. The combined flow races along the Sonora Island shore at five knots and increases to nine knots in the constriction of Dent Rapids. At Stuart Island the waters divide, south through Gillard Passage and the Yuculta Rapids to Georgia Strait, and north, where I was headed, through the Arran Rapids into Bute Inlet.

The wall of Sonora Island is straight the whole way, without so much as a pimple to create a helpful backeddy. Bucking the current was out of the question, except by steering so close to shore that there was no room to paddle on the inside. More than once the foot of the motor hit bottom with an alarming clunk. At times I travelled in a tunnel under overhanging branches festooned with dry kelp bulbs, dangling like Christmas tree decorations, where they had snagged at high tide.

Although it certainly didn't seem like it, I was running against the ebb tide to save time. My plan was to pass through the Arran Rapids on the slack, just after noon. If I waited here for the flood to whisk me through Dent Rapids, I could not catch another slack tide at Arran Rapids until early evening. That would leave me racing darkness to find a campsite in Bute Inlet, where I had never been. And the chart was not encouraging; the contour lines crowded on top of one another, right down to the water. There didn't appear to be any beaches.

At Dent Rapids I squeezed past along the shore and ran on for a ways, before angling out to cross to the north side of Cordero Channel. The current was faster than it looked, and I was swept back into the rapids. Fortunately, with less than an hour to slack, the boils and whirlpools had dwindled, letting me pass with nothing more than a shot of adrenalin. My timing was better at the Arran Rapids: the last of the ebb strolled disarmingly through a passage as straight and placid as a canal. Within three hours the flood tide would transform Arran into a wild chute of white water. Yawning near its west entrance would be a ship-swallowing hole where many a feckless boater has come to grief.

From the moment I entered it, Bute seemed to dwarf every other inlet I had been in. Past Turnback Point at the inner end of the rapids, it spread three miles wide and reached away so far inland that I could see no land in the trench between the mountains. There was smoke in that direction, blotting out the horizon. Somewhere ahead a forest fire was burning.

Nowhere on the coast had I been in country so dry. The grass on the rock bluffs was seared to straw and the moss was lifeless grey. On the lower slopes, maples were turning yellow and brown a month before their time. The water was an uncreased sheet of blue-grey steel, blinding in the noonday sun. After baking for an hour, I turned into Leask Cove, the only likely looking camping spot on the chart until Orford River, much farther on. Anchoring the canoe, I retreated to the woods to wait for the cool of the evening before unloading and making camp. Meantime, the tide would do the work of carrying everything up the beach.

My notebook from that interminable afternoon reads: "All life is stunned by the heat. Nothing moves, except dead leaves that fall ticking down through the trees. The cove is a furnace. Twice I've ducked in the water – so cold my temples ache. And I'm sweating again before I sit down here. The only coolness is the sound of the creek at the end of the cove."

The rising tide brought the sun with it, hammering full into the cove. Glancing light needled into the pockets of shade where I had spent the afternoon, driving me deeper into the woods. A half-hour before sundown the tide drew back from the hot boulders, and a tension seemed to drain from the air. Herring began dimpling on a line between the points. A smoke-bloodied sun slipped down the north face of Mount Estero, and cool air dropped from the ridge at my back, fragrant with the resin of scorched firs. At the creek I washed away the salt of sea water and sweat, then cooked on the smallest of fires and sat very still for an hour, awaiting the cool of evening.

Far inland the night wind from the glaciers was already shunting smoke ahead of it down the inlet. At dusk the smoke severed the land from the sea, hanging mountains in misty space, like the peaks of a Chinese watercolour.

By morning the inlet was plugged with smoke. Rounding Fawn Bluff long before the sun broke over the mountains, I could follow its progress in shafts of light, tilting steeper and steeper down through the haze. For a time after sunup, windlines sparkled on the black water against the shaded side of the inlet, and I had hopes that the air might clear. But when the shadows retreated into the ravines, the breezes died away.

There was little to see. Across the inlet in the logging camp at Moh Creek, a windshield flashed in the sun. Twice, boats appeared miles ahead, shimmering in the hot air, and dissolved as I approached into logs with upthrust branches and roots. The points I steered for began as vague lines on the horizon. An hour, sometimes two, dragged past before I rounded them and looked ahead as far again into the smoky distance. All through the morning the haze grew thicker and the light turned bleary orange. Close to shore, the air smelled acrid.

Just after noon wind leads began to stir in the middle of the inlet. Within half an hour a breeze had filled, moving the burnt air at last. As the smoke thinned, the mountains leaned forward and stood taller, guarded by glaciers whose winter snowfields had collapsed into black crevasses. Snow cornices drooped from the rims of granite walls, filtering sunlight into caves of cool aqua. On the right Superb Mountain and Mt. Sir Francis Drake soared nearly 9000 feet out of the inlet. Between their twin spires, drifting cloud drew a pattern of sun and shadow on a vast bowl of snow. A river of ice snaked from a cave which gaped from the face of a glacier like the vault of a domed stadium. At the base of a cliff looming dizzily over the water, I stopped to gas up on a ledge and looked straight down into black depths between the toes of my boots. Just a few paddle strokes from shore, the canoe floated in water a thousand feet deep.

Gradually over the past hour the sea had been taking on the pale green of the glacial creeks that tumbled down every ravine. At Purcell Point, ten miles from the end of the inlet, the canoe cut through a tideline into milky, silt-laden water. It was cold – so cold that I could feel its chill in the air – and came from two rivers, the Homathko and the Southgate, emptying into the head of the Inlet.

On the chart the end of Bute looks something like a mushroom, with the cap formed by alluvial flats and muddy littoral between the Southgate on the right and the larger Homathko on the left. Inland, the flats are walled by peaks and glaciers, forming the southern perimeter of the Homathko Snowfield, which smothers all but the tallest mountains for thirty miles to the north. And beyond, in the headwaters of the Homathko, was Mt. Waddington, the loftiest peak on the coast at 13,260 feet.

A couple of miles before the Southgate I pulled in at a float below three houses huddled together behind a knoll. No one had been here for some time; beans had gone unpicked in the garden and overripe tomatoes were dropping from the vines. A gyppo logger lived here (I was told later), and he had taken his family to Vancouver for a holiday. Nor was there anyone on the Southgate River. The last of several logging camps had shut down a few years before, and the settlers who once farmed the fertile riverbottom land had been gone for two generations.

Turning towards the Homathko, I wallowed uncomfortably across open water, with a rising swell on the beam. Far short of the rivermouth the canoe ground to a stop on a sandbar. I backed off and detoured one way and another, stranding repeatedly in water so silty I couldn't see bottom just an inch or two beneath the canoe. Eventually, fast water revealed the channel, far to the right against the flats.

Once into the rivermouth I was astonished by the strength of the Homathko. While streams all over the coast had dwindled to a trickle in the drought, it was charging out to sea, bank-full with the meltwater of glaciers and snowfields. Despite the tide flooding into the river and slowing the current, the Homathko was still much too fast for me to meet head-on. Keeping to the slower water along the mud banks, I inched past overhanging willows and stranded logs that forced me out into the current. The riverbottom bristled with snags. Some showed themselves as a bulge or line of turbulence at the surface, while others gave no warning before the canoe or the motor struck. If the propellor hit hard enough to stall, I had to swing away into deeper water to restart and then work back up the bank, trying to remember where the snag lay waiting. The worst hazards were stumps, upturned on the bottom and trailing fibrous roots that wound in a knot around the propellor. To clear these tangles, I had to go ashore and use a knife.

Twice I investigated back channels, looking for a place to camp, and grounded almost immediately in boot-sucking mud. Slogging up to the flat ground under the trees, I found only underbrush, alive with mosquitoes. No grasslands awaited the traveller here as on the delta of the Kingcome River; only willow growing down to tidewater, grading inland to alder and cottonwood. The crown of one bar offered thinner brush and a breeze to move the bugs, though not a stick of firewood.

Eventually a logging camp appeared on the right bank – a float and a log dump, enclosed downstream by a boomstick jutting out into fast water and held in place by cables. I nosed out into the current and drew even with the end of the log. The canoe slowed and stopped, and I held there for a moment, paddling like mad. But it was no go; I let the bow fall off to the left and ferried across the river, losing a lot of headway before fetching up under the bank. Working upstream beyond the camp, I crossed again, falling back in the fast water but catching an eddy above the float. It was a maneuver I would have to repeat many times in the next few days.

I called my wife on the camp radiophone – she worried about me in Bute Inlet, for good reason, as it turned out – then went on upriver. I camped on a sandbar overgrown with young alders, not far above the float. Solitude it was not, but after thirteen hours of swinging a paddle, I'd have gladly camped on a parking lot.

Until dark it was a noisy camp. Just beyond the trees on the riverbank, helicopters were landing with men who had been fighting the forest fire. I could see it now, an insignificant patch of black and a thread of smoke, high on a mountainside across the river. It seemed too small to pall an entire inlet with smoke.

The Homathko once had an unsavoury reputation, in part from the killing of fourteen men in a work party building a wagon road up the river to the interior gold fields in 1864. Chilcotin Indians did them in for molesting their women and withholding food when the Indians were starving. Old photos show the road's wooden trestle clinging to

215

the walls of the canyon that begins thirty-two miles upstream. In more recent times a number of trappers and travellers have been swallowed in its gorges or drowned beneath its many logjams.

The British Columbia government recorded the Homathko's flow for several years to assess its hydro-electric potential. The numbers, when I looked them up, meant little to me. But when I compared them with the Missouri, a river which drains more than half a million square miles, I got some sense of the Homathko's scale. Although it drains an area 250 times smaller than the Missouri, the Homathko puts out an eighth of the Missouri's water. And in flood, the rampaging Homathko has one-and-a-half times the average volume of the Missouri. The difference is precipitation – dry country over much of the Missouri's watershed and, in the Homathko drainage, sixteen feet of snow on top of the Tiedemann Glacier.

Upstream from the sandbar the river made a sharp turn to the right. According to the rules I would find the slowest water on the inside of the bend. When the river changed direction, I would change sides, keeping always to the inside. But the Homathko doesn't abide by rules; half-way round the turn the way was blocked by a logjam, and across the river by another jam and an impassable curl of white water shearing off the logs. Short of a nightmare portage through the wreckage behind either jam, my only hope lay in beating the current around the logs on the near side of the river.

Little is ventured in such an attempt, as long as you are below the jam. You simply edge out from shore and do your damnedest to make headway. Above the jam it's a different story. If your motor quits and you are carried back against the logs, the canoe will be pinned sideways by the current. With dexterity and luck, an empty canoe might be worked free. But a heavily loaded canoe will capsize – always upstream, never down – taking you under with it, unless you are nimble enough to scramble up on the logs the instant the canoe hits. If you miss, you are all but certain to be trapped underwater in the jam, and neither you nor the canoe is likely to be seen again, except in small pieces downstream.

When the bow was almost to the end of the outermost log, I opened the throttle and started digging. At first the canoe swung too wide and dropped back a half-length before steadying and moving ahead. I nosed up beside the jam and then slowly past it, gaining a few inches with each stroke. Now time became a factor; I could beat the current, but how long could I keep it up? I had no ironman illusions about my endurance. A canoe length above the outside of the jam, I began to angle cautiously for slower water. This was the dicey part. If I kept to the fast water too long, I would tire and drop back; turning too sharply for the bank, I risked an encounter with the jam. I settled for a compromise, crossing about fifty feet upstream. If I had needed a spurt of strength, there was plenty of incentive at my back; even over the motor I could hear the awful sound of the river hissing down under the logs.

Above the bend the Homathko's muddy banks and enclosing forest gave way to open bars of gravel and glacial sand as fine as flour. The river split often, dividing and re-dividing around sandbars formed on the downstream side of logjams. Everywhere there was stranded wood: logs; whole trees; giant, contorted roots and wind-rows of smaller drift, washed ashore in backeddies. All through the warm, hazy afternoon I followed the river, tracking the canoe up gravel bars and ascending deep reaches through the forest. I lost count of the jams I passed and the sweepers I skirted or slipped under close to shore, sometimes by chopping a gap in the branches. Soaked to the waist and utterly absorbed in the riddles of river travel, I paid little heed to the passing hours and miles.

At length, when the sun was a handspan over the mountains, I came to a place that could not be passed without portaging. There seemed no point in keeping on; I had no objective except to see a bit of the Homathko, and that was well satisfied. Tilting the motor up out of the water, I let the current sweep the canoe away downstream. For an enchanted hour I flashed past the jams and sweepers and down the splits that had taken six hours to ascend.

In the middle of the open section of river I camped where two deer and three wolves had left their tracks in the damp sand since last night's high tide. (There is only about a foot of rise and fall at this point on the river.) I put on dry clothes, made a pot of soup and sat atop a drift pile, watching the river roll by. A breeze was blowing upstream, bearing the perfume of cottonwood and damp silt, the archetypal scent of northern rivers. Inland, as the evening air cleared, I could see a black needle, too sheer to hold the summer snow, and a flat-topped tusk, lifted on vertical walls, high above the sea of peaks. My charts offered no names, only heights of 11,000 feet and more.

The Homathko retains an ineffable wildness, despite more than half a century of logging. Alder and cottonwood have long since replaced its original stands of fir, and logging roads reach inland for miles on both sides of the valley. And yet the river rolls on, undammed and undyked, seemingly oblivious to the human presence. Its mountains stand remote and untouched as ever, walling the valley in immutable ice and stone.

In the afterglow I cut poles and pegs from the alder thickets behind the camp and set up the tarp in the open, rather than in a more sheltered spot. It was a mistake I would regret.

Around midnight the snapping of the tarp rousted me out of bed. The alders were bent low in the wind. Blowing sand stung my bare ankles. I considered moving to the shelter of a dry flood channel, but rejected the idea (the mistake compounded) in favour of snubbing up the ropes and anchoring the tent pegs with rocks. Hunting stones in the dark, I built cairns around the pegs and crawled shivering into bed, pulling the blankets over my head to muffle the din of the storm. Sleep was impossible. The wind rose higher and higher, screeching through the ropes like the rigging of a ship. The tarp cracked gunshots, and sand sifted into the crack beneath the blankets. There was grit between my teeth. I lay tense and waiting; surely something would have to give way to the strain.

It was not the tent pegs but the tarp itself which let go with a bang and a rip, tearing the grommets out of its windward side. One of the poles came down across my shoulders, and the tarp, which was still anchored on two sides, enveloped me in flailing ropes and sheeting. I clawed out from under the tangle and stood up into a searing blast of sand. The river, not thirty feet away, had disappeared in the blizzard. With a shirt tied over my nose and mouth and eyes squinting nearly closed, I set to work like a naked Lawrence of Arabia making a place to wait out the night. Setting boxes and fuel cans in parallel rows, I pulled the tarp over the top and managed, after an infuriating struggle, to pin it down with boulders. Frozen half to death, I crawled into the narrow space. The blankets were full of sand, but so was I, in every pore and orifice. Inside the mouth of my cave, miniature dunes were forming. By morning they would be a foot deep.

At dawn the wind eased back a little and the choking clouds of sand subsided to dust devils swirling along the riverbank. A quick tally of the damage found the boxes tight and free of sand inside and the motor protected by a garbage bag. But everything that wasn't in a box was full of sand – packs, charts, clothes, boots, binoculars, cameras. The canoe (which would likely have rolled into the river, had it not been tied) was drifted a third full, and had to be shovelled out with a paddle before I could sluice the rest. I would need half a day to clean up the mess and this was no place to do it. The valley was capped by cloud blowing in from the inlet; rain and even more wind would not be far behind. I had to move to a more sheltered place, downriver in the trees.

In mid-stream the headwind whipped the crests off the current waves, rattling spray like pellets against my rainjacket. I fought to keep the canoe pointed downstream, scared silly of being blown sideways and hitting a snag on the beam. In water this fast, the canoe would flip in an instant. A gust on the bend above the twin logjams knocked the bow off to the right, giving me a lively time getting straight and clearing the jam on the outside. But that was the last of it; downstream between the high banks, the wind tore through the treetops and eddied down to the river in harmless puffs. I sat back and drifted, weary to the marrow of my bones.

21

With the helicopters gone, the sandbar upstream from the logging camp was peaceful. Stoked with coffee and porridge, I slept, showered the sand from my hide (thanks to the kindness of the logging camp) and slept again into the afternoon. Between times I repaired the tarp and began the painstaking task of cleaning the sand out of my cameras. It was extremely fine and sharp, mostly silica, and apt to scratch glass under the slightest pressure.

All through the morning drenching squalls slanted down from clouds rolling up the valley from the inlet. The land gratefully drank up the long-awaited rain; mossy bluffs on the mountainside turned from grey to green within hours. In mid-afternoon rents of blue tore open the clouds. Sun patches raced over the ridges, striking snowfields and walls of ice. Above the river to the west, black crags cut their tethers to earth and ploughed through seas of flying mist.

Revived in body and spirit I hiked up the valley on a logging road. On the way back I turned in at a track leading across a rough clearing and over a log bridge to three small buildings of weathered shingles. I'd been told I would find two women living here, Liz Carr-Harris and Lynne Siebert. It was Liz who came to the door – short white hair, a round, florid face and eyes that crinkled nearly closed when she smiled. They were in the middle of canning green beans. Jars were stacked on the counter, and Lynne was readying another batch to put on the stove. I offered to come back at a better time.

"No, no, the bloody beans can wait," Liz insisted. "Come in, we'd love to have a talk."

Lynne joined us in a little three-sided alcove at the front of the cabin. She was thin and tanned, with close-cropped salt 'n pepper hair. Like Liz, she wore blue jeans and a plaid shirt, both faded from many washings. They sat up straight as if a banquet were about to begin; visitors were a rare event, and conversation was something to be taken seriously.

From the outset it was apparent that, despite their isolation, they knew far more about what was going on in the world than I did. "Politics is one of the best spectator sports there is," Liz said. "I'm a political junky. We listen a lot to CBC radio, which makes us more politically aware than almost any Canadians who don't. If we could afford it, we'd have a computer and a satellite dish and we could tap into just about anything we wanted. The information age is upon us – even here."

"We didn't come here for isolation," Lynne said. "We came for independence, and technology is part of that, whether its our radio, the chain saw, or our generator. We've got no hang-up about technology."

"But the trouble is that our technology has been hijacked by the wrong people," Liz said. "The militarists and industrialists have taken off with our best technology, and the universities spend their time developing it for them. Think what could be done if technologies were developed for our kind of lifestyle: intensive agriculture, communications, photo-voltaic cells for electricity, fish culture, recycling wastes – that's all technology. We burn wood for heat all winter and we ought to be able to generate electricity off that."

Liz's idea is that people need what she calls an agribase on the land. "Independence is what it's all about, self-sufficiency. To behave responsibly, autonomously, you have to provide your basic life support systems. Working for wages, sooner or later you have to do things you disagree with."

To supplement the agribase, she believes, a person would have to work for wages about one-third of their time, sharing a permanent full-time job with two other people. "That would solve structural unemployment right away because one job would serve three people. At the same time, if people were encouraged to establish an agribase, you'd be stimulating a whole array of research and manufacturing of the bits and pieces and gadgets for doing this kind of thing. So you'd have a vigorous domestic market going in Canadian technologies that could also be sold all over the Third World."

"The assumption in this country is that technology has to be market-driven," I said. "Do you really think there are enough people willing to move out to places like this?"

"Well, to begin with, the military hogs the best technology and it's certainly not market-driven. But to answer your question, yes, I do. More and more people, starting with single mothers who are in the worst crunch, are realizing that this kind of life means a substantial increase in the standard of living they could otherwise expect. That's the first huge potential market. And when I say 'women' I don't mean gender so much as family people, including single men with children and family men who consider fathering to be part of their job."

I was having trouble placing single parents on the Homathko River. Liz read the skepticism in my face.

"Sure, moving back to the land has been given a bad name. Some people in the hippy movement got in beyond their capability. And earlier, there was a pattern of failure amongst the settlers on the coast. But it needn't be that way. The settlers failed because they were trying to follow a frontier model of the nuclear family making it on the land. It was an aberration, a recipe for failure because they were cut off and alone. Today, only someone in the Bronx would consider trying to live entirely off the land. You have to make money away from your agribase and you have to have a network of friends and support. Modern communications, technology, makes all that possible."

In some ways, Liz and Lynne's experience replicates the frontier pattern because they pre-empted Crown land, though with a great deal more difficulty than the pioneers. In the mid-1970s, when they were living in a teepee on Salt Spring Island, they began pouring over government maps, looking for a place to homestead. Almost everything south of Bute Inlet was privately owned or in forest reserve. After a long search they found vacant land, but were made to jump through bureaucratic hoops for five more years before they got their pre-emption.

"The government and the forest companies don't like people in the woods," Lynne said. "They make it very difficult and they are incredibly rude when they know you want to pre-empt."

In 1975 Liz went north to look at twenty-five acres they had located on the Homathko River. With a borrowed canoe and a couple of hours of instruction, she set out from Quadra Island in April. Crossing the open water at the top of Georgia Strait, she was caught by a squall and nearly swamped. Slowly and painfully (sitting on the beach for three days with arms too sore to paddle) she made her way to the logging camp at Orford River, half-way up Bute Inlet. From there she hitched a ride on a tug and camped near the mouth of the Homathko. Wading creeks "boob deep" with her clothes in a bundle on top of her head, she set off up the valley. "I explored all up through here. It was spring and the cottonwoods were coming out and the valley was full of sunshine and there were no loggers and there was no logging camp. The minute I walked into the valley, I loved it."

Back on Salt Spring she reported that she had found the promised land. But of the ten people who were originally interested in the venture, only Lynne decided to make the move. Over the next four years they came many times to the Homathko, locating and staking their parcel of land, clearing a tiny opening in the bush and building a primitive shelter. Each winter they grubstaked in the Northwest Territories, cooking in oil exploration camps. In 1978, when they returned to the Homathko, a logging camp was locating on the river just downstream from their pre-emption. They struck a deal with the company: an acre of their land would be cleared and two old camp houses moved onto it in return for giving up enough of their pre-emption for a road and airstrip. It was a mixed blessing for Liz and Lynne: their bit of heaven had been invaded, but they had a roof over their heads and a link with the outside world.

After working in the north for another winter, they moved to the Homathko to stay in the spring of 1979. That fall the logging company offered them a job looking after the camp during the eight-week winter shut-down. Ever since they have lived on their pre-emption year-round, except for shopping trips to Vancouver in the spring and fall.

"We usually argue about who has to go to town," Lynne said, "because it's such a culture shock. It takes two days just to get used to the exhaust fumes. And we're always amazed how much prices have gone up in six months. We buy only milk, cheese, flour and a few other staples. I go to a movie or two, visit with friends – do the things we miss in the city. But I'm always glad to leave."

Liz and Lynne live on about $2,000 a year. Most of their food comes from their garden, plus venison and fish given to them by men from the logging camp. They keep no animals because of the high cost of bringing in feed. "We eat wonderfully and enjoy a varied diet," Liz said. But they also put up with inconveniences few people would tolerate. The cabin is a cramped two rooms, without electricity, an indoor toilet or running water. Liz makes light of the hardships. "Water is no problem, except in cold weather. Usually we can break through the ice where the waterfall comes over the bluff. But sometimes it freezes right down to the gravel and we have to look for chunks of ice we can melt."

The Bute, as Liz calls it, is colder and windier than any inlet on the coast. When the northeasters stream over the Tiedemann Glacier and down the valley, the Homathko freezes in a single day. Sixty-knot gales drive dangerous seas down the inlet to Stuart Island. In many ways, it's the best time of year for Liz and Lynne.

"The loggers are all gone and we have the valley to ourselves," Liz said. "Before the last plane, we lay in a big stack of books from the Open Shelf [the B.C. government mail order library] and send out our Christmas letters. There will be no more mail for two months. We settle down by the fire for great days of reading. When the wind lets up, we go cross-country skiing, often down along the river. The coming and going of the tide freezes the river in layers of thin ice until it looks like a Danish pastry. It crinkles and crackles and talks to you; it's kind of nice."

For the past three years many of Liz's winter days have been taken up with a book she is writing on social philosophy. "It's feminist theory. I'm thinking of calling it *Motherhood Issues* because the consciousness that gave rise to pagan religion and the concept of a mother goddess is returning." Although a publisher had shown interest, there was as yet no certainty that she would ever see the book in print.

There were other uncertainties in their lives. A new logging camp superintendent had cut them out of their camp-watching work for three winters, and it could happen again. "I guess his macho image of loggers out in the bush was threatened by two little old ladies doing the same thing," Liz chuckled. In the longer term, within five or perhaps eight years, the camp is expected to run out of timber and shut down permanently. There was no sense of impending crisis when Liz talked about these things; she was secure on her agribase. "We've gone as long as three years with no money coming in. Sure, we need a more reliable income. We'd like to learn computers; there's always work in that field. But what we really need is that third person so that we can split a job three ways and always have two people on the place. So far, we haven't been able to find anyone."

Lynne was less sure of the future. "I don't want to go back to town, but I can see if there's just the two of us and we get creakier and creakier, we'll have to do something."

They took me out to see the new shed they were building with poles and cedar shakes. We toured the extensive vegetable garden, cultivated right to the toe of the mountain. Many things were doing well, though the beets were as small as radishes for want of fertilizer. "We do our utmost; we even pee in a bucket and lace the compost with it," Liz laughed. "But the soil is pretty sandy." Occasionally, animals get into the garden. One year they lost nearly all their parsnips to a grizzly with three cubs before they went out and chased it away.

We stood in front of the cabin, talking for a long time, as if they were storing up conversation against the winter. "Living here has given me a marvellous sense of my own perspective," Liz said. "I'm a lot more confident than I used to be and a lot more humble. The mountains give me humility. And the woods make me feel that I have as much right to be here as the wolves."

When I left they pressed a loaf of bread and some tiny, delicious tomatoes on me. I felt strange accepting food from people who get to a store only twice a year.

By morning the wind was up again and clouds were clamped down tight over the valley. I cleaned the last of the sand from the gear, gathered a mound of firewood against the coming rain, and walked four disappointing miles through brushy country that shut out all view of the inlet. Nonetheless, I needed the exercise; two months in the canoe had restored the arms and washboard belly of my twenties and left my legs feeling like dead stumps.

In the logging camp I had a lame conversation with Bruce Germyn, a bald, barrel-chested man whose father ran a logging company on the Homathko for many years. I couldn't decide whether he was simply bored by me and my questions or naturally phlegmatic. But when I asked about log driving in the river, I touched a nerve and he came to life.

"We had the cheapest logging in British Columbia. From eighteen miles up, we pushed logs straight into the river and drove them down. No trucks; we did it all with cats and arches. But when all this ecology business came along in the 1960s, the fisheries department started getting on our backs. Hell, we weren't doing any harm to the salmon, but they kept at us and at us until we had to quit. Just a bunch of goddamned do-gooders."

I let it pass. But a month or two later in Vancouver a different picture of the log drive emerged from files in the fisheries department archives. Year after year thousands of logs stranded on the banks and bars of the Homathko. The company was permitted to bulldoze them into the river during the summer months when there were no salmon eggs in the gravel. But the water was too high at that season, so they waited for low water in winter and early spring. Then eight bulldozers rumbled over miles of spawning beds, killing untold millions of eggs in the gravel. When they were ordered to stop the drive in 1963, the company defied a vacillating fisheries department for three more years.

More than twenty years after the last drive, the Homathko salmon runs are a mere remnant, though it's impossible to say how much of the damage is attributable to stream damage and how much to overfishing. The reports of fisheries officers who witnessed the drive were clear enough: the drive, they said, was ruinous. Its cost to the fishing industry is likely in the millions. The company's only penalty was a $250 fine for taking roadbuilding gravel from the river without a permit.

The rain came an hour before dark – no wind, no preliminary shower; just a few fat drops plopping on the tarp and then the deluge. It fell straight down, pattering through the alders and dancing on the river, raising mist over the water. I made a comfortable place among the boxes and watched the drops hissing into the fire. I thought of Carole and my family, wondering as I often did, what they were doing and why I had taken myself away from them. I thought of turning south and how long it would be until I hauled the canoe out at the end of the road.

This was a fall rain, pressing down on the earth with the dead weight of coming winter. For hours I lay awake, listening to it pounding on the tarp. I slept and when I woke again in the dark, the fire was out and the blankets were wet with drifting spray. Dawn came slowly through the downpour. Overnight, the clouds had dropped almost to the valley floor, shrinking the mountains to mere weeping hills.

Although I was loath to get up, conditions were right to move on; after a windless night, the inlet would be calm. And the high tide near noon would be ideal for running out of the river. On low tides below four feet, the Homathko builds a nasty sea on the drop-off into the inlet.

Half-blinded by smoke, I cooked spread-eagled over the fire to keep the rain out of my breakfast. Still, rain drops spat hot fat out of the frying pan, burning my hands. And when I sat under the tarp to eat, water poured from the brim of my hat, making a soup of congealed bacon grease and eggs in my plate. Loading the canoe, everything was wet before the spray tarp was snapped down. Then, just as I pushed off, the rain stopped.

Around the first bend a crack opened in the clouds and a bar of sun struck the brown river. For a moment the Homathko resembled some humid branch of the Amazon, roiled with sticks and leaves, slipping along beneath dripping alders and cottonwoods. Downstream, the river vanished under rolling mist, as if it had plunged over a waterfall. Keeping to the fast water, I avoided the snags and passed out of the river's mouth without touching a sandbar.

I had in mind to look for a camp on the Orford River, twenty-five miles ahead. To put myself on the east side of the inlet while the going was good, I made the long crossing to the base of Mt. Rodney, which lifts its symmetrical cone high over the mouth of the Southgate River. The inlet was calm and mottled with islands of crinkled silver, drifting inland under holes in the clouds. But before long, conditions began to change. Clouds bunched around the peaks and joined in an arch spanning the inlet. High in the heads of valleys, snow squalls and then curtains of rain moved lower. The sun blinked at the edge of the cloud and disappeared. Light rain ringed the glassy water. The mountains turned green-black, veined by white torrents.

The wind arrived with a rip and a snort off the mountainside, bitterly cold and charged with big drops that stung my face like hail. It was a capricious wind, raging then dying to faint puffs and thin, chilling rain. After several of these squalls I discovered a pattern: I hit them usually at the northern end of bays and ran out of them again at the southern end. Although the storm was moving generally up the inlet, some quirk of temperature or pressure snared the wind in the scooped land above each bay and sent it plummeting down the mountainside. It fell with a counterclockwise twist that brought it tearing around the curve of the shore and out over the water. For some time lightning had been flickering over the peaks. Now the storm broke right above me, unleashing sheets of rain and wind which sent the canoe skittering sideways over the water. Running as close as I dared to the cliffs, I still caught the blast sheering off the rock. For mile after mile I went on, looking for a place to haul out, but finding not a single break in the rain-slick walls of the inlet.

Trouble, when it arrived, was a total surprise. I was coming up on the bluff outside Orford River, staying close to shore. I expected the water to be rough around the point on the north side of Orford Bay, just as it was on the north side of every bay I'd crossed for the past two hours. But well short of the bluff the canoe began to pound into a heavy chop bouncing back off the rocks. I moved out to what looked like smoother water. The tide was ebbing fast against the wind, which was dead ahead now, slapping rain and spray into my face. By the time I saw the breakers, I was into them and it was too late to turn back.

There is a certain regimen to meeting danger in a canoe: sizing up the difficulty, making a considered decision, and then pumping yourself up physically and psychologically. But when you are taken by surprise, none of this happens. There is only fear and a rush of adrenalin so overwhelming you can barely keep your arms from thrashing the paddle pointlessly.

There was time only to make a grab for the throttle and slow the motor before the canoe buried itself in the first wave. It came up sulkily, pouring green off the spray tarp, and plunged again. The waves were being undercut by the tide and knocked down from behind by the wind. As I came abreast of the point, they were hit from the side by a cross-current from the outflow of the rain-swollen Orford River. Where wind, current and tide collided, the sea went wild. Breakers tumbled in from every side, crashing down into yawning holes. Peaks of water erupted without warning out of the troughs, flinging spray up into the wind. The canoe bucked and corkscrewed sickeningly, pointing to the sky and plunging half its length into the bottom of the holes. In the troughs I could see only water and sky; from the crests the sea looked like heavy rapids in a big river. As the canoe lifted to each wave, the stern wallowed deeper and deeper. Twice the motor coughed seawater through the carburetor, then backfired and died.

I had never been in a sea such as this with a canoe. It seemed only a matter of time before a wave broke into the stern behind the spray cover, or I was knocked off balance and capsized. The tide was sweeping me out into the inlet faster than I could paddle against it, and turning around to start the motor was out of the question. And yet there was nothing I could do, except keep the paddle deep in the water and risk a few quick strokes to hold the canoe into the wind.

Certain that I could not stay afloat, I thought ahead to what I would do when I was in the water. There were two distress flares in the outside pockets of a pack. But who would see them? There was not a soul in the inlet behind me. And ahead were only breaking seas and empty miles of grey water. Only one man could help: the watchman at the logging camp in Orford Bay. But even he wouldn't see me because the camp was inland beyond the trees. I thought of the paralyzing cold and the survival suit I'd considered bringing. No, I was right to leave it behind; I would never have got it on.

I had no sense of time. After what seemed only minutes, I glanced back to find the bluff a half-mile behind. Without the forward motion of the motor, the canoe was less inclined to bury its stern when it came down off a wave. And the cross-current from the river had turned and aligned itself with the tide. Ahead, the seas looked as big as ever, though they were running in one direction now. Cautiously, I began to paddle at an angle to the waves, edging towards shore in Orford Bay. I could see floats now in the right side of the bay and a gap in the marshy shore a half-mile to the left, where the river entered. Mountains crowded close behind, momentarily hard-edged in the lightning, then blurred by driving rain.

It was slow work, making a few strokes landward and turning the canoe back to take the biggest whitecaps bow-on. Before long it was obvious that the tide would carry me well past Orford Bay. Then I would have to work back and risk taking a breaker into the stern.

Already, a lot of water was sloshing in the bottom. I would have to try to start the motor.

The spark plug was soaked. At least a dozen times I squared the canoe to the waves and managed a quick wrap and pull with the cord before the bow fell off the wind. Twice the motor coughed and died. At last, it fired and started, belching steam into the wind. I turned and ran in the trough with the seas on the beam, slowing or speeding up to avoid the breakers. Occasionally, a wave spilled into the stern, but it mattered little, now that I had one hand free to bail.

Towards the head of the bay, the waves lost their momentum in the brown flood fanning out from the river. The Orford was over its banks and sweeping a tide of sticks and leaves out to sea. Feeling drained and in no mood to fight my way upstream to a sodden camp, I turned in at the wharf. I would take my chances at the logging camp.

Outside a cavernous truck shop, a man was working on his back under a battered van with his legs sticking out in the rain. Len Hrechka wriggled out, black with grease, clutching a fist-full of wrenches.

"Sure, I don't see any problem with that," he said when I asked if I could sleep on a floor somewhere in the camp. "Can you cook?"

"After a fashion."

"That's good enough. There's lots of food here but I don't much care for cooking." He was the camp mechanic, monkey wrenching and batching until the first shift of men arrived in a few days to start logging.

I trudged back to the wharf and dug my pack out of the canoe, after a furious battle with the spray cover (it shrank drum-tight when wet). When I came up the ramp, Len was waiting with the truck.

Keeping well within my culinary limits, I fried potatoes, bacon and eggs, spiced up a tin of baked beans, and made toast and a great vat of coffee. We ate sitting across from one another at a long table in a cookhouse meant for fifty men. And then we stayed on through the evening, talking politics, ecology, logging and fishing. Rain drummed on the roof and lightning strobe-lit snapshots of the camp, framed in the windows. I thought of the inlet and the overturned canoe and waves charging out of the dark; I grew colder and weaker, my hands lost all feeling and I slipped down into the black water. But Len was still there across the table, talking quietly. I basked in the comfort of the cookhouse and the company of a considerate man.

In the morning, on the road to the wharf, I met five Indians from the Homalco Band that once made Bute Inlet their home. They had come to look for salmon in the river, and one carried a rifle to hunt deer. The chief, Richard Harry, a bulky, round-faced man with a deep voice, asked about the canoe and where I'd been.

"The Homathko."

"When did you come down?"

"Yesterday afternoon."

"How was it, a little rough?"

"Very rough."

They all burst out laughing.

"When I saw that damn little canoe," the chief explained, "I said to these guys, 'I'll bet somebody's had the shit scared out of him.'" More laughter. "Everybody around here knows Orford River is a bad place."

From the wharf I could see fresh snow plastered to the windward side of the peaks around the head of the Orford valley. Below the cliffs frost had touched the alpine meadows, igniting the reds and golds and russets that would fire all of the high country in another few weeks.

Down in the inlet broadleaf maples showed dull yellow and brown, and close to the water the vine maples were turning scarlet. It was a day of heavy overcast and grey stillness. Off Fawn Bluff soft rain began to dimple the water. In Leask Cove a lens of mist hung stationary over the trees where I had sweltered less than a week ago.

Almost imperceptibly summer had turned into fall.

22

Stuart Island and the rapids at the mouth of Bute Inlet seem to be a dividing point between a wet, densely forested coast to the north and a drier, more open country around Georgia Strait. As I moved south the evergreens pulled back from the water's edge, the undergrowth thinned and red ochre-barked arbutus trees, which reach the northern limit of their range beyond Stuart Island, became commonplace. The water was warmer, and oysters made their first appearance, growing so thickly within a few miles that their shells turned the shore chalky grey. Seabirds of many kinds were more numerous than they had been since Queen Charlotte Strait. These changes were gradual but marked, so that by the time I reached the islands enclosing the top of Georgia Strait, I was unmistakably in a different country.

The people, or at least their lifestyle, changed as well. Just about everyone lived within a half-hour of a ferry by boat or car. They shopped in Campbell River and sent their kids to regular schools. Many of them worked for wages on fish farms or in town. And many others were retired on secure pensions. They were preoccupied, not by the isolation that dominates the lives of coast people to the north, but by a mushrooming population and the attendant ills of pollution, rising taxes and dwindling privacy.

Another change was the proliferation of salmon farms. To the north, I had passed no more than two or three. Here it seemed that almost every bay was filled with net pens and buoys, floating feed sheds and crew quarters. I'd been steering clear of the farms, just as I would rather not hang around a broiler factory or feedlot. Even so, the reek of dead fish came often across the water, and the acres of pens cut off access to many beaches and coves.

Burton Wohl, a retired Hollywood screenwriter, spoke with rage and sadness about a salmon farm that was about to be built on his Read Island doorstep. His cove, looking out on the exquisite King Islets, would be nearly blocked by net pens, spewing tons of fish shit,

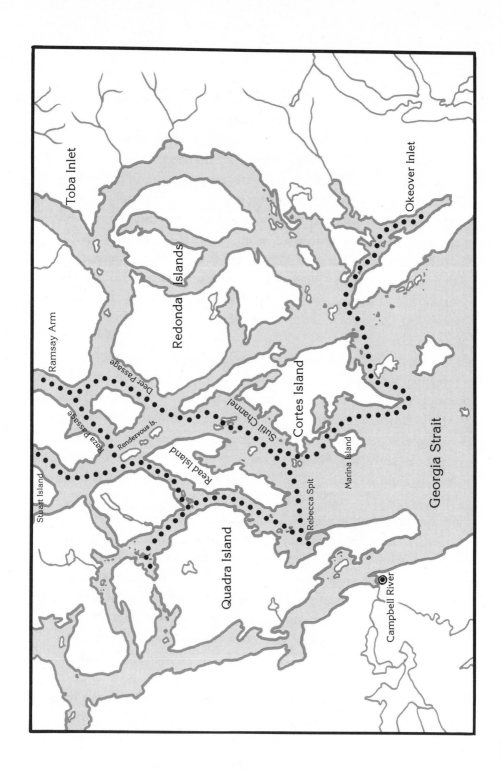

antibiotics, red dye (added to feed to tint the fish's flesh a more marketable colour) and caustic net cleaners into the water. The silence would be shattered by motors and the incessant chatter of two-way radios amplified through speakers. His attempts to have the farm located elsewhere had come to a dead end; the owner was a Swiss pharmaceutical baron who proved to be about as accessible as a numbered bank account.

Swallowing my scruples, I spent an evening on the Cortes Island fish farm of Tom Pedersen, a Danish immigrant logger who had sunk his life savings into 36,000 Chinook fingerlings and the feed and equipment it would take to raise them. He said his money would run out before the fish were ready to sell in about eighteen months. He would have to borrow. But no Canadian bank would take the risk; too many farm salmon have succumbed to disease, bad food, predators, plankton blooms, oxygen starvation and innumerable other failings of an infant industry. Small fry like Tom Pederson were doing the risky pioneering, while multinational corporations circled like sharks, ever ready to offer emergency financing in return for control of the farm. With luck, Tom Pedersen would sell his fish and pay off his debt. Or, given a bad break or two, he could lose the farm and end, like dozens of other fish farmers, working as a sharecropper for absentee owners. (Some time after my visit farm salmon prices fell by fifty percent, bankrupting many small operators.)

I wished Tom Pedersen well, though my true sympathies were with the fish. While their wild brethren passed their lives on a wondrous North Pacific odyssey, they swam round and round in crowded pens, waiting for the next feeding of pellets. By selective breeding, the industry intends to create a farm salmon, domesticated and docile as a dairy cow.

Camping in a busy provincial park on Rebecca Spit across from Heriot Bay, after two months on an all-but deserted coast, I suffered culture shock. A woman impassively watched her Dobermans piss on my grub box, cooing from the path, "Oh, they just want to be friends!" A lost soul named Tom moped about the camp, telling me how he had wrecked the sailboat he lived on and didn't know what to do. For hours a woman with a voice like a bullwhip harangued a man who was trying to drown himself in a case of beer.

That night, by the fire, I resolved to keep the last days of my travels for myself. Early the next morning I left Rebecca Spit. Georgia Strait lay serene under pearly haze, stretching a hundred horizonless miles to the south. If the day remained calm, there would be mirages in the afternoon, hanging mirror images of the islands upside down in the sky. Following Sutil Channel past the the granite and arbutus shores of Cortes Island, I made a day-long circuit through Deer Passage, Ramsay Arm and Raza Passage, arriving late in the afternoon at an unnamed islet off the north end of the Rendezvous Islands. And there I stayed for the next three days.

Mornings I watched the birds and poked about on the tidal isthmus to the next island. The harlequins were back from a northern summer of feeding at the bottom of mountain streams, like the torrent ducks of the Andes. Two drakes preened on the same boulder each day, dazzling in their slate blue, chestnut and white. The western grebes had also returned, winging through the mountain passes from prairie lakes. They rafted offshore, diving with graceful arcs that lifted them clear of the water. From the high side of my islet I looked down on seventeen red-breasted mergansers herding a school of herring into the cove. When they dove, I could see them lancing through the fish, driving them to the surface in silver boils. Many other migrants passed through the cove – greater yellowlegs, sanderlings, black turnstones and flocks of tiny treetop birds that swooped and twittered between the islands. Once, with my inept whistle, I called a loon so close that I could make out its ruby eye.

Afternoons I left the motor behind and paddled, light and easy, through the islands. In a cod hole on a sunken ledge that had escaped the notice of commercial fishermen, I caught and released in rapid succession three rock cod, a dog fish, and a pair of whopping lingcod as long as my leg, before a young ling of the right size came to the gaff. I returned to the camp in the dusk, slipping quietly into the cove to see what was there. Three days running, a seal and her pup lay quietly in the kelp, and once a feeding mink gave up its fish and loped over the neck of sand.

With the red tides behind me I made up for a summer without oysters, downing them fried, stewed in milk and raw on the half-shell, with Tabasco, lemon and Scotch on the side. And when I tired of oysters, I gorged on steamed clams, combining the surplus with cod and potatoes to create a chowder of rare distinction.

Evenings I sat by the fire with my notebooks, sorting through impressions of people and places that had melded together over the past months. One thing that had come clear was my old ambivalence about moving upcoast. I had met a few young couples on my travels who were doing the latter-day pioneering that I had only dreamed about. While I envied their energy and the keen intensity of their lives, I could see now beyond the heady days of designing and building to years of unremitting toil. Settling on the coast beyond roads and electricity meant stepping back two generations into a ceaseless round of chopping, digging, fixing. Buildings, wharves, fences seem to rot away almost overnight in the rain, and every hard-won clearing has to be defended constantly from the invading forest. Twenty or thirty years ago I would have welcomed such a challenge. Now the time had passed.

Often on some deserted shore I came upon a moss-covered house foundation or the decayed stumps of a former clearing, overgrown already by towering trees, though the people had been gone for only fifty or at most seventy years. Everywhere an air of impermanence pervades the lives of coast people. They seemed to me like perennial floatcamp dwellers, knowing that one day they would have to cut their ties and move back to town. Except in the Indian villages, no one is born out there. And no one dies out there, if they can avoid it. Even after decades in their cove, Merril and Edie Hadley accepted the inevitability of old age driving them away. If no one takes their place, their house, gardens, even their clearing in the forest will vanish in a few years.

What is it about this coast that sooner or later defeats the people who love it most? Isolation and the lack of a local economy were obvious causes before I set out, and nothing changed that view. Groceries, machine parts, sending kids to school, trips to the doctor – all increase their cost in direct proportion to the distance from town. And there were other factors that I hadn't anticipated.

Settling on the remote coast had always seemed to me an individual undertaking, a personal quest for independence and privacy. But I realized now that the single family against the wilderness is a nineteenth-century frontier aberration which never worked, at least not here. The terrain and climate are too hostile and the isolation too complete for families, especially women with young children, to contend with alone. And yet nearly every family I met had set out on their own and still maintained a distance in their dealings with their neighbours, even when they lived miles apart. Despite work swapping or occasional visiting, they never comprised a mutually sustaining community.

Elsewhere, seacoast people face their hardships and isolation together in communities. For Newfoundlanders, the outport is the model, not the embattled family. They do not live alone, or at least not by design. Their closest equivalents on the West Coast were the native Indian people who survived for generations in isolated villages, sustained by their extended families, clans and tribal connections. Rugged individualism had no place here.

I had become convinced that there was no place here either for the landsman. The Indians succeeded because they were sea people who lived entirely without agriculture, venturing inland only to hunt or forage. The forest to them was a kindly presence, the haunt of spirits and source of building materials, food and medicinal plants. To the settler the forest was the enemy to be thrown back in the struggle to create a farm. Perhaps we Europeans lack the genetic or cultural conditioning to live like the natives in tiny clearings scratched at the margin of forest and sea. In the deep, rainy inlets, especially north of Vancouver Island, I felt as if the trees and swarming undergrowth were forever at my back, pressing towards the water. Only in a few river valleys did I find room to stretch and breathe.

What is it, then, that brings a new wave of would-be settlers with each generation? Aside from those who are simply running away from something (I met many), people have always been drawn by an aura of lost Eden that hovers like sea mist over the islands and inlets, promising a free life on a starkly beautiful shore. It's an elusive thing, hard to find and harder still to hold onto. The first settlers touched it when land was free and the coast's natural abundance was rich beyond imagining. But the hopes of many died stillborn within a few short years of hardship and disillusionment. The loggers knew it, too, glorying for a generation in the power of muscle, steam and steel to lay low the greatest crop the world has ever known. But all that ended when the environmental bills came in. And in the hippie time young people made their own bohemian paradise along the summer beaches, only to have it slip away in the autumn rains.

Often as I travelled, I felt the tug of the coast's seductive magic, just as the first settlers must have known it, or the Indians long before them. It beckoned from the light beneath the waves, from mist on the ridges, from the sky at dawn, and from a thousand other sun-shot images that flicker still behind my eyes. But for me it is a seasonal thing that retreats into the dank November woods. Winter works a darker magic. Surf rages beneath the seaward cliffs and cloud hangs low on the inlet walls. It is the time when spawned-out salmon are dying along the creeks and the whispering dune grass of the estuaries lies flattened in the rain. I am content then to lay up my canoe and make the journeys of maps and dreams.

I built up the fire against the autumn chill and sat long after dark, thinking back through the beautiful places I had camped. In Blunden Harbour, Burdwood Cove and Grappler Sound, winter storm tides would soon efface the last traces of my fires. No one would walk those beaches again until summer. I wondered what would become of the people I had met. How many grey winters would Charlie Chilson's sons endure in Seymour Inlet before they left their father to his antiquated logging? What chance, if any, did Milan Pesicka have of protecting his livelihood from marauding prawn boats in

Drury Inlet? I thought of Jan and Maria Laan struggling to resurrect their Cracroft Lagoon resort from years of neglect. They were in for a tough winter. And Glenn Shuart, alone as anyone on the coast, waiting for the return of the wintering swans of the Apple River estuary. On the Homathko, Liz and Lynne would be preserving the last of their venison and vegetables, watching the snowline edge lower on the mountains. When it reached the flatlands by the river, the logging camp would shut down and the silent valley would be theirs again.

Many of the people I met promised to write or phone if they came to Vancouver. Few did, and it was just as well. My trip was a snapshot of a moment in their lives; what happened to them afterwards could have no place in what I wrote. Although I wished them well, I came away certain that most of them would eventually give up their remote homesites for an easier life in town.

No doubt others will come to take their place. But life beyond the towns becomes more costly every year. And the base of natural resources – fish, timber for the small logger, unattached land – is shrinking. Travelling as I did at the water's edge, it was possible to believe otherwise. Much of the shoreline, where the most accessible timber was logged long ago, has regrown. A seamless mantle of green has closed the gaps left by countless logging camps, canneries and homesteads. But the absence of people is misleading. It is no longer necessary to live on the remote coast in order to extract its natural wealth. Technology has made it possible to reach out from the towns to log remote valleys and comb the coastal waters with freezer ships.

And yet no matter how scarce the once-great abundance becomes, each new summer will bring its would-be pioneers, heading up-coast to try their luck where so many others have failed. Over the past century the tide of settlers has slowed to a trickle. But the islands and inlets that attracted them are still there in all their splendour, remote and beautiful as ever.

During those last evenings by the fire, I came to one other conclusion about my journey: everything I had seen and done would have been enhanced by sharing it with someone else. Although I had proven to myself that I could travel alone, solitude for me was more penance than pleasure. Without regret I struck myself from the company of lone adventurers.

For my last night I moved south to an old haunt on Shark Spit, jutting like a double-edged dagger from the north end of Marina Island. Except for mussels and oysters encroaching on the sandflats, little had changed since I first came here as a youngster in 1951. The craggy old firs were still there, cloaking the base of the spit in hushed twilight. And the dune grass rustled in the evening wind, just as I remembered it. Even the sunset was the same, red now with the smoke of slash fires (lit since the recent rains) and red in that long-ago summer when no rain fell for two months, and forest fires ran wild all over the coast.

In the night a wind from the southeast moaned through the firs. By morning there was rain, mixed with blowing fog. I'd have stayed put, but Carole would be waiting with the pickup at the wharf in Okeover Inlet. After nearly three months on the water, I intended to be there.

A heavy swell was breaking on the long reef off the southern end of Cortes Island. Sneaking through on the inside, I stayed dry until I swung inland with the waves on the stern quarter. Green water broke over the gunwale, forcing me to turn upwind and bail.

The wind died away as I crossed the bottom of Cortes. Over the entrance to Malaspina Inlet the cloud was thinning and flecked with blue. In the narrows between the islands the tide flooded pale jade over a bar of shell sand. Gulls stood in the stream, trailing slender wakes from their pipestem legs. Rounding the last point, the wharf came into view and then the flash of Carole's jacket, red against the dark of the trees.

APPENDIX

Equipment Used on This Trip

Canoe

The canoe was fibreglass, taken from a mould off a Peterborough rib canoe, which was built in 1912. (This Peterborough model went out of production in the 1930s, due to the expense of fitting together its scores of tongue-and-groove ribs, which were unsupported by either planking or canvas.) My fibreglass copy was made with a keelson (but no external keel) and an extra layer of roving in the bottom for strength. It measured seventeen feet, four inches long, thirty-four inches wide and weighed ninety-five pounds. The gunwales were made of white oak, seats and thwarts of maple, and the traditional long decks of red alder. Flotation tanks fore and aft were fitted with screwtop hatches for storage.

Without its canvas spray cover, the canoe would have been uncomfortable and, at times, dangerous. The cover snapped under the outside of the gunwales and was pulled taut by a rope that passed over three posts, forming a ridge that shed even the heaviest wave.

Gear

Much of the gear and food was carried in watertight boxes which fit snugly fore and aft of the center thwart, keeping the load from shifting in rough weather. One, the grub box, was divided into compartments for standard size jars and tins. A smaller box for cameras, charts, binoculars and other articles needed on the water fit tightly in front of the back thwart, within reach of the stern seat. Clothes, bedding and foam mattress went into large bags, custom-made from tough nylon-reenforced poly tarp material, which were stowed behind the front seat. To raise the load above water in the canoe, I put the cooking grill and my sleeping pallet on the bottom. This consisted of four one-by-six pine boards, bolted together by stainless steel rods which could be removed for travelling. On the few occasions when I used the pallet, it made the difference between a good sleep and a miserable night on a log boom or rock pile. The cooking grill, incidentally, had its own canvas bag to contain soot, as did the pots, which were stored in the bow, together with five-gallon plastic containers for water and outboard fuel. Stowed beneath the front seat was the ten-by-twelve-foot poly tarp that I made into a lean-to by suspending one edge from poles and anchoring the opposite side with stakes. I prefer a lean-to to a tent for its roominess and open view, but it is also open to insects. A fine-weave mosquito net is a must.

As for safety, there isn't much in the way of equipment that will augment your own caution. I carried a light aircell life jacket but never wore it; the water in most places was too cold to withstand for long. Although there is rarely anyone around to see them, flares are still worth taking. A lightweight waterproof two-way radio would be of real value, though its battery would need frequent charging.

The charts I used were a constant headache because of their cumbersome size and penchant for disintegrating in the damp. A better choice would be to cut or copy the relevant pages from a B.C. coast marine atlas (there are two on the market) and have them waterproofed with plastic coating.

If you are travelling on the open coast, a heavy sweater, rubber boots and raingear are essential to cope with the fog and cold, even in mid-summer. I prefer thigh-length boots which are high enough to keep out water and easier to walk in than floppy hip waders. Fisherman's raingear is heavy but preferrable to fabrics such as Gore-Tex which leaks after a day or two of steady rain.

The menu is a matter of personal preference. For those who can get by on a spartan diet, it is possible to live largely on fish and clams (red tides permitting), augmented by rice and perhaps bannock. But this is monotonous fare, and fishing is time-consuming and unreliable. I carried tinned tuna and salmon as a protein backup, along with rice, bannock, oatmeal, raisins, nuts, dried fruit, dehydrated soups and Surprise peas, which can be found in most supermarkets at prices much below those charged by outdoors stores. Most other freeze dried foods seem to me denatured and overpriced. But again, it's a matter of taste.

Finally, a few items that really matter: waxed nylon string and a stitching awl for repairs; a light anchor; plenty of quarter-inch rope; at least six cod jigs of various sizes; a good axe (not a hatchet), together with file and stone to keep it sharp. (My choice is the Hudson's Bay style axe with a tomahawk head.)

SELECTED
BIBLIOGRAPHY

Bigg, Michael, et al. *Killer Whales. A study of their identification, genealogy and natural history in British Columbia and Washington State*. Nanaimo: Phantom Press, 1987.

Cail, Robert E. *Land, Man and the Law – The Disposal of Crown Lands in B.C., 1871-1913*. Vancouver: University of British Columbia Press, 1974.

Collison, Henry William. *In the Wake of the War Canoe*. Toronto: Mission, 1915.

Drucker, Philip. *Indians of the Northwest Coast*. Garden City, New York: The Natural History Press, 1963.

————. *Cultures of the North Pacific Coast*. New York: Harper & Row, 1965.

Duff, Wilson. *The Indian History of British Columbia. Vol.1. The Impact of the White Man*. Victoria: B.C. Provincial Museum, 1964.

Dunae, Patrick A. "Promoting the Dominion: Records and the Canadian Immigration Campaign, 1872-1915." *Archivaria* 19:73-93.

Durham, Bill. *Canoes and Kayaks of Western America*. Seattle: Copper Canoe Press, 1960.

Ellison, Rev. W. G. H. *British Columbia and Vancouver's Island*. London: Arthur Chilver, 1890.

Gunther, Erna. *Indian Life on the Northwest Coast of North America*. Chicago: University of Chicago Press, 1975.

Haig-Brown, Roderick. *The Western Angler*. Toronto: Totem Books, 1981.

Halliday, William May. *Potlatch and Totem, the Recollections of an Indian Agent*. Toronto: Dent, 1935.

Hart, J. L. *Pacific Fishes of Canada*. Ottawa: Minister of Supply and Services, 1973.

Holm, Bill. *Crooked Beak of Heaven*. Seattle: University of Washington Press, 1972.

————. *Northwest Coast Indian Art*. Seattle: University of Washington Press, 1965.

LaViolette, F.E. *The Struggle for Survival – Indian Cultures and the Protestant Ethic in B.C.* Toronto: University of Toronto Press, 1973.

Marchak, Patricia. *Green Gold*. Vancouver: University of British Columbia Press, 1983.

Maser, Chris. *The Redesigned Forest.* San Pedro: R. & E. Miles, 1988.

Menzies, Archibald. *Menzies' Journal of Vancouver's Voyage.* Victoria: Government Printer, 1923.

Pérouse, J.F.G. de la. *Voyage Around the World Performed in the Years 1785-88.* Vol. 1. London: G.G. and J. Robinson, 1799.

Peterson, Lester R. *The Cape Scott Story.* Vancouver: Mitchell Press, 1974.

Poole, Francis. *Queen Charlotte Islands – A Narrative of Discovery and Adventure in the North Pacific.* Vancouver: J.J. Douglas, 1972.

Robin, Martin. *The Rush for Spoils.* Toronto: McClelland and Stewart, 1972.

Rushton, Gerald A. *Whistle Up the Inlet.* Vancouver: Douglas & McIntyre, 1990.

Sproat, Gilbert Malcolm. *Scenes and Studies of Savage Life.* London: Smith, Elder and Co., 1868.

Stock, Ralph. *Confessions of a Tenderfoot.* London: Richards, 1913.

Thomson, Richard E. *Oceanography of British Columbia.* Ottawa: Minister of Supply and Services, 1981.

Walbran, Capt. John T. *British Columbia Coast Names, 1592-1906.* Vancouver: J.J. Douglas, 1971.

White, Howard, ed. *Raincoast Chronicles First Five.* Madeira Park: Harbour Publishing, 1976.

——. *Raincoast Chronicles Six/Ten.* Madeira Park: Harbour Publishing, 1983.

ACKNOWLEDGEMENTS

First, let me thank Captains Jim Power and Dick Hansen of the Canadian Fishing Company, who carried my canoe and gear north to begin this journey. And my brother Noel for his advice on constructing the craft that was to serve me so well.

Generous assistance with research was provided by Ann Yandel and George Brandak, Special Collections, University of British Columbia; Francis Gundry, British Columbia Archives and Records Service; Bennett McCardle and Carolyn Heald, Public Archives of Canada, and the staff of the Northwest History department at the Vancouver Public Library. Robert Davidson, Simon Dick, Graeme Ellis, John Ford, Bill Holm, Harold Phillips, David Suzuki, Michael Trew and Jane Watson also contributed valuable information. I wish to acknowledge, as well, the help of Gary Logan, Paulette Westlake and Gordon Miller of the Department of Fisheries and Oceans, and especially the late Michael Bigg, a scientist of rare wisdom and conscience.

While I researched in Ottawa, Ralph Torrey and Judy Smith kindly kept a roof over my head, and in Victoria, so did Sheanne and Alan O'Sullivan. For their many helpful suggestions on the manuscript, I am indebted to Robert and Annette Jack and to my father, Ted.

Everywhere on the coast I was met with great kindness from people who took me into their homes or helped me in some way. My thanks to:

Bruce Bennett, Hamish Bruce and Mara Gagnon, Jim and Anne Borrowman, Dane and Helen Campbell, Charlie Chilson, Bruce Davies, Alf Didriksen, Jean Haddinott, Merril and Edie Hadley, Olie Hansen, Colleen and Bob Hemphill, Len Hrechka, Richard Harry, Jan and Maria Laan, Dennis and Cathy Langtry, Len McAfee and Debbie Nishakowara, Chris and Sharon McCready, Alexandra Morton, Milan and Pam Pesicka, Mike and Joy Rodway, Glenn Shuart, Paul and Helena Spong, Dave Thomson and Peggy Sowden, Brad and Anne Wilson.

Finally, my thanks to Marilyn Sacks for her firm and tasteful editing. And to my wife Carole and daughter Ashely, who kept the faith when I had doubts.

GEOGRAPHICAL INDEX